D1558875

Persuasion
and
Soviet Politics

For June

Persuasion
and
Soviet Politics

David Wedgwood Benn

Basil Blackwell

Copyright © David Wedgwood Benn 1989

First published 1989

Basil Blackwell Ltd
108 Cowley Road, Oxford, OX4 1JF, UK

Basil Blackwell Inc.
432 Park Avenue South, Suite 1503
New York, NY 10016, USA

British Library Cataloguing in Publication Data

A CIP catalogue record for this book is available from the British Library

Library of Congress Cataloging-in-Publication Data

Benn, David Wedgwood, 1928–
Persuasion and Soviet politics/David Wedgwood Benn.
p.   cm.
Bibliography: p.
Includes index.
ISBN 0-631-15639-9
1. Communication in politics—Soviet Union.   2. Persuasion
(Psychology)   3. Public opinion—Soviet Union.   4. Soviet Union—
Politics and government—1953-1982.   5. Soviet Union—Politics and
government—1982—   6. Propaganda. Communist—Soviet Union.
I. Title
JN6581.B45 1989   88-7579
303.3'75'0947—dc19   CIP

Typeset in 10 on 12 pt Ehrhardt
by Photo·Graphics, Honiton, Devon
Printed in Great Britain by
T.J. Press (Padstow), Ltd., Padstow, Cornwall

2 - 5 - 91

Contents

не психология, а тоталитаризм

Preface

This book is addressed both to specialists in Soviet affairs and to a wider audience. The subject will, I hope, be self-explanatory as the chapters proceed. But it may be helpful at the outset to say something about the underlying theme and conclusions of what follows.

The book sets out to explore the traditional Soviet approach to propaganda, persuasion and public opinion. My research was originally prompted by curiosity as to whether, or how far, the Soviet approach to propaganda had been influenced by a concern with psychology. I came to the conclusion that psychology, very far from having been harnessed by the Soviet authorities for political purposes, had been seriously hampered by political constraints in the USSR. It was the official disregard for, rather than reliance on, psychology which characterized Soviet thinking in the past. This has had a number of significant consequences. In particular, it led the regime to misundersand or overrate the power of propaganda; and the disregard for psychology can, I believe, provide a more general insight into Soviet politics.

When I began my research, there seemed to be little likelihood that the Soviet system would change. But Mikhail Gorbachev's accession to power gave a new topicality to the subject of Soviet persuasion. For Gorbachev, regardless of whether his ideas ultimately prevail, is the first Soviet leader to embark on radical reform by largely *non*-coercive methods. That alone will earn him a place in history. However, although I am among those who have strong hopes that he will succeed, the present book is not, in the main, concerned with Gorbachev. It attempts to look at Soviet persuasion in a historical perspective.

It is usual for authors to accept responsibility for the shortcomings in what they have written. I have special reasons for doing so. During the early stages of my research – in the Brezhnev period – one had to contend with a mass of Soviet literature on propaganda which was often unrevealing and contained more verbiage than meaningful information. Then, with the gradual advent of *glasnost'*, the opposite difficulty arose: a steady stream of new, interesting information which threatened to make any manuscript out of date. In the event, it was necessary to be firmly selective and to omit a great deal. In particular, I have made no attempt to discuss in any detail the constitutional and legal reforms in the USSR, many of which were still being debated when this book went to press. Nor have I tried to describe in any detail the restructuring of the apparatus and departments of the Communist Party Central Committee which were in some state of flux when this book was completed. The account given in chapter 2 of the control over propaganda therefore relates mainly to the recent past.

In preparing this book, I have had help from a number of people. Professor John Erickson encouraged me to pursue this project in its earliest stages. I am indebted to the Alexander Baykov Library of Birmingham University, and especially to its former librarian, Jenny Brine, for valuable assistance in locating Soviet publications. Special appreciation is due to Stephen White, who not only read the manuscript but drew my attention to Soviet sources which I would otherwise have missed, and helped to locate most of the pictures. And my particular thanks must go to Margot Light, who read successive drafts of the manuscript and made detailed comments on all of them.

Some of the material presented here first appeared in *The World Today* in June 1985 and in *The Journal of Communist Studies* for September 1987. I am grateful for permission to make use of it. Except where otherwise indicated, all the translations in this book are my own.

David Wedgwood Benn

The author and publishers are grateful to Dr Stephen White of the University of Glasgow for permission to reproduce plates 1, 2, 3, 4, 5, 6, 7, 9, 10, 11, 14, 16, 17, 18, 20, 21, 22, and to the Novosti Press Agency for plates 8, 12, 13, 15 and 19.

— канал (secondary) primary) sources?
в архиве, repuqueka?
— использование

Note on Sources

Most of the Soviet books in the notes to chapters are cited under the name of their authors or editors. In some cases they have been cited by their title alone, either because they do not have an author or editor (as for example with the *Programme of the Communist Party of the Soviet Union*) or because they are normally traceable in libraries through their titles.

A number of the Soviet publications referred to have rather similar titles and some of them form part of an annual, or occasional, series. It may therefore be helpful to mention some of the publications which have been most frequently quoted:

Spravochnik propagandista (A propagandist's handbook). This is an annual publication.

Spravochnik sekretarya pervichnoi partiinoi organizatsii (Handbook for a secretary of a primary party organization). This appears irregularly; quotations are from the editions of 1977 and 1980.

Since 1968 an annual publication concerned with propaganda has appeared in Moscow under the auspices of the Academy of Social Sciences attached to the Central Committee of the Soviet Communist Party. The first three volumes, for 1968, 1969 and 1970, appeared under the title *Voprosy teorii i praktiki massovykh form propagandy* (Questions of the theory and practice of mass forms of propaganda). The fourth volume, in 1971, appeared under the slightly different title *Voprosy teorii i praktiki massovykh sredstv propagandy* (Questions of the theory and practice of the mass media of propaganda). The series was then continued under the title *Voprosy teorii i metodov ideologicheskoi raboty* (Questions of the theory and methods of ideological work), of which volume 1 appeared in 1972. From 1983 the series was renamed *Voprosy teorii i praktiki ideologicheskoi raboty* (Questions of the theory and practice of ideological work).

In addition, the following abbreviations have been used:

LG   *Literaturnaya gazeta* (*The Literary Gazette*). Weekly organ of the Board of the Union of Writers of the USSR.

PS, PO   *Politicheskoye samoobrazovanie* (*Political Self-Education*). Journal of the Central Committee of the Communist Party of the Soviet Union. As from October 1987 it was renamed *Politicheskoye obrazovanie* (*Political Education*). Until the end of 1987 it appeared 12 times a year. Since the beginning of 1988 it has been published 18 times a year.

BSE   *Bol'shaya Sovetskaya Entsiklopedia* (*Large Soviet Encyclopedia*).

PSS   V. I. Lenin, *Polnoye sobranie sochinenii* (Lenin, *Complete Works*, 5th Russian edn, Moscow, 55 vols).

CW   V. I. Lenin, *Collected Works* (English edn, Moscow, 1960–70, 45 vols).

1

Persuasion, Soviet Politics and Reform

заагач

The ideology and psychology of stagnation affected many aspects of our lives.
From a Soviet journal, April 1987, *PS*, 4 (1987), p. 16

The question is of the sincerity of our policy.
Mikhail Gorbachev, April 1987, *Pravda*, 17 April 1987

This book sets out to explore some of the interconnections between persuasion and Soviet politics. It aims, more specifically, to examine the Soviet approach, both past and present, to the question of *method* in relation to propaganda, persuasion and the influencing of public opinion. It also has two other purposes: to draw attention to specialist literature in this field which has appeared in the USSR over the years; and lastly, to explore, at least in a preliminary way, the relationship between two vast and extremely complex questions, namely the nature of Soviet beliefs and the nature of persuasion.

All these questions are, needless to say, intimately bound up with the changes which began in Russia in 1985 following the accession to power of Mikhail Gorbachev - changes which became associated with the term *glasnost'*, or 'openness'. We will return to those changes in a moment. But this book is not about the reforms of the 1980s as such: it concentrates on the long-standing problems which led up to those reforms. For if it can be shown that the earlier Soviet approach to propaganda was not working well, then this in itself helps to explain the pressure for change. Much of the initial research for the chapters which follow was done many years ago – at a time when the name of Mikhail Gorbachev and the now famous expression *glasnost'* were virtually unknown in the outside world. And when explaining the purpose of this book, it may be helpful, first of all, to explain how the idea behind it originated.

For many years prior to November 1982, when Leonid Brezhnev died, the USSR was widely regarded in the Western world with a considerable degree of cynicism – as a repressive, inefficient, partly corrupt and, of course, notoriously secretive society, ruled by an elderly, conservative leadership, assumed to be mainly interested in the preservation of its own power and motivated by expansionist aims in foreign policy. The Soviet system was widely depicted abroad as a failure in virtually every field except that of military power. Its prolonged survival was often explained (at least by implication) as being due to nothing much more than coercion – combined with an elaborate system of censorship, secrecy and propaganda (sometimes referred to by such expressions as 'thought control' or 'indoctrination'). Furthermore, the Soviet regime, so it appeared, was not merely able to disregard the public opinion of its own people: it actively sought – with a considerable degree of success – to shape that opinion in accordance with its own wishes. Indeed, the regime's preoccupation with propaganda was seen as one element in the Soviet threat. The regime was even more to be distrusted when it preached detente than when it preached confrontation.

The idea behind this book originated from an attempt to probe this stereotype, insofar as it related to propaganda. It was not a question of wanting to show the Brezhnev regime in a more 'charitable' light: but simply of trying to understand the Soviet mind better. For if propaganda or 'indoctrination' really did play such a key role in Soviet political thinking, then this naturally raised the question: what exactly did the methods or techniques of such indoctrination consist of? What was the recipe, real or supposed, for success? And did Soviet specialized literature throw any light on this? Hence our concentration on the Soviet approach to propaganda *method*, which takes up the major part of this book. The problems of getting to understand this subject will be discussed in more detail in the next chapter. But the initial research suggested that the subject was vastly under-explored; and that Soviet propaganda was far more beset with problems than was often realized.

Meanwhile in the mid-1980s the USSR (as well as the Western image of the USSR) began to show signs of change. Information from Russia became far more readily available; and much of it confirmed the earlier tentative conclusions of this inquiry. Soviet spokesmen increasingly emphasized that the previous system had created a mass of difficulties – not least in the media. Soviet society, after a long period of stagnation, showed signs of approaching a crossroads and of entering a period of what might be called 'creative flux'. Reform was still very far from being an irreversible, accomplished fact: indeed there was repeated talk of domestic opposition to reform. At grass-roots level, life in the USSR may not have changed very much; and there was no sign that the country was moving towards political democracy of the Western type. Nevertheless, the change at the top had been dramatic. The accession to power of Mikhail Gorbachev immediately destroyed the image of a 'gerontocratic' Soviet leadership. Nor did Gorbachev or his advisers fit the stereotype of narrow-minded, undynamic, conservative bureaucrats. Gorbachev became personally involved in launching the most radical changes in the USSR since the Stalin era - changes which, if carried through to completion, would go a long way towards undoing the Stalin legacy.

Gorbachev's programme of *perestroika*, or restructuring, was set out at length in a series of resolutions approved by the special conference of the Soviet Communist Party held in Moscow from 28 June to 1 July 1988.[1] These resolutions envisaged not only a drastic reform and decentralization of the economy, but a no less basic reform of the political system. Abuses of personal power by leaders - which had characterized Soviet politics ever since the Stalin era - were to be curtailed by a new rule to prevent any individual, including the General Secretary of the Communist Party, from holding any one elective office for more than two five-year terms. (One delegate pointed out that such a rule would have obliged Stalin to retire in 1934 and Brezhnev to do so in 1974.)[2] The Communist Party itself, whilst retaining its ultimate supremacy, was to devolve many of its powers concerned with the everyday running of the country to a new two-tier of Supreme Soviet, or parliament; and the powers of the President were to be strengthened. Elections to these bodies, as well as elections to posts in the Communist Party, were generally to be held with a choice of candidates. A far-reaching reform of the legal system was to be embarked upon - based on the principle that 'everything is permitted which is not forbidden by law'. Among the stated aims of this reform were the protection of the independence of judges and the safeguarding of the rights of the individual against the state. (Gorbachev had earlier said that a new law on freedom of conscience and the right of religious believers was being prepared.)[3] In relation to foreign policy, the conference endorsed Gorbachev's concept of 'new thinking' - a concept which laid great stress on interdependence rather than confrontation in East–West relations, in the age of nuclear weapons.[4] Over and above that, the celebrated principle of *glasnost'* was to be embodied in a new law which would, for the first time, define what was secret and what the Soviet citizen was entitled to know.

In the autumn of 1988 the Soviet Constitution was amended to provide a framework for these reforms. They were criticized, even in the USSR, for falling short of democracy. But it became increasingly difficult, even for the sceptics, to dismiss the reforms as being purely cosmetic. Nowhere was change more striking than in the Soviet media - the subject which directly concerns us here. Unsolved problems and open clashes of opinion were paraded in public in a manner totally unknown in Russia, at least since the 1920s. Nationalist grievances - in Kazakhstan, in the Baltic republics and, above all, in Armenia and Azerbaijan - were no longer treated as taboo subjects. The Stalin era was opened up to scrutiny. Some of Stalin's most prominent victims (including Nikolai Bukharin, one of the most prominent Soviet leaders of the 1920s) were officially rehabilitated. And a new precedent was created when, on 16 May 1988, Moscow television carried a long documentary programme which included film of a notorious show trial of the 1930s.[5] At the party conference itself, a delegate got some applause when he called for the resignation of, among others, President Andrei Gromyko and the Editor of *Pravda*, Viktor Afanasyev. *Pravda* duly reported both the speech and the applause; although Afanasyev later got the chance to reply.[6] The Soviet media also reported a highly critical speech delivered by the former Politburo member Boris Yel'tsin who had, less than a week before, attacked his former Politburo colleague, Yegor Ligachev, in an interview on BBC television. But Yel'tsin's critics, including Ligachev, also spoke.[7]

These examples did not stand alone; and they seemed to indicate not just a change in the current party line but a much more profound change in the whole Soviet intellectual climate. Thus, early in May 1988, the Moscow *Literaturnaya gazeta* had reported a conference on religion where one of the official speakers had talked about removing what he called 'the halo of infallibility from scientific atheism' and had urged a dialogue between believers and communists.[8] In the same month, the paper had, for the very first time, published a lengthy extract from George Orwell's *1984*, which was scheduled for publication in Russia in its entirety. The paper reprinted Orwell's chapter on 'The Ministry of Truth'; and advised its readers to study the book 'in a thoughtful and unprejudiced way'.[9] In the meantime, Soviet foreign policy came to be officially regarded as a legitimate subject for criticism. At a press conference in Moscow in June, the then Chief of the Soviet General Staff, Marshal Sergei Akhromeyev, indicated that his country's military build-up in the 1970s and 1980s might have been mishandled. Another speaker on the same occasion criticized Brezhnev's foreign policy for its 'total absence of *glasnost'* and disregard for public opinion.'[10] The press also published the views of those who held that the Soviet intervention in Afghanistan in 1979 had been a mistake.[11] Such criticisms had never been reported before.

The momentum of *glasnost'* in the media accelerated dramatically in the summer of 1988. But it had begun to be visible quite some time earlier. Already in the autumn of the previous year, *Literaturnaya gazeta* had printed a virtually unprecedented article on how Americans perceived the Soviet Union. The article explored the perceptions underlying the 'evil empire' rhetoric; and it went on to say that this rhetoric could more or less be paraphrased in the following words:

> The Soviet Union is a totalitarian state. Its entire life is regulated from above: which factories and collective farms are to produce what, what clothes people are to wear, what music they can listen to, what pictures they can paint, who can and cannot travel abroad, and so forth. Elections are only a formality because only one candidate is nominated per seat, criticism of the government or of particular leaders is forbidden, newspapers print only articles and letters which contain praise of the existing system ... The socialist economic system has not vindicated itself: economic growth rates are low, the standard of living lags far behind that of most Western countries, the country faces constant shortages of food and industrial products. Finally, since the country is a godless one, and religion is placed under pressure, moral standards are low, hypocrisy and double standards are widespread.

'This grim picture or parts of it exists in the minds of many Americans,' the author observed. Yet - and perhaps most remarkably of all - he did not dismiss it as preposterous but made the comment that 'if we look once again at this list and attempt to translate it into more decorous language, then we see many things which are familiar to us from present-day material in our press, describing ... the "period of stagnation"' (the now conventional name for the Brezhnev period). They were things, he said, against which the Soviet Communist Party and government were now campaigning. The article did, indeed, refer to what it called American paranoia and quoted polls which showed Americans to be very poorly informed about the USSR. All the same, the author insisted that 'we cannot brush aside foreign public opinion, particularly mass attitudes in the US' and that 'it would be wrong to ignore the influence of our internal affairs on world politics'.[12]

Events in the Soviet Union in the late 1980s therefore suggested at least the possibility of a major shift in the power-base of the system – away from coercion and in the direction of persuasion. Hence their relevance to the subject of this book. At the same time it would be far too simplistic to portray all these changes as a steady onward march towards politics of the Western type. To take only one example, Soviet dissidents opposed to the system as such were accorded no legal status and, even up to the present, are still sometimes arrested. The momentum of reform was subject to ebbs and flows, although it would no doubt be unwise to unduly influenced in one's judgement by short-term trends. However, the real question at issue is not a short-term one: it concerns the overall strategy of the reformers among the top Soviet leaders which began to evolve from 1985 onwards. And here, one has to make at least two important qualifications.

For one thing, and quite obviously, none of the reforming leaders showed any intention of abandoning the Soviet system as such. Gorbachev himself insisted that the Communist Party was 'the ruling party' and that 'we shall permit no one to go against socialism'.[13] Secondly, and perhaps a little less obviously, the Soviet reforms gave no sign of any 'end of ideology' of the kind so often predicted by Western observers in the past. Gorbachev, very far from de-emphasizing Marxism-Leninism, repeatedly spoke about the need for its further development. In 1986, in a speech to a conference in Moscow on the social sciences, he said that: 'Theory . . . is necessary for literally every forward step that we take. No practical question of any major importance can be resolved unless it is understood, and given a basis, in theory'.[14] This statement was more than a formality: it is not irrelevant to mention that the vast Soviet political education system was, at this time, not dismantled but re-organized and consolidated.

Given the commitment to the system and to the ideology, how were the ideas of the Soviet reformers to be interpreted? On this point the evidence is less than totally complete; and there were signs of disagreement – as well as 'creative flux' – in the thinking of the leaders themselves. But the outlines of a new approach were at least becoming discernible. The Soviet leaders had no desire to imitate either Western political institutions or Western capitalism. But they did appear to agree that the existing system in their own country was functioning badly; and that it required radical reform – but *within* the framework of its own principles. Gorbachev himself apparently kept an open mind about how deep this 'reform from within' would have to go: he spoke of the need 'to remove, layer by layer, the problems which have accumulated in all spheres of social life'.[15] But he also insisted on the need for a coherent, as opposed to a purely piecemeal, approach, saying that in the late 1970s and earlier 1980s 'the question acutely arose of devising a *strategy* for the development of Soviet society'. (emphasis added).[16]

The Soviet reforms, in their early stages, were generally seen in the outside world as nothing more than a renewed drive for economic modernization and efficiency. Subsequent events showed that this was an inadequate interpretation. One essential element in the proposed reforms consisted in encouraging greater initiative at grass-roots level. One of the most dangerous enemies, Gorbachev had said, was 'the habit of working "according to instructions"'.[17] He developed this argument further when, in a speech about economic reform, he told the Communist Party Central Committee that:

> We must realize that the time when management consisted of commands, prohibitions and exhortations has vanished into the past. It is now already clear to everybody that it is no longer possible to work with such methods. They are simply ineffective. To create a powerful system of motives and incentives . . . that is the imperative of the time.[18]

The incentives, Gorbachev also said, must be 'more powerful than under capitalism'; and must entail not only a restructuring of the centralized planning system but, it appeared, a new element of industrial democracy, involving, among other things, the right of the workers to have a voice in the selection of their managers.[19]

There was therefore a movement away from the old system based on commands from above. And it marked a radical innovation in strategy. The whole purpose of the reforms, so it was said, involved 'taking account of [people's] interests, influencing their interests, managing them and managing through them'.[20] This once again enhanced the role of persuasion and public opinion in Soviet politics. Furthermore it was increasingly being argued in Soviet pronouncements that openness and public accountability were inseparably connected with efficiency: indeed, the Chernobyl' nuclear power station disaster in April 1986 had been used to drive that point home. The reforming Soviet leaders also appeared to agree that economic stagnation could not be overcome unless the parallel problems of public apathy and intellectual stagnation were tackled at the same time. At all events, the issue of economic reform soon became linked to reforms of a much wider kind, embracing not only greater cultural freedom, but politics and ideology.

The summer of 1986 saw a markedly new atmosphere of debate at the congress of the Writers' Union.[21] Soon afterwards, Gorbachev publicly raised the question of political reform by saying that the *perestroika* (or 'restructuring') must extend to 'the democratization of society, of all spheres of our life – state organs, the economy and the social and cultural spheres'.[22] This was followed by proposals in the Soviet press – soon endorsed by Gorbachev himself – for the ending of one-candidate elections.[23] In the summer of 1987, a *Pravda* article took the argument even further. It referred to 'a transition from power in the name of the people to power exercised by the people itself' and went on to refer not only to the possibility of 'real choice' between candidates at elections but to the possibility of the Soviet public being able to make 'a comparison between opinions and

points of view and, in consequence [a comparison] between alternative
solutions to one or other problem'. This was a further sign of an intention
to give the Soviet public a greater voice in politics.   Yet another sign in
the same direction was the increasing emphasis in the Soviet press at this
time on the need to develop what was called 'a culture of discussion', that
is, the art of courteous, reasoned debate between people of different
opinions. In the words of this same *Pravda* article:

> It is important ... for the state and the collective to show toleration
> for different, or sometimes even mistaken points of view; and to
> provide guarantees for the protection of those who find themselves
> in a minority when some question is being discussed.
>
>   The point, in other words, is that the democratic principle of
> subordination to the majority should be implemented in a civilized
> manner, by methods which are ethically above reproach and which
> do not run counter to political honesty, social justice or elementary
> human decency.[24]

Yegor Ligachev, widely regarded as one of the more conservative
members of the ruling Politburo, had made a very similar point some
months earlier. A culture of discussion, he said 'is incompatible with the
sticking on of labels, with accusations of supposed deviations from socialism.
None of these methods have anything in common with true science or true
creativity or true Marxism-Leninism'.[25] However, the encouragement of
dialogue was apparently easier said than done. According to the then
editor-in-chief of the party's theoretical journal *Kommunist*: 'It must frankly
be said that the holding of discussions under conditions of extended
democracy and openness is very, very far from being a simple matter. We
had forgotten how to debate; and a great deal had to be started, so to
speak, from scratch'.[26]

Diversity of opinion was therefore, within limits, to be not merely
tolerated but actively encouraged. Gorbachev himself gave it the name of
'socialist pluralism'.[27] Although, in principle, all debate had to be within
the framework of support for the system, considerable grey areas existed.
Even openly anti-communist views were allowed – as, for instance, when
the Soviet authorities organized a television link-up with the US, in which
the American speakers said some hard-hitting things about communism.[28]
Gorbachev himself insisted that democracy must not be confused with
anarchy and that 'demagogues' must be resisted; but he added that it
would be wrong to 'succumb to the temptations of prohibitionism'.[29]

All this provided the theoretical underpinning for a deliberate decision
taken at the top to foster debate at lower levels. But reform appeared to
extend not only to economics, culture and politics. It was also reflected in

ideology. In 1986, Gorbachev expressly abandoned any claim by the Soviet Communist Party to absolute infallibility. In a speech in Moscow to a visiting Yugoslav communist delegation, he said that 'no party possesses a certificate to the absolute truth'.[30] This came close to saying that Marxism-Leninism was itself open to more than one legitimate interpretation. In a speech the following year delivered to an international gathering of communists to mark the 70th anniversary of the revolution, Gorbachev attacked what he called 'the arrogance of omniscience' from which 'neither dialogue nor productive discussion results'. It was, he went on, impossible to assess the contemporary world 'on the basis of postulates which arose in the fifties and sixties or even in the thirties.' 'It is necessary to make a fresh reading of the theoretical heritage of our predecessors for the sake of the social emancipation of man.'[31]

The evidence adduced so far would therefore seem to suggest not an abandonment of the system or the ideology but an all-out effort to revitalize both – with a distinctly new reliance on dialogue, debate and public opinion. It appeared that the Soviet reformers, far from seeing ideology as an obstacle to reform, believed on the contrary that *only* Marxism–Leninism – properly applied – could provide the essential long-term strategy for creating a society with a permanent mass appeal. That appeal would, presumably, be based on an appeal to people's interests; and this, so it seemed, was the way a reformist leadership sought to reconcile the pursuit of democratization with the continuance of one-party rule. The reformers appeared to see the coercive methods of Soviet rule in the past not as proof that the system could not work, but as something which had prevented the enormous potential of the system from being fully realized. As Gorbachev expressed it: 'We shall not sacrifice the true values of socialism by one iota. On the contrary, we shall enrich them by freeing ourselves of everything that distorted the humanistic purpose of our system.' At the same time Marxism–Leninism – like much else in Soviet society – was to undergo a fundamental restructuring (or *perestroika*) within the framework of its own tenets.[32] The reformers appeared to regard ideology not so much in a dogmatic sense – as a set of propositions which it was forbidden to challenge – but, rather, in a heuristic sense – as a method of inquiry and as a key to the working out of a strategy. Gorbachev himself deplored the 'deficit of new thinking' in the modern world,[33] and condemned 'the ideology and psychology of stagnation'.[34] That being so, his disclaimer of infallibility becomes easier to understand.

It could of course be objected – both by Western sceptics and by Soviet conservatives – that this new approach marked a tacit abandonment of the traditional ideology and an admission that Marxism–Leninism had been wrong. The matter is not, however, quite so straightforward; and the rightness or wrongness of communist ideology is less relevant than might be supposed. For the writings of Marx, Engels and Lenin had to a large extent concentrated on an analysis and critique of the old order and (in Lenin's case) on the strategy of revolution. None of them had contained any very detailed guidelines as to the running of a future socialist, or communist, society. It would therefore be difficult to show that the reforms in the USSR in the 1980s were specifically incompatible with the ideas of the founding fathers of Marxism. The new Soviet emphasis on dialogue rather than confrontation certainly marked a change from earlier times. But this change could itself be defended – even on purely ideological grounds. It could be argued that the earlier, more confrontational approach was no longer capable of solving current problems; that it had failed to halt the stagnation of Soviet society, that it had contributed to the escalation of the international arms race, and therefore that it was not furthering the Soviet or communist cause. It may lastly be noted with regard to ideology that much of the thrust of the Gorbachev reforms consisted not in renouncing traditional Soviet ideas – but in trying to put into practice some of the ideas that had always been proclaimed in theory. The Soviet leaders in the later 1980s had much to say about the harm caused by 'the gap between word and deed'. This was not just a cliché: for it should be remembered that terms like 'democracy', 'legality' and 'peace' had been very much part of the vocabulary of Stalin. The very term *glasnost'* had been used by Lenin;[35] and the principle of 'the broad extension of *glasnost''* and 'constant responsiveness to public opinion' were expressly incorporated into article 9 of the 1977 Soviet Constitution, adopted in the Brezhnev era.[36] To some extent, then, the 'restructuring' of Soviet ideology simply involved attempts to translate theory (or fiction) into reality.

This book is not primarily concerned with discussing whether the Soviet reformers will succeed. The purpose above was simply to try to make their thinking intelligible. It need hardly be pointed out that the problems which they face could be formidable; and these problems can be stated quite shortly. How far, even in principle, is the pursuit of democracy compatible with one-party rule? What would happen if the will of the voters were seen to be at loggerheads with the will of the ruling party? This is the most fundamental difficulty of all – and is likely to be emphasized both by Western sceptics and by Soviet conservatives. But it has to be considered alongside certain other difficulties. How far, for instance, is it possible for Soviet society to become more pluralistic without the risk of becoming centrifugal – bearing in mind that the USSR is made up of more than 100 nationalities and that the Russians make up only about half the total population? How much public consensus is there in favour of a radical economic reform programme, with all its attendant risks of drastic price rises and higher unemployment? And supposing, just hypothetically, that the Soviet system were to collapse or disintegrate, where is the guarantee that it would be replaced by a more democratic system? Even to mention these questions may be enough to show what enormous issues they raise. We shall not try to answer these questions in what follows here. Indeed, it would be unwise to do so because the questions are likely to be answered in practice, by events in the years immediately ahead. We need only note that the feasibility of reform of the Soviet system from within – which was previously a matter of concern to no more than a narrow circle of scholars – has now, thanks to changes in the Soviet leadership, been moved close to the top of the international agenda.

But these reforms – even though they are not the prime concern of this book – do have the most direct connection with this book's theme. Attempted reforms, whether ultimately successful or not, almost always generate discussion and produce new information. This is what happened in the Soviet Union after the mid–1980s and it helps to illuminate the problems which we shall be examining. Those problems – concerned with the roles of coercion, persuasion, propaganda and public opinion – will inevitably subsist in the Soviet Union in one form or another, whatever the political future may hold. But they raise a number of very basic issues – and it is to these that we shall turn in the next chapter.

Notes

1 These resolutions were printed in *Pravda*, 5 July 1988.
2 Ibid., 30 June 1988, p. 7 (Georgii Arbatov).
3 Ibid., 30 April 1988, p. 2.
4 The development and implications of this 'new thinking' are analysed in Stephen Shenfield, *The Nuclear Predicament: Explorations in Soviet Ideology* (Routledge & Kegan Paul and the Royal Institute of International Affairs, London, 1987).
5 See *Pravda*, 17 May 1988, p. 6.
6 Ibid., 1 July 1988, p. 7 (V. I. Mel'nikov) and 2 July 1988, p. 12 (Afanasyev).
7 Ibid., 2 July 1988, p. 8 (Yel'tsin) and p. 11 (Ligachev). Yel'tsin's BBC interview was broadcast on 30 May.
8 *Literaturnaya gazeta* (hereafter *LG*) 4 May 1988, p. 7: (quoting V. Zots, of the Higher Party School of the Communist Party of the Ukraine).
9 *LG*, 11 May 1988, p. 15.
10 *Pravda*, 26 June 1988, p. 4 (quoting *inter alia* Marshal Akhromeyev and G. A. Borovik).
11 See, e.g., *LG*, 16 March 1988, p. 10, where Academician Oleg Bogomolov disclosed that he had signed a protest to Brezhnev in January 1980 regarding

the Soviet intervention. See also ibid., 29 June 1988, p. 14 (quoting Professor N. Molchanov).

12 *LG*, 28 October 1987, pp. 14–15 (Nikolai Popov).

13 See, e.g., *Pravda*, 1 July 1988, p. 8 (as to 'the ruling party'); ibid., 30 September 1987, p. 2 (as to socialism).

14 Ibid., 2 October 1986, p. 1.

15 Ibid., 2 August 1986, p. 1.

16 Ibid., 20 September 1986, p. 1.

17 Ibid., 5 December 1986, p. 1.

18 Ibid., 26 June 1987, p. 5.

19 Provision for the election of managers, generally through competition, was made in article 6 of the Law on the State Enterprise published in *Pravda* and other Soviet newspapers on 1 July 1987. The same article provided, however, that the Communist Party committee at the enterprise was to have a supervisory role.

20 *Politicheskoye obrazovanie*, (hereafter *PO*) 10 (1987), p. 108 (V. Ivanov).

21 An extensive, although abridged, verbatim report of the congress debates appeared in *Literaturnaya gazeta* on 25 June and 2 July 1986.

22 *Pravda*, 20 September 1986, p. 2.

23 See, for example, *LG*, 17 September 1986, p. 10 (V. Vasilyev); also *LG*, 1 January 1987, p. 11, *passim* (D. Likhachev).

24 *Pravda*, 24 August 1987, p. 3 (E. Kuz'min).

25 Ibid., 2 October 1986, p. 2.

26 V. I. Zubarev, et al. (eds), *XXVII s"yezd KPSS i zadachi kafedr obshchestvennykh nauk* (Moscow, 1987), p. 77 (I. T. Frolov).

27 *Pravda*, 30 September 1987, p. 1.

28 For example, during one Soviet–American television exchange which was broadcast live and seen by a mass audience, the US Senator Daniel Moynihan told his Soviet listeners that they lived in a 'human rights hell' where restrictions on emigration and press freedom were worse than those imposed in Tsarist Russia: see *The Times*, 16 October 1987.

29 *Pravda*, 14 October 1987, p. 2.

30 Ibid., 11 December 1986, p. 2. A joint communiqué issued at the end of these Soviet–Yugoslav talks affirmed the need for 'a constructive dialogue based on equal rights and excluding the monopoly by any party of the truth'; ibid., 13 December 1986, p. 4.

31 Ibid., 5 November 1987, pp. 2–3.

32 See ibid., 2 August 1986, p. 1, where Gorbachev said that the *perestroika* must extend to 'the spiritual-ideological sphere'.

33 *LG*, 5 November 1986, p. 1.

34 *Pravda*, 18 January 1987, p. 1.

35 For example, Lenin had once described *glasnost'* as 'a sword which heals the wounds that it inflicts': see V. I. Lenin, *Polnoye sobranie sochinenii* (*Complete Works*, 5th Russian edn, Moscow; hereafter *PSS*), vol. 23, p. 53.

36 *Konstitutsiya (Osnovnoi Zakon) Soyuza Sovetskikh Sotsialisticheskikh Respublik* (Moscow, 1977), article 9. In English-language editions of this document, the term *glasnost'* was at first translated by the not entirely appropriate word 'publicity', rather than by the word 'openness' which became the standard English rendering of *glasnost'* later on.

2

How to Persuade?

I think these elements of failure are less attributable to faults of detail than
to an impatient philosophy, which aims at creating a new world without
sufficient preparation in the opinions and feelings of ordinary men and
women.

> Bertrand Russell, in *The Practice and Theory of Bolshevism* (1920, p. 7),
> after a visit to Soviet Russia

Introduction

The subject of persuasion and Soviet politics is far from new – as the
above quotation demonstrates. And the kinds of question which underly
this book can perhaps most simply be explained at the outset by three
specific examples.

Let us take, first of all, a serious social problem, non-political in itself,
and in no way peculiar to Russia – namely alcoholism. Doctors in the West
generally assume, both on pragmatic and on moral grounds, that the
treatment of this disease, if it is not based on seeking to win the patient's
co-operation, is likely to be ineffective. The Soviet authorities, however,
have traditionally set out from rather different assumptions: *their* system
has been much more ready to override the wishes of the individual for his
own, or the collective, good. So the compulsory treatment of alcoholism
(by order of a court) has been attempted for many years.[1] The evidence,
however, indicates that this has been far from an unqualified success.
According to the view of a Soviet judge in the 1970s: 'Life demonstrates
that it is not always highly effective. Few people are successfully cured.'
He then quoted figures showing a much higher success rate from voluntary
treatment.[2] Compulsory treatment has continued to remain one of the

instruments for attempting to combat alcoholism. But a Soviet Minister of the Interior and former Chairman of the KGB, General Vitalii Fedorchuk, himself went on record as saying that the success rate from compulsory treatment was low and that 'the results of voluntary forms of treatment . . . are much more significant.'[3] The high incidence of alcoholism in the USSR led, in May 1985, to new and much more stringent measures to curb alcohol sale and distribution; but it is noteworthy that these new measures also envisaged an expansion of facilities for confidential treatment at places of work.[4] Meanwhile, a Soviet psychologist argued in 1987 that experience had shown that 'attempts to solve the problem of eradicating drunkenness mainly by administrative methods or methods of prohibition do not produce lasting results but, on the contrary, drive the disease inwards.'[5] This approach indicated a change in Soviet thinking; and at about the same time, it became known that the Soviet authorities were seeking to learn from experience in the United States and that a Soviet branch of 'Alcoholics Anonymous' had been founded with American co-operation.[6]

Let us now turn to a different kind of problem, which is also bound up with the problem of persuasion: the birth-rate. The Soviet authorities, faced for many years with a slowing-down of the birth-rate (especially among the European populations of the USSR) and concerned that this will lead to a future manpower shortage, have over a long period been trying to persuade their citizens to have larger families. The 1980s did in fact see the beginnings of an upturn in the birth-rate. But the response to official propaganda seems to have been small. It has been suggested that this is because many Soviet married couples, precisely because they want to protect their newly-won living standards, are unwilling to shoulder the burden which a larger family entails. Therefore, official exhortations have hardly provided any solution. Indeed, in the view of one Western specialist writing in the 1970s, the Soviet authorities have little scope for engineering an increase in the population and would do better to tackle the manpower shortage in some other way, such as using the labour-force more efficiently.[7]

Our third – and even more familiar – example concerns the much-publicized official campaign in recent years to improve labour discipline by eliminating absenteeism and slacking and improving overall work performance. There is, at the time of writing, every sign that the Soviet leadership is displaying a political will over this problem, which was not seen in the Brezhnev era, and that 'discipline' has been elevated into a priority of the first order. But it does not follow that this goal can be achieved – or that the Soviet leaders think it can be achieved – by compulsion alone. Public support may prove essential, if results are to be lasting. Thus, one Soviet industrial relations specialist, writing in the mid-

1970s, stressed the need to create a positive motivation among the work-force and noted that 'It is in practice impossible to achieve good results at work in a modern enterprise if the mass of workers do not want this'.[8] Evidence was published in the Soviet press, also in the 1970s, showing that whereas encouragement led to an improvement in discipline in about 87 per cent of cases, punitive measures produced an improvement in only 9 per cent of the sample.[9] Even when Yurii Andropov embarked on his celebrated discipline campaign after succeeding to power on Brezhnev's death, articles in the Soviet press continued to note that mere coercion would not solve the problem. 'Bad organization' was frequently blamed as one of the reasons for poor work performance.[10] 'Administrative methods alone' (that is, coercion) would not suffice, according to a writer in *Pravda* who also noted: 'The sternest measures ... will prove ineffective unless the causes and conditions which give rise to these violations are removed.'[11]

The problems of alcoholism, the birth-rate and industrial relations are not the main theme of this book. They are quoted mainly as a useful starting-point for our discussion; each illustrates on a small scale certain issues which are basic to any examination of propaganda or persuasion. In all these cases the real issue – and the one which will concern us throughout this book – is not the laudability or otherwise of the particular goal, but the realism or otherwise of the method chosen to achieve it. The three examples have been chosen so as to bring this into relief. There is nothing dishonourable or indeed peculiarly communist or 'totalitarian' about a government trying to combat alcoholism, influence the birth-rate or improve labour productivity. The crux of the matter in each case is: what methods are in practice likely to succeed? How, in general, does a government get its citizens to moderate their drinking habits, have larger families or work more conscientiously? Regardless of whether coercion is a morally acceptable approach, will it actually work? Does mere exhortation offer a better prospect of success? And if the answer to both these questions is negative, what is the moral which ought to be drawn?

Closely bound up with this question is another one, already touched upon, namely the question of consent. This again emerges from our three examples. They each underline the (rather obvious) truth that even in a Soviet-type society, which has sometimes been described as 'totalitarian', the authorities are far from being all-powerful. That is to say, like their opposite numbers in other countries, they will, under certain circumstances and for the attainment of certain goals, be obliged to rely on winning their citizens' co-operation as a matter of sheer practical necessity. Failure to get such co-operation may, at least in the long run, jeopardize the achievement of the goals.

The winning of consent is sometimes a matter of basic importance.

Nowhere is it more directly relevant than in relation to the subject under discussion in this book, political propaganda. This, by definition, is intended to make an impact not just on behaviour but on attitudes and opinions. But one then has to ask: how far and under what conditions is it practicable to get an individual or group to adopt a set of opinions against their will or without their co-operation? And even if coercive or other techniques exist for moulding opinion, whilst so to speak 'by-passing' the need for consent, what are they?

It is useful to keep such questions in mind when embarking on our main theme, which is the approach to propaganda and public opinion adopted by the Soviet leadership. The general Soviet standpoint in the past on these issues has been officially expounded many times. The following statement, made during the Brezhnev era by Viktor Afanasyev, who in 1976 became the Editor-in-Chief of *Pravda*, is probably as clear as any:

> Our enemies not infrequently criticize the Communist Party for monopolizing the guidance of the political information system . . . However, the guidance of this important sphere of public life is both the party's right and its obligation . . . Our party is the ruling party; and it is therefore called upon to carry out the guidance of all spheres of life in a socialist society, including the ideological sphere . . . the defence of the party's policy and ideology is at the same time also the defence of the most sacred ideas and interests of the people.[12]

So, according to this view, the guidance of public opinion from above is absolutely necessary. It is also quite feasible, as another Soviet writer, V. K. Paderin, once argued: 'The formation of public opinion is a process amenable to management. Here an enormous role is played by the ideological activity of the CPSU [Soviet Communist Party] – by a systematic, well-thought out influence on people's awareness and behaviour.'[13]

Statements of this kind are certainly not new and indeed Soviet-style persuasion has already been analysed from a number of different angles. A good deal has been written about what Soviet communicators are trying to do and why they are trying to do it, about the illiberal aspects of the system and, not least, about the censorship. More recently a number of previously unavailable sociological findings have been published in English about the impact which official propaganda makes on the Soviet citizen. All this, needless to say, is highly important and closely related to but distinct from the subject of this book, the question of propaganda *method* – or what one might term the '*how*' of persuasion in general and Soviet persuasion in particular. Quite regardless of whether the 'guidance' or 'management' of public opinion is a good or a bad thing, how if at all can it effectively be achieved? Have Soviet persuaders worked out a clear strategy for this purpose, and if so what is it? This is the crux of the problem.

There was a time, during the Stalin period and immediately afterwards, when the answers to such questions might have seemed relatively simple – both to the Soviet leaders and to their opponents. It could have been argued in the light of the evidence then available that any authoritarian regime which possessed a monopolistic control extending to education, information, the media, literature, the arts, the police and the armed forces as well as most of the rewards and penalties in society, possessed virtually all the tools it needed for the shaping of individual or mass opinion, at least in the long run. The 'method' of persuasion might have appeared to consist precisely in this monopoly (to which Afanasyev alluded). And there is no reason to doubt that control of the kind just described can indeed, under certain conditions, be a major factor in the shaping of opinions.

More recent experience has however shown that this is by no means always the case; and that public attitudes are not nearly so pliable as might once have been supposed. The history of Spain under Franco and of Iran under the Shah are two illustrations of how a prolonged censorship of the media (even if sometimes in a mild form) totally failed to make the intended lasting impact on public opinion. Sustained and coercive indoctrination campaigns in China under Mao Zedong did not prevent the later emergence of dissident protests. The Dubček reform movement in Czechoslovakia in 1968 came as the sequel to 20 years of propaganda, censorship and control on the Soviet model, which evidently did nothing to make the population any better disposed towards the system. The same thing applies with even greater force to the events which precipitated the rise of Solidarity in Poland in the summer of 1980. In this case, censorship of the media, very far from saving the then Polish leadership, merely compounded the leadership's loss of credibility and, from the latter's point of view, proved positively disastrous. It is therefore apparent that no system of purely external controls imposed from above will, by itself, guarantee successful indoctrination.

Any discussion of propaganda method in a Soviet context therefore has to go further. One has to ask what methods or techniques the Soviet system had evolved which went beyond the controls just described. It becomes relevant to look at a sizeable, although often little known, volume of Soviet literature on this subject – much of it dating from the Brezhnev era. What assumptions did these writers make about the role of propaganda in relation to public opinion? What practical advice did they offer specifically about propaganda method? How did it tally with the Soviet sociological findings about the impact of the official message on the Soviet public?

How did it compare with the sort of advice on persuasion techniques given by Western specialists in this field? And how, taken together, did all this tie up with the crucial issue of consent already mentioned?

A discussion of these questions forms the main core of this book; and is, I believe, relevant to a number of wider issues. First, it can perhaps help to demythologize the subject. It has not been unknown for propaganda itself to become a cause of myth and misunderstanding. One has only to recall the celebrated Nazi claim that Germany lost the First World War, not because her armies were defeated, but because her morale was sapped by the techniques of British propaganda.[14] It is sometimes useful to credit an adversary with skills he does not possess. And it is particularly important to bear this in mind in view of some of the traditional Western stereotypes about the Soviet Union. The Soviet Union is, in some contexts (such as its military power) commonly presented as a formidable danger. In other contexts (such as its agricultural performance) it is presented as not merely inefficient but inherently so. Without entering into a general discussion about these two images – of Soviet threat and Soviet failure – one might still ask: which of these two images is, or was, more apposite when assessing the Soviet propaganda effort? The question is all the more relevant because of the conflicting answers which are sometimes given. Soviet propaganda has sometimes been described as a 'secret weapon' or as an instrument of 'thought control', which implies a substantial degree of official success in shaping public opinion. At other times (especially in the past) Soviet propaganda has been regarded as both inept and dreary; and it has been claimed that hardly anyone in the USSR in fact believes in the Marxist-Leninist ideology any longer. It may at least contribute to clarification if one looks at what Soviet communicators have themselves had to say about propaganda.

Secondly, as to Soviet thinking on this subject, there are further questions which may usefully be asked. Did it have a hidden rationale which has perhaps been imperfectly understood? Or was it perhaps characterized by a lack of realism? Closely related to this is the relationship in Soviet society between coercion and persuasion. How far are they, or are they not, complementary? The ruthless and sometimes vicious way in which force was used under the Soviet system in the past should not be ignored or minimized. (Indeed, it was hardly a matter for suprise that the 'human rights' issue in Russia attracted so much international attention. The Soviet leaders were hardly in a position to object to such scrutiny, having so often held up their society as a model worthy of imitation by others.) But this still leaves unanswered the question as to the relationship between propaganda and force. According to one possible line of interpretation, it is precisely the blending of coercion and persuasion which has given the system its peculiar strength and which provides one of the keys to an understanding of Soviet politics. A slightly different perspective would suggest, however, that the use of crude coercion in the past may to some extent have been symptomatic of an official inability to persuade; and that *this* is one of the keys to Soviet politics. For example, incarcerating dissidents in psychiatric hospitals is not in itself evidence of a method of indoctrination: it may simply have been a sign of powerlessness when attempted indoctrination failed.

A further question – peripheral, although not unrelated to the theme of this book – is that of East–West communication. What bearing does propaganda have on the issues of negotiation, bargaining, dialogue, 'ideological struggle', detente or possible nuclear confrontation between the opposing sides? Should it be seen as a partial substitute for the use of force, which can perhaps offer one side of the prospect of 'victory on the cheap'? Should it be seen as an added source of danger which makes confrontation more likely? How far is it simply a sterile exercise? Might it perhaps be made to serve a more constructive, even therapeutic, international purpose? We shall briefly return to this topic in the final chapter.

The questions just listed deserve to be more carefully scrutinized, even if they cannot be definitively answered. All of them are bound up with the narrower theme of this book, namely the 'how' of propaganda, the problem of method. And this in turn hinges very largely on perhaps the most basic issue of all – that of the power of propaganda in general. Under what circumstances can it be of crucial importance? And how far do people tend to be autonomous and resistant to persuasive manipulation? No persuasive 'method' is likely to be very realistic if it ignores these last questions. And they are also relevant to our inquiry for a quite distinct reason. Even if (as may well be possible) the Soviet system does enjoy a substantial degree of popular acceptance or support, it would not automatically follow that this was the result of official indoctrination. It must therefore be stressed at the outset that when this book examines the strengths and weaknesses of the Soviet approach to propaganda, it does not seek to draw any direct conclusions about Soviet public attitudes towards the system as such.

It remains to deal with one final preliminary point – as to terminology. This raises problems which go beyond mere semantics. The words 'propaganda', 'persuasion', 'indoctrination' and 'communication' recur in the pages of this book. None of them is ideally tailored to convey the intended meaning. Sometimes in everyday usage the first two terms are treated as near-synonyms. At other times they are used for the purpose of contrast, to refer to two fundamentally different kinds of activity: one might say, for instance, that the Nazis were obsessed with propaganda but indifferent to persuasion. The difference of meaning here is a real one.

But it is part of the subject to be explored and cannot, therefore, be disposed of by prior definition.

The expressions 'attitude-formation' or 'attitude-change' would be more precise, although perhaps less elegant, for our purpose. A rough definition of the activity which this book sets out to discuss would be: 'ways of attempting to influence people through their opinions and attitudes by means of communication not involving threats or inducements, fraud or concealment'. There may be room for disagreement as to whether fraud or concealment can be considered as methods of persuasion; it has been pointed out that the giving of false information or the withholding of true information is not a 'true' form of influence.[15] What is obvious, however, is that we are talking about something quite distinct from bribes, threats or force. As to this last point, it has succinctly been said that 'Propaganda does not change *conditions* but only *beliefs about* conditions.'[16] One might perhaps amend that statement to the effect that propaganda changes only 'beliefs about, and attitudes towards, conditions'; and it would then serve for the purposes needed here.

The concept of propaganda just outlined is not essentially different from the one now current in the Soviet Union. In the past, terminology was prone to get confused because of the traditional Bolshevik distinction between so-called 'propaganda' and 'agitation' – the former referring to complex theoretical ideas addressed to small groups; and the latter to a small number of simple ideas, or calls to action, addressed to the masses. This distinction, originally coined in 1892 by the Russian Marxist Plekhanov, was taken up ten years later by Lenin in his much-quoted pamphlet 'What Is to Be Done?';[17] and it was seen by the Bolsheviks as being of key importance at a time when the gap between committed party supporters and the population as a whole was wide. Today, despite vastly changed conditions, the distinction is still made by Soviet writers, between propaganda (concerned with explaining basic theory and long-term goals) and agitation (concerned with action to implement immediate policy goals) although it is said that the two 'are intimately fused and interwoven'.[18] But this distinction does not much matter for our purposes – because 'propaganda' is now used much more loosely by Soviet writers to refer to persuasive activities of all kinds. In its widest sense, according to a Soviet textbook of the 1970s, it denotes 'a special kind of social activity whose basic function is to disseminate knowledge, ideas, artistic values or other information for the purposes of moulding definitive views, notions or emotions and thereby exerting influence on people's behaviour'. In a slightly narrower sense, the term is used to mean 'activity aimed at spreading amongst the masses the ideologies of certain classes, parties or states'.[19] The necessary aim, in other words, is to influence opinions. It will be seen,

both here and later, that in the Soviet view propaganda is not in itself a
pejorative term. It is good or bad depending on the cause which it serves.
But that is a matter of attitude, not definition.

Soviet communication and its problems

Let us now turn to some of the more familiar features of Soviet
communication. We shall concentrate more on the past than on the present
– since the final shape of current reforms has yet to be determined.
Nevertheless, so far as the past is concerned, there are at least two
propositions which seem to command general agreement. First, ideologically
orientated propaganda under Communist Party direction was intended to
function as one of the key elements in the Soviet political system. Secondly,
the actual quality of the propaganda output was often poor; it was by no
means always calculated to win hearts and minds; and, particularly towards
the end of the Brezhnev era, it led to open expressions of concern on the
part of the Soviet leadership. Neither of these propositions is new. What
matters here is the possible interconnection between them.

The organization of Soviet propaganda

As to the first of these two points – the key role assigned to official
propaganda – the facts are not really in dispute. The traditional Soviet
propaganda effort was always extremely ambitious in its declared aims. It
was rigidly controlled, elaborately organized, conducted on a vast and
increasing scale and intended, in theory to reach every citizen without
exception. Its professed goals were (and perhaps still are) extraordinarily
far-reaching; and they went well beyond particular objectives, such as the
fulfilment of the five-year plan. From the early years of Bolshevik rule the
declared purpose was to educate a 'New Man' with a moral code superior
to that of any previous society. This was expressly stated in the 1961 party
programme and was substantially repeated in slightly different words in
the revised programme adopted at the party's 27th congress in March
1986, which declared it to be one of the party's tasks 'to educate the
working people in a spirit of high ideological integrity and dedication to
communism'.[20] If this means what it says, it presupposes the success of
persuasion, or attitude-formation, on a very large scale indeed.

The leadership's commitment to these goals at all times went hand in
hand with the running of a large propaganda apparatus with ramifications
extending to virtually all areas of Soviet society – not excluding members
of the Bolshoi Theatre, who themselves were reported to attend political

education classes.[21] For our purposes it will be enough to recall the basic principles of this apparatus rather than its details, which have been described many times before. As we have already seen, the principle of Communist Party guidance or control, very far from being concealed or played down by the authorities, was repeatedly and emphatically proclaimed. And this remains true, even though the methods of guidance or control have, since the mid-1980s, been undergoing substantial modification.

Certainly in the past, censorship of the media was extensively resorted to, even though the mechanisms of that censorship were largely kept secret. The very first Soviet decree on the press, which empowered the authorities to close newspapers, was passed only two days after the November 1917 revolution and was then said to be temporary. In fact, censorship was soon intensified and was quite publicly referred to until the early 1930s: the last known law on the subject was published in 1931.[22] In later years, the authorities became less open. But the existence of a censorship agency (the Main Directorate for the preservation of state secrets in the press, usually known by its abbreviated name, *Glavlit*) was repeatedly referred to over the years: it certainly existed as recently as August 1986, when a group of *Glavlit* officials received state decorations.[23] In February 1986 Gorbachev himself said that censorship existed – in order, as he put it, to prevent the publication of 'state and military secrets, the propaganda of war, violence and cruelty, personal insults or pornography'.[24] However, in the past, as can be seen from recent admissions in the Soviet press, the definition of secrecy was widely drawn. One example was the ban, later repealed, on any public mention of the existence of drug addiction in the USSR. The ban was said to have been imposed on the insistence of the Soviet Ministry of Health.[25]

To all this it should be added that censorship in the narrowly formal sense was only part of the story. Informal censorship was just as important. For example, as the Soviet press now frankly says, writers were often subject to interference and pressure to change their manuscripts.[26] Journalists would resort to self-censorship mainly, as one of them said, out of fear.[27] One notable challenge to censorship came in June 1986 just after the 7th congress of the Writer's Union, when a group of Soviet writers, including Yevgenii Yevtushenko, publicly insisted that in literature 'there were no forbidden subjects' and that every literary piece of work had the right to life except for writings 'which provoke war, violence or chauvinism'.[28] Meanwhile in September 1986 it was announced that a new 'Law of the USSR on the press and information' was to be drawn up.[29] In the summer of 1988, as we saw in the last chapter, a law on *glasnost'* was promised. It remains to be seen how this will eventually operate – although as we have already seen the Soviet press under Gorbachev became much more outspoken and diverse in the views it reflected.

But censorship in the negative sense was itself only one aspect of traditional Soviet propaganda, which was always geared to a number of positive objectives. What was (and perhaps still is) basic to Soviet thinking was not merely an emphasis on what may be termed 'indoctrination' (which arguably takes place to some degree in all societies, usually by indirect rather than direct means) but an insistence that 'indoctrination' is something which must, at all costs, be organized. Hence the existence in the USSR of a whole number of agencies which have no real counterpart in other types of political system and which are involved in what is termed 'ideological work', an expression which includes both the formulation and the spreading of the party's ideas.[30] Particular mention should be made here of the Academy of Social Sciences attached to the Communist Party Central Committee, originally founded in 1946 and upgraded in 1978.[31] Its functions were then said to include carrying out or supervising the political training or retraining of senior officials; the undertaking of research on 'current problems of Marxism-Leninism'[32] and the organization of research into the theory, methods and effectiveness of propaganda work, of which more will be said later.

The day-to-day supervision and control over 'ideological work' is exercised by a highly complex network of institutions. According to a Soviet book of 1984 they include, among others, the Ministry of Culture, the Ministry of Higher and Secondary Special Education (as it was then called), the State Committee on Television and Radio and the TASS news agency.[33] However, as this author also observes, the ultimate control rests with the Communist Party Central Committee which in practice, of course, means the party leadership. Day-to-day party control is undertaken through one of the appropriate departments of the Central Committee Secretariat. These departments were in the throes of re-organization in 1988[34]; but in relation to propaganda, the following have a special role: The Department of Culture, which supervises the theatre and the arts; the Department of Science and Educational Establishments, which supervises schools, universities and other institutes of higher learning; and the Chief Political Administration of the Soviet Army and Navy, one of whose functions is to conduct political education in the armed forces. Finally, and of most direct concern to us is the Propaganda Department founded originally in 1920 and known by its present name since 1966.[35] This, like many other departments (including those of Science and Education) is replicated at lower levels.[36] All these are divided into more specialized sub-units known as 'sectors'. The Propaganda Department contains (or contained during the Brezhnev period) sectors responsible for 'party study' (of which more in a moment) and for newspapers as well as other sectors not publicly identified.[37] The Propaganda Department is one of the channels, although not the only one, through which party directives are conveyed to the media. It appears that the Propaganda Department also has at least some share of responsibility for presenting the Soviet case abroad. Between 1978 and 1986 the latter function was dealt with by a Department of International Information headed by Leonid Zamyatin.[38] However, this department was abolished as a separate entity and subsumed under the Propaganda Department when Zamyatin was appointed Soviet ambassador to Britain in the spring of 1986.[39]

This enormous apparatus of communication has, needless to say, produced one very predictable result. Soviet citizens have been massively and increasingly exposed to the Communist Party's message. The USSR, like virtually all other countries, has – especially since the Second World War – seen a vast expansion of the media. Radio in the USSR has, of course, become virtually universal. Television, which barely existed at all before the 1950s was by 1984 said to be available to 95 per cent of Soviet families.[40] The increase in newspaper circulation has been just as enormous. Average daily newspaper circulation amounted in 1940 to 38.3 million copies. By 1986 it had risen five fold to a total of 198.1 million – thus providing more than one copy of a newspaper for every adult inhabitant.[41] Beside all this, it need hardly be added that virtually all the population of the USSR have been educated in Soviet schools.

But quite apart from its obvious concern with education and the media, Soviet 'ideological work' has always had yet another vast dimension which deserves special mention. The Communist Party has relied heavily – and under Khrushchev and Brezhnev to an increasing extent – on so-called 'oral propaganda', that is, on the communication of the party's message through the spoken word. In 1986-7, as explained below, the Gorbachev leadership carried out a radical overhaul of the entire 'oral propaganda' system. The aim, however, was to revitalize, not to abandon the system. At the time of writing it consists, as in the past, of the following elements:

1   A system of *party study* involving regular courses (usually held between one and four times a month except in the summer).[42] Adult political education in the USSR originated in the 1920s.[43] The number of pupils vastly increased between 1953 and 1964 when Nikita Khrushchev was in power. Numbers were drastically reduced immediately after Khrushchev's departure, but were then slowly increased until 1981, when the expansion was, for a time, halted. A three-tier system of courses was created in 1965, to correspond with the pupils' level of knowledge,[44] but in 1981 this was again altered.[45] Political education is also organized in the form of so-called 'mass study' as well as 'party study'. Both members and non-

members of the Communist Party are included in these courses.

2   A network of *economic education* first inaugurated in a comprehensive form in 1971 for the express purpose of embracing the entire working population.[46] The educational year appears to be broadly the same as for party study. Courses have been very diverse, depending on the type of pupil (for example, collective farmer, engineer, etc.) Until the reform of 1987, these courses were quite separate from professional training: they were largely intended to teach the audience the principles and objectives of the party's economic policy. Some pupils have taken these courses under the party study system.

3   Other politically-orientated courses of part-time study including, in particular Komsomol study; and people's universities (founded in the late 1950s,[47] a form of adult education covering a wide variety of subjects, not all political).[48] Both these networks have been partly involved in economic education.

4   A system of ad hoc public lectures, mainly organized by the *Znanie* (or 'Knowledge') Society, founded in 1947 and concerned with political, international, social, economic, scientific and atheist themes.[49]

5   A system of regular lectures and informal talks at places of work. These are delivered, as circumstances require, by managers of enterprises or their deputies, by rapporteurs (*dokladchiki*), or by 'political informers' (*politinformatory*), a relatively new type of speaker, inaugurated in the 1960s, who specializes in particular topics (politics, economics, culture and communist morality, international affairs); or by the much more traditional agitator who usually belongs to the work group and who is responsible for persuasive activities at grass-roots level and may also hold chats on a one-to-one basis.[50] Since the 1970s, the practice has gradually been introduced of holding what are termed 'set political days' (*edinye politdni*) which means that in each locality a particular day in the month is specially set aside for the delivery of political reports, usually at places of work.[51]

6   A system of 'propaganda and agitation' in residential areas. This was energetically pressed by the authorities in the 1960s, particularly after the introduction of a five-day working week in 1967, which left less time for lectures at places of work.[52] However, propaganda in residential areas appears to be conducted in many places only 'from time to time'.[53]

Closely related to this kind of 'oral propaganda' is another very well-known type of activity, called 'visual agitation' – a term which includes films and more recently video-tapes, although it has been associated above all with political posters and slogans. Posters are elaborately planned by committees of activists at local level; and the main theme of this 'visual agitation' has been said to be 'an appeal for enthusiastic and highly productive labour, the mobilization of working people for the successful fulfilment of production plans and socialist commitments, the bringing to the awareness of every worker of the most important political and economic tasks and the news of the day'.[54]

We have so far concentrated on the traditional aspects of this system. However, at the time of writing, there were signs of significant innovation, or indeed flux. As already noted, the entire system of political and economic education was radically overhauled under the Gorbachev leadership in 1986–7, partly with a view to making it simpler and more flexible.[55] The structure of party study was to be based on the following components:

1 Universities of Marxism–Leninism (a long-established institution), which were to concentrate on the training and retraining of propagandists and of party workers included in the *nomenklatura* (the reserve list of those deemed fit by the party to fill certain key positions);

2 Political seminars intended mainly for professional people (engineers, doctors, teachers, managers, members of the intelligentsia), who were to be grouped together largely according to their professions;

3 Philosophical (methodological) seminars intended for scientists and teachers in universities and other higher educational establishments. These seminars were to concentrate on studying the social and natural sciences, ecology and other global problems 'on the basis of dialectical-materialist methodology';

4 Political schools intended mainly for communists and non-party activists who have no more than a secondary, or incomplete secondary, education;

5 Study according to individual plans but subject to party supervision. (This kind of study was itself a long-established practice.)

The 1987 reform provided that universities of Marxism–Leninism were to work from 1 September until 1 June; and that political schools and seminars were normally to work in urban areas from 1 October until 1 June and in rural areas from 1 November until 15 April.

The 1987 reform also laid it down that Komsomol study should be based on political schools and seminars and on political discussion clubs. Economic education was, for the first time, to be combined with professional training, instead of being confined as in the past to expounding the principles of economic policy. The current economic reforms, so it was said, necessitated the retraining of millions of workers who would combine 'high professionalism with political maturity and economic literacy'. The main institutions of economic education were to be 'schools of socialist management' (*shkoly sotsialisticheskogo khozyaistvovaniya*), mainly for workers and collective farmers, etc.; and, at a more senior level, 'production-

economic seminars' and 'universities of technical-economic knowledge', for
engineers, specialists, managers, etc.

The flavour of the system can be judged from the basic courses – which
were to be planned over a span of five years, to cover the period between
party congresses. For the period 1986–90 the course for party study
included, for example: 'The CPSU [Soviet Communist Party], the leading
and directing force of the revolutionary renewal of society'; 'The country's
new system of economic management,' 'The all-round development of
socialist democracy, the deepening of popular self-management and the
strengthening of the legal foundation of Soviet society'; 'The ideological
struggle in the contemporary world'; 'The foreign policy strategy of the
CPSU and new political thinking in the nuclear age'; as well as a number
of other courses dealing, among other things, with cultural policy, atheism
and relations between the nationalities in the USSR. Courses were also to
be planned on more theoretical topics such as 'Marxist–Leninist philosophy
and social progress' and 'Scientific communism and current problems of
the perfection of socialism'. So far as economic education was concerned,
the planned courses covered such subjects as 'The radical reform of
economic management' and 'The socialist enterprise: autonomy, responsibility and self-management'.

Changes in organization and syllabus were in themselves nothing new.
But the 1987 innovations did nevertheless go considerably beyond anything
ever done before. The previous system, so it was now said, had been
'divorced from life, cumbersome and excessively regulated' and 'the absence
of creative discussions and of a frank exchange of opinions substantially
reduced interest in study and undermined its authority.' In 1986, when
the decision to change the system was first announced, it was decided that
the proposed changes were to be published in draft in the press and
submitted for public discussion.[56] This was duly done and a number of
amendments were in fact made and accepted[57] – something which had
never previously happened where political education was concerned.
Furthermore, the new system provided for a substantial – and entirely new
– measure of decentralization. Local parties were authorized in principle
to introduce their own courses and no longer had to use only those
prescribed from above.

Quite clearly then, the 1987 reform was not intended to dismantle or
de-emphasize the existing sytem. Indeed it was expressly laid down that
party first secretaries down to the lowest level were to bear 'personal
responsibility' for the theoretical training of cadres. The changes seem to
be a clear example of the more general attempt, mentioned in the last
chapter, to reform the system from within. It was stipulated in particular
that those responsible for political and economic study must regularly take

account of pupils' suggestions; and that the teaching process must be based on 'dialogue' and on 'the comparison of different points of view'.[58] This point was almost brand new; and it was later authoritatively underlined in a party journal which stated that henceforward discussions must be guided 'by the power of arguments, not by the arguments of power'.[59]

To describe all the minutiae of this highly elaborate organization would be outside the scope of this book – all the more since the system seems to be in the throes of change. Nevertheless, the system – now as in the past – does possess three characteristics of particular importance for our purposes. First, it has a strongly ideological content and aim, especially in the case of party study. Secondly, it entails a substantial degree of active and sometimes obligatory participation by the ordinary citizen. Thirdly, it has always existed on a large scale. But from the 1960s onwards it was, in certain areas, expanded on a vaster scale than ever before. Each of these three points calls for a brief explanation.

First, as to ideology. In February 1976 Leonid Brezhnev told the 25th Communist Party congress that 'The mass study of Marxism–Leninism is a most important characteristic of the development of public awareness at the present time.'[60] Ten years later, the revised edition of the Soviet Communist Party programme also stressed ideology though in a slightly different spirit. It declared that: 'The CPSU will work unremittingly so that all Soviet people can thoroughly study the Marxist–Leninist theory, raise their political awareness, consciously participate in the shaping of the party's policy and actively implement it.'[61] There are grounds for believing that such statements were not mere rhetoric. The political education system built up by Khrushchev prior to his removal in 1964 was publicly criticized for having allegedly de-emphasized ideology and concentrated too heavily on purely practical economic tasks (sometimes merely 'providing people with narrow professional knowledge without any link with revolutionary theory', as one Soviet official later wrote).[62] Under Brezhnev this changed. This is not to suggest that the curriculum became scholastic; on the contrary it was very much 'action-orientated' and geared to the party's current priorities. Nevertheless the emphasis on ideology was unmistakable. To take one of many possible examples, it could be seen from a glance at the intermediate stage of party study as it existed in the early 1970s. In a course scheduled to last 256 hours and to be spread over five or six years,[63] the syllabus was: party history and political economy, 72 hours each; philosophy, 48 hours; and 'scientific communism', 64 hours. The philosophy section included four hours of discussion on such questions as 'What is matter? Movement, space and time – objective forms of the existence of matter' and 'The significance of the Marxist understanding of the material nature of the world for the struggle against idealism and religion'.[64] This formed part of a course which was being taken by between 6.5 and 7.5 million people;[65] and as many, or more, at that time were taking similar subjects at a more advanced level. In the economic education network the curriculum always was, of course, much more practical; but even here, the study sessions were officially criticized in the Brezhnev era for sometimes giving too little attention to what were termed 'the fundamental conceptions of revolutionary theory, the methodological conclusions of Marxism–Leninism'.[66]

The stress laid on ideology in the 1970s can also be seen from the amount of prescribed reading of 'primary sources', which usually meant Marxist–Leninist classics. Thus, within the then economic education network, even collective and state farm workers taking a 64-hour course (apparently spread over two or three years) on 'Socialism and Labour' were expected to read some 80 pages of Lenin.[67] Over 250 pages of Lenin's works – together with extracts from Karl Marx – were prescribed in what was then the primary stage of party study in the 1970s.[68] Apparently this prescribed reading was widely disregarded, as a party handbook complained in 1980:

> there is evidence which shows that some pupils merely confine themselves to attending study sessions or at best to reading the textbook and do not study primary sources. This inevitably results in the pupil merely 'scanning' the material, as they say, without profoundly grasping its meaning. It is essential resolutely to fight against such an attitude towards study.[69]

The full syllabus for political and economic study under Gorbachev is still unobtainable. However, for reasons already given, there is every sign that ideology (although of a much less dogmatic kind) will retain its importance.

Secondly, as to participation. The pupil in the party study and economic education courses was in theory certainly not supposed to play a passive role. The latter courses regularly included so-called 'problem' subjects such as analysing the potential for raising labour productivity.[70] In the party study system pupils were expected to present papers (*referaty*) for comment and criticism in class.[71] An element of compulsion has thus been involved – and not only in the instances just given. Party study is, in some form, obligatory for party members. This was re-affirmed in 1987, though the choice of subjects was made voluntary.[72] In August 1971 economic education was officially declared to be obligatory in the long run for the entire work-force; and study performance was to be taken into account in relation to pay, grading and promotion.[73] In 1987 it was recommended to carry out a 'universal economic instruction' (*ekonomicheskii vseobuch*) in 1987–8.[74] Quite apart from the political and economic study network, pressure may exist in other areas of oral propaganda. Talks and lectures at work-places may be difficult to avoid. Furthermore, managers and other senior officials in enterprises and institutions are expressly enjoined to deliver 'regular speeches' on political topics to their staff.[75] That is not necessarily to say that all participation is unwilling; but merely that difficulties are liable to arise for anyone who is unwilling to participate.

Thirdly, as to the scale of the effort. Under the post-Khrushchev leadership, propaganda and agitation at places of work were both consolidated and expanded. Tentative moves to get rid of the old-style agitator, as being too unsophisticated, were firmly rejected by the authorities.[76] Murmurings in some quarters in the 1960s and 1970s to the effect that the whole oral propaganda system had been made obsolete by the rise of the mass media were no less firmly condemned.[77] But it was in the areas of party and economic education that the expansion was most dramatic. Comprehensive Soviet figures giving detailed breakdowns are not available for the whole period which concerns us. There are discrepancies in the official figures given at different times; and in any case the oral propaganda system underwent a number of fluctuations and re-organizations. Nevertheless, the enormous long-term expansion of this system is not open to doubt.

In 1954, the year after Khrushchev's accession to power, the number of pupils said to be involved in party study stood at 4 million – equal to just over 3 per cent of the then adult population aged over 18.[78] By 1964, the year when Khrushchev fell, these numbers had soared to levels variously given as 30, 35, or 36 million[79] – equal to between 21 and 25 per cent of the adult population at that time.[80] Following Khrushchev's removal, his successors reduced the number of pupils in party study by about two-thirds in an evident attempt to improve the quality of instruction. The number of pupils for the year 1966–7 was given as 13.5 million, but it was then gradually increased so that by 1970–1 it had reached 15.3 million. The introduction of economic education in the following year meant another huge increase of the groups in adult study. Party study in the narrower sense also continued to expand: towards the end of the decade, in 1978–9, it was said to include 23 million pupils.[81] Only in 1981 were there signs that the expansion was, once again, to be halted. The party study system was further re-organized and it was said that 'There must be no formal mass "enrolment" of pupils.' This was a clear reversal of earlier policy, according to which 'The constant increase in the number of pupils in party study is a law-governed phenomenon.'[82] But this cutback, like others before, seemed to reflect adjustments of tactics rather than changes of aim. Meanwhile, under Gorbachev, the overall numbers embraced by politically-orientated adult study continued to expand, despite

TABLE 1   *Number of pupils in the party, Komsomol and economic study networks during selected years 1975–87 (millions)*

Pupil group	1975–6	1980–1	1985–6	1986–7
Party study	19.5	22.6	13.3	14.4
Komsomol study	6.8	8.7	10.3	7.9
Economic education	20.6	26.3	33.0	37.2
Mass political study	—	—	8.0	6.9
Totals	46.9	57.6	64.6	66.4

In 1975–6 and 1980–1, pupils in 'mass political study' were included among the pupils in 'party study' and were not separately classified. The figures for 'economic education' are said not to include those taking short-term courses to raise their qualifications.
Source: Fartiinaya zhizn, 21 (1987), p.19

important changes in the style and content of political education. It will be seen from the table 1 that in 1986–7, the overall numbers involved in adult study of this kind was said to be 66.4 million. That would amount to approximately 36 per cent of the Soviet adult population at the relevant time[83] – an enormous increase on the levels of the 1960s.

When discussing the scale of the 'oral propaganda' network it only remains to mention the large and increasing numbers of the 'propagandists' or lecturers involved in operating the system. These fall into several sub-groups. The so-called 'rapporteurs' (*dokladchiki*) were said, both in 1977 and 1985, to number 300,000[84] There were reported to be over 3.5 million 'agitators' in 1973 and about 3.7 million in 1985[85] The number of 'politinformers' (*politinformatory*) was given as over 1.3 million in 1971 and as 1.8 million in 1977 and 1985.[86] The sharpest numerical increase occurred, however, among the 'propagandists' (those most directly concerned with systematic courses of political and economic study). They were said to number over 1.2 million in 1973, but more than twice as many, 2.5 million, in 1986–7.[87] This once again demonstrates the long-term trend of the oral propaganda system towards expansion.

This brief survey of the traditional Soviet propaganda apparatus has deliberately emphasized 'oral propaganda' for the reason that whereas the supervision of the media involves no more than a few thousand party officials, the system of lectures, talks and courses necessarily involves the time and effort of tens of millions of people. There is no reliable way of calculating how much time is spent as a result. But if one were to assume

– purely notionally – that every pupil engaged in study spent an average of one man-day per year attending a class (that is, one hour per month for eight months in the year) then this alone would mean a national total of 66.4 million man-days for 1986–7. The actual total may well be several times higher. In any case this calculation takes no account of the time involved for the 'propagandists' themselves; or of the man-days spent on *ad hoc* lectures and talks outside the network of systematic study. Even in the Brezhnev era, the disruptive effect of 'oral propaganda' sometimes gave rise to complaints. *Pravda* once printed a story of how patients at a polyclinic were kept waiting because doctors were attending a political lecture.[88] Another contributor to the paper voiced what must have been a widely held sentiment when he wrote: 'In the factories we fight to save minutes, sometimes even seconds. But when we have a badly organized conference or lecture, then a multitude of people waste their time by the hour. In some places this is regarded as normal.'[89]

   The rationale underlying this enormous effort in 'face-to-face' communication has usually been explained (both by Soviet and Western writers) on several grounds. First, it gives the citizen the chance to ask questions and voice complaints, and so helps the authorities to gauge public opinion. Secondly, it forms part of a system not just of persuasion, but of social control. Thus, as late as 1980 the functions of the 'agitator' were said to include the following: 'to draw the attention of the collective to every instance of a breach of discipline, to show the harm caused by absentees, to give in his talks an angry, principled assessment of private-property psychology, consumerism, acquisitiveness, hooliganism, drunkenness, bureaucracy, indifference, philistinism and vulgarity'.[90] Both at work and in places of residence oral propaganda has traditionally been supposed to go hand in hand with sanctions – backed up if need be by informal comrades' courts against deviant behaviour.[91] To all this we shall return later on. A third and perhaps more convincing explanation for oral propaganda is that it has provided a channel through which the authorities can communicate with their own public in relative privacy, without being overheard by the outside world. Khrushchev's denunciation of Stalin in 1956 and Khrushchev's own dismissal in 1964 are known to have been explained in some detail at closed lectures, though never really explained in the Soviet mass media. Furthermore, in the 1970s when many Soviet citizens listened to Western broadcasts, lectures no doubt became a useful way of replying to these broadcasts in comparative privacy. A senior party official, writing in 1975, made precisely this point about privacy. Oral agitation and propaganda, he wrote, 'provide an opportunity to talk to Soviet people *frankly and confidentially* about many domestic and international questions which, for various reasons, cannot be covered to the same extent

in ... the press, radio and television' (emphasis added).[92] The additional
(sometimes more up-to-date) information which these talks contain is one
of the reasons why they sometimes appeal to the audience.

But these explanations, however true, are obviously inadequate. They
fail to account for the gigantic *increase* in the propaganda effort since the
1950s, especially where the teaching of ideology is concerned. This leads
to the last, and most basic, reason for this vast expansion, namely the
party's long-established belief that it must aim to carry its message to the
entire population.[93] As one Soviet communications specialist observed in
1984 – a few months before Gorbachev's accession:

> The principle of embracing the entire population in a single ideological
> influence continues to be of pressing importance during the period
> of mature socialism. An important factor in the building of a
> communist society is the ideological-political unity of the people. It
> cannot be ensured if the party's influence is confined to some
> particular strata or groups of the population. In our country, the mass
> mastery of Marxist–Leninist theory is a distinctive characteristic of
> the development of the social awareness of the Soviet people.[94]

The rationale of negative censorship, or even of positive propaganda, is
not so hard to understand. Indeed, it is perhaps the least illuminating
feature of the traditional Soviet communications system. There are many
authoritarian regimes – and not only in the communist world – which ban
the expression of opposition views and try to project themselves in a
favourable light. The really unique feature of traditional Soviet persuasion
is precisely the goal of saturation coverage, with the implication that even
outright opponents have got to be converted. It is, in any case, quite clear
that propaganda in the Soviet Union, including the propagation of ideology,
is not just an empty ritual, nor is it confined to some small elite. And this,
whatever else it may prove, certainly demonstrates the importance attached
to propaganda by Soviet leaders in the past.

But the fact of this vast effort does raise one further, and potentiallly
very important, question. Is all this effort to be taken as a sign of massive
effectiveness? Or is it a sign of massive overkill? If the 'overkill' interpretation
proves correct, it will throw an important light not only on Soviet thinking
in the past but also on the perennial problems of Soviet propaganda which
later necessitated the Gorbachev reforms.

Problems and criticisms

So much for the (real or ostensible) role of Soviet propaganda. But what about the other side of the coin: its quality? Where this was concerned, there was growing evidence, especially in the late Brezhnev era, that all was not well. This became particularly apparent when the Soviet Communist Party in April 1979 adopted a strongly worded and widely publicized resolution on the subject. The resolution called attention to the existence of 'quite a few weaknesses and shortcomings, some of them extremely substantial' in the propaganda output. One of the most serious failings was said to be 'that the quality of this work by no means always corresponds to the enhanced educational and cultural standards and requirements of Soviet people'. Among a great many other shortcomings which the resolution listed were 'a tendency to gloss over, to avoid unsolved problems, acute questions', 'an inclination towards verbal waffle, towards all kinds of propaganda clichés, the grey "official" style of material' and 'the mechanical repetition many times over of well-known truths'. Henceforward, so the resolution said, 'it must become a rule that no question which worries working people goes unanswered'; and there should be greater concern about 'promptness, persuasiveness and intelligibility' (*dokhodchivost'*).[95] In an apparent reference to the impact of Western broadcasts beamed into the Soviet Union and at that time unjammed, the resolution also warned that 'imperialist propaganda' (said to be acting in collusion with Peking) 'is incessantly waging a furious offensive against the minds of Soviet people'. There is little doubt that the political competition from these broadcasts was one of the main reasons why such a resolution was promulgated.

Nearly two years later, in February 1981, when Mr Brezhnev addressed the 26th congress of the Soviet Communist Party, he returned to the subject of propaganda and made the following, even more outspoken, comment:

In fact it is a question of restructuring [*perestroika*] – no, this was not a slip of the tongue, I said restructuring – many sectors and areas of ideological work. Its content should be more topical and its forms should fall in line with the present-day requirements and needs of Soviet people.[96]

It is clear that in the late Brezhnev era the whole propaganda effort was undergoing re-appraisal. It should be added, however, that the defects complained of were not new; nor, in the pre-Gorbachev era, were they rectified. Soviet political rhetoric (especially in the past) has had its own easily recognizable style; and one of its most striking features was, very often, an apparent *lack* of any genuinely persuasive purpose, in the sense of an attempt to appeal to the unconverted. It contained much that an outsider would find hard to accept at face value. The old and all too familiar claim that the Soviet public unanimously supported its government might be cited as an untruth. But it could also be seen as the sort of statement which was likely not so much to deceive as to provoke disbelief or puzzlement. A Soviet interest in convincing the doubters was by no means always in evidence. The doubters would hardly have been impressed, for instance, by the statement by a senior party leader in 1978 that 'NATO and the US are in reality alone responsible for the arms race ... The Soviet position in international affairs rests on the fact that there are no classes or social groups in our country which would profit from war production. We have banned war propaganda by law.'[97] Statements of this sort were noteworthy because of their almost total failure to grasp the point of view which they were seeking to rebut. Nor was the persuasive power of Soviet arguments necessarily reinforced by its sometimes harshly polemical style; or by the constant use of the word 'struggle' even when there was no visible opponent (for example, 'the struggle for the fulfilment of the five-year plan'). Furthermore, Soviet communication was almost certainly handicapped by its terminology. Words like 'bourgeois', 'imperialist', 'revisionist' and 'reactionary' are neither attractive nor always fully intelligible to those not already versed in Soviet political ideas.

Jargon was one familiar feature. Another was the tendency of the Soviet media to be dreary. To a considerable degree the newspapers until the early or mid-1980s still lived up to their reputation of neglecting human interest material which could attract their readers, of preaching sermons and of giving high priority to purely economic news about such things as plan fulfilment. There was the authenticated story of a Soviet local newspaper which was found to be devoting 80 per cent of its contents to items about production work; 19 per cent to items about 'social work', meetings and political study; and only 0.2 per cent to problems of the family and everyday life.[98] Such a case may have been extreme; but it was not altogether uncharacteristic.

Two other attributes of Soviet persuasion were also extremely well known: intrusiveness and, of course, secretiveness. As we have already noted, every effort has traditionally been made in the USSR to get the official message across, even if it is unsolicited. As a party handbook explained in 1980:

Chats within the home itself make it possible to reach everyone. There are people who have not as yet developed a sense of the need to attend lectures and reports. Agitators ... and others talk to them in their homes, inculcate into them a taste for political information and dispel philistine notions and rumours.[99]

The spreading of a sometimes unsolicited message nevertheless often went hand in hand with the failure to provide information which the public might want to know. This takes us to one of the central features of the traditional system – namely the absence of openness or *glasnost'*. It may be pointed out that excessive secrecy occasionally gave rise to Soviet newspaper complaints even in the Brezhnev years. For instance, in 1973 *Pravda* reported the difficulties of a journalist who had been unable to get information from a ministry about the progress of socialist competition.[100] Four years later a writer in the paper complained that 'brushing aside inquiries by journalists . . . an unwillingness or inability to give explanations on questions which might be of interest to readers has for some managerial officials become almost the norm'.[101] But only under Gorbachev did the extent of the secrecy begin to be revealed. Thus, many of the country's effective laws were not accessible to the public because they were contained in departmental directives which were classified as 'sub-legal' acts and were confidential.[102] Local Soviets were often in the habit of recording their decisions in documents marked 'for official use only'.[103] Yet another, even more remarkable, example of secrecy was to be found in the country's main library – the Lenin Library in Moscow – which in 1987 was publicly accused of concealing at least one and a half million Russian-language books from its readers' catalogue.[104] In some cases (for example the refusal to publish the views of dissidents) there were obvious political reasons for the secrecy. But in many other cases – for example the unwillingness to report crimes or air crashes – the secrecy seemed to spring from sheer habit.

It might thus appear that the traditional Soviet propaganda output showed little concern for the tastes of those to whom it sought to appeal. And it is indeed worth recalling that the official style of communication was the subject of repeated self-criticism over the decades. To take only a few random examples: as long ago as 1926 it was observed: 'The dryness of our newspapers has been repeatedly noted in our press'; 'Readers demand more liveliness and vividness.'[105] In 1935, the then Secretary of the Communist International, Georgii Dimitrov, spoke pungently about the propaganda shortcomings of foreign communists; but he did so in terms which could have been taken as applying also to the Soviet Union:

> We do not always know how to speak simply, concretely, in images which are intelligible and familiar to the masses . . . As a matter of fact, if you scan our leaflets, newspapers, resolutions and theses, you will find that they are often written in a language and style so heavy

that they are difficult for even our party functionaries to understand, let alone the rank and file workers.

If we reflect, comrades, that workers, especially in fascist countries who distribute or only read these leaflets, risk their very lives by doing so, we shall realize still more clearly the need of writing for the masses in a language which they understand, so that the sacrifices made may not have been made in vain.[106]

Concern about the inability to communicate was, over the years, a recurrent Soviet theme. Ivan Maisky, when describing his work as Soviet ambassador in London during the Second World War, recalled how virtually none of the propaganda material he got from Moscow was in a form suitable for transmission to the British press.[107] On the same theme, but this time in reference to Soviet domestic propaganda, Aleksandr Chakovskii a future Editor-in-Chief of the Moscow *Literaturnaya gazeta*, recalled, in 1961, that 'An acquaintance of mine once taught me how to deliver a speech. "Better dull, but correct," he said. And a great many of us followed that advice'.[108]

A campaign to 'brighten up' the media in the USSR was a constant preoccupation during the Khrushchev period in the 1950s and early 1960s. Improvements, then and later, certainly occurred. But in the early 1970s the problem was still being spoken about. In 1972 a Soviet journal could observe that 'propagandist articles on theory in the newspapers often remain unread because their language is dry and grey . . . As a result, one of the most important tasks of the Soviet press – the raising of the social activity of the masses, goes unfulfilled'.[109] And late in 1974 a secretary of the Moscow Communist Party made comments which in many ways anticipated the more high-level criticisms which were to be levelled five years later:

Attention should be drawn to the not always sufficiently high standards of information in our propaganda, to the superficial, prosaic and grey quality of the speeches of some lecturers and propagandists, to their inability to explain acute, sensitive questions. *Incompetent propaganda is as harmful as the absence of any propaganda at all* [emphasis in original].[110]

Four years after that, in November 1978, Leonid Brezhnev criticized the Soviet media for often being 'overloaded with general phrases which offer nothing either to the mind or to the heart';[111] and the Politburo set up a commission which eventually produced the resolution already quoted. In October 1979, Mikhail Suslov, a well-known Soviet conservative and one of the leading ideological authorities in the Brezhnev Politburo, addressed a conference convened to discuss the implementation of this resolution. He then stressed the fact that the problems were not new: 'It cannot be said these shortcomings were insufficiently spoken about in the past. The misfortune lies elsewhere: in the fact that some [propaganda] workers are utterly unable to proceed from general discourses about shortcomings to concrete activity for the removal of these shortcomings'.[112]

When trying to interpret traditional Soviet thinking about propaganda one therefore comes up against a dilemma. If the leadership did *not* care about public opinion, then why all the gigantic effort? If on the other hand it *did* care, then why this persistent and self-confessed difficulty in communicating? Why the adherence to a style which, fairly obviously, was not calculated to have a mass appeal? Why, on so many non-sensitive issues such as air crashes or train crashes and much else, did the leaders simply not bother to keep the public informed? To reply that the Soviet leadership was not interested in persuasion but only in maintaining its own power is to miss the point. For the leadership's power-base could hardly be strengthened by a highly organized propaganda apparatus which lacked credibility or mass appeal. It is no doubt the case that many of the defects in the traditional propaganda system stemmed from the political system as a whole, since controls over the media are not conducive to an interesting or lively style. Furthermore, the Soviet ideology – particularly in the form which prevailed between the Stalin and Gorbachev eras – was not one which lent itself to easy or simple exposition. Over and above that, there was the whole history of Soviet society in which coercion had, at various times, loomed very large; and this must have left its mark. Again, there were the inherent difficulties in producing the kind of unanimous public opinion which the authorities said they wanted.

Factors such as these were undoubtedly important. But this leads on to the further question with which this book will be concerned – namely how far these factors served in the past to blind Soviet official thinking to the psychological realities of the persuasion and communication process. This brings us still closer to the core of our subject. For the necessary aim of persuasive activity of any kind – whether political, religious or indeed commercial – must of course be to stimulate motivation in the audience. Soviet propaganda is no exception: it is aimed, as we have already seen, at 'the raising of the social activity of the masses'. It is therefore highly relevant to ask: how far did traditional Soviet thinking show any concern with motivation in relation to propaganda?

At this point it also becomes relevant to mention one other aspect of the discussion which follows – namely the radically different approaches to propaganda in Russia on the one hand, and in Western Europe and the United States on the other. The difference lies not just in the frequently-drawn contrast between 'control versus freedom' or 'democracy versus dictatorship'. An equally important difference lies in the psychological *methods* employed. For it would be a mistake to regard propaganda as in some way the brainchild of dictatorships. Mass persuasion in the West has for many decades been a highly professionalized activity – as can be easily seen from the role of advertisers and public relations consultants in Western election campaigns. Indeed, the period from the 1920s saw a vast proliferation in the West and especially the United States of literature concerned with propaganda and persuasion – stimulated both by domestic factors (advertising, growth of the media) and by international developments (notably the two world wars and the rise of totalitarian regimes). The appearance of a bibliography on propaganda in America as early as 1935 was one sign of this interest in the subject.[113] Public opinion polls of a reasonably reliable kind appeared in the USA in 1936 and they soon spread to other parts of the Western world.[114] The Second World War gave another powerful impetus to the study of propaganda in the West. Since then the development of mass persuasion in the West has steadily continued.

But this brings us to an even more specific difference between the Western and Soviet approaches to the subject. In the United States, in particular, propaganda became closely linked with the social sciences. It became a sub-branch of 'communication research' which, according to a much-quoted definition first propounded in 1946, involves the study of '*Who* says *what*, through what *channels* [media] of communication, to *whom*, [with] what ... results.'[115] Communication research has been an interdisciplinary activity – embracing, among many other things, the findings of psychology, sociology and, not least, opinion surveys. In the West today, a political propaganda campaign would be unthinkable without the involvement of pollsters. And whatever the objections to that approach, it at least makes it possible to test theories about persuasion by empirical means.

What light does all this research shed on the notion of propaganda as a highly powerful instrument for the shaping of public opinion? One of the best-known findings is, of course, that the impact of propaganda and mass communications is more complex and as a rule more limited than was once supposed. Mass persuasion can indeed have a powerful impact. But it is only one of a number of factors which contribute to the formation of opinion; and its influence depends not only on the content and flow of information (important as they are) but also on the predispositions of the audience. According to this view, audiences are not the defenceless targets of propaganda. On the contrary, they are selective, they have their own autonomous purposes and will tend to ignore messages which they see as irrelevant to their needs.[116] This approach to the subject easily explains why, for example, Soviet-style indoctrination failed in Czechoslovakia in the years before 1968. It also explains some of the familiar methods of mass persuaders in the West. Their messages are usually targeted on minorities – such as marginal voters. They make no attempt to 'reach everybody' as Soviet propagandists have tried to do. One of the main results of this propaganda research has been all those familiar 'techniques of persuasion' – techniques which are meant to get an audience to *want* to comply with the persuader's wishes. Techniques of this kind are essentially manipulative and sometimes cynical. But they have no necessary connection with coercion, censorship or the monopolistic control of information. And, most important of all, the findings of communication research have – by clarifying the conditions under which propaganda is likely to succeed or fail – helped to underline some of propaganda's inherent limitations, thus making for realism.

In the Soviet Union, on the other hand, communication research (including the use of opinion surveys) never developed on anything like the same scale. It did make an appearance in the early years of Bolshevik rule; and there was an official interest at that time in its relevance to propaganda. This research and the circumstances of its later suppression under Stalin are discussed in a later chapter. More recently, from about the early 1960s, it re-appeared with official encouragement; and its impact on propaganda method is described in the latter part of this book.

Few would dispute that even in the Brezhnev years propaganda was to some extent 'modernized'; and one proof is the greater degree of frankness – as exemplified in the sometimes hard-hitting criticisms quoted in this book. Nevertheless, certainly in the Brezhnev era, practical results were belated. In 1967 – already fifty years after the revolution – a Soviet psychologist could complain that 'the psychological problems of agitation and propaganda are touched upon only casually in our literature; no really serious efforts to investigate them have yet been made.'[11] And the author went on to contrast this state of affairs with the 'exceptional interest' shown in these problems in the West and especially the United States. During the Brezhnev era, as we shall see later, the situation did, to some degree, change. Nevertheless as late as 1980, another prominent Soviet psychologist indicated that progress had been very slow:

It should be admitted, to our great chagrin, that our psychology has up till now devoted unjustifiably little attention to the psychological aspects of propaganda and agitation. When it is remembered that Western psychologists have devoted very considerable efforts, particularly over the last 30 years, to . . . investigating the psychological aspects of propaganda activity, it is essential for us within the shortest possible time to make up the loss and to fulfil the public duty placed upon the science of psychology.[118]

So far as the psychology of propaganda is concerned, the literature in the West is far more extensive and far more profound than anything which has ever appeared in the USSR. The lack of communication research development in the Soviet Union is, of course well known to Western specialists.[119] One of the aims in the rest of this book is to examine its implications in greater depth. I am certainly not suggesting that the use of Western 'techniques of persuasion' would have been of much use in the context of Soviet society. Nor am I suggesting that persuasion can only succeed with the help of the social sciences; nor that the unsolved problems of the Soviet leadership are mainly problems of public relations. What I am, however, suggesting is that the leadership's frequent indifference to public relations in the past, as well as the past neglect of psychology and communication research, *does* tell us something about the traditional Soviet approach to propaganda. It is paradoxical, to say the least, that a leadership which expended so much effort on seeking to win converts to its cause should have devoted so little attention to these highly relevant areas of inquiry. This of itself should lead one to re-examine the lingering stereotype of Soviet indoctrinators as skilful psychological manipulators. Soviet propaganda as an *activity* has been the subject of many books by non-Soviet writers. The focus of attention here, however, is on the *disparity* between the vast scale of the activity ostensibly aimed at proselytization and the remarkably small amount of thought which seems to have been given to the psychological processes involved. If this disparity is explored, it should provide an insight into some of the thinking which underlies Soviet politics.

Notes

1 Compulsory treatment for alcoholism (subject to a court order and to certain other conditions being fulfilled) was authorized by a decree (*ukaz*) of the Presidium of the Supreme Soviet of the Russian Republic, dated 1 March 1974: see *Vedomosti Verkhovnogo Soveta RFSFR*, 10 (1974), p. 287. Similar legislation was introduced in all other republics of the USSR. See, for further explanation of these laws, B. M. Lazarev (ed.), *Grazhdanin i apparat upravleniya v SSSR* (Moscow, 1982), pp. 246ff.

2 *Pravda*, 24 March 1976, p. 6 (article by A. Likas, Chairman of the Supreme Court of the Lithuanian Republic).

3 *LG*, 29 August 1984, p. 10.

4 The measures were summarized in *Pravda* and other Soviet newspapers on 17 May 1985.

5   See B. Bratus', 'Alcoholism in the light of psychology', *PS*, 7 (1987), pp. 110–18, esp. p. 115.

6   See *The Times* 2 February 1988 ('Russians dry out the American way'; report from Christopher Walker in Moscow).

7   See Jeff Chinn, *Manipulating Soviet Population Resources* (Macmillan, London, 1977), esp. pp. 129–30. More efficient use of the labour-force was, of course, one of the major elements in Gorbachev's economic reforms.

8   Viktor Mikheyev, *Sotsial'no-psikhologicheskie aspekty upravleniya. Stil' i metod raboty rukovoditelya* (Moscow, 1975), p. 338.

9   *LG*, 27 September 1978 p. 10 (V. Nikitinskii and V. Glazyrin).

10 *Pravda*, 18 March 1983, p. 2 (S. Ivanov).

11 Ibid., 26 May 1983, p. 2 (A. Stavtseva).

12 *Problemy nauchnogo kommunizma*, 8 (1974), p. 93.

13 Valerii Paderin, *Obshchestvennoye mnenie v razvitom sotsialisticheskom obshchestve: sushchnost' i zakonomernosti formirovaniya* (Kazan', 1980), p. 90.

14 For an account of this see Lindley Fraser, *Propaganda* (Oxford University Press 1957), ch. 3.

15 W. J. M. Mackenzie, *Politics and Social Science* (Penguin Books, Harmondsworth, 1967), p. 225.

16 See Daniel Lerner, 'Effective propaganda: conditions and evaluation', reprinted in *The Process and Effects of Mass Communication* (University of Illinois Press, Urbana, 1954), pp. 480–8, esp. p. 482. This article originally appeared in Daniel Lerner (ed.), *Propaganda in War and Crisis* (George W. Stewart, New York, 1952).

17 See Lenin, *PSS*, vol 6, pp. 66–7. See also, article on 'Agitation' in *Bol'shaya Sovetskaya Entsiklopedia*, (hereafter *BSE*), 3rd edn, vol. 1 (Moscow, 1970), pp. 181–2. See, for the original reference to the distinction between propaganda and agitation, G. V. Plekhanov, *Sochineniya*, vol. 3 (Moscow, 1928), p. 400, quoted in the *BSE* article.

18 See P. K. Kurochkin et al. (eds), *Kommunisticheskaya propaganda: voprosy teorii i metodiki* (Moscow, 1974), p. 26.

19 V. G. Baikova et al, (eds), *Osnovy kommunisticheskoi propagandy* (Moscow, 1978), p. 6.

20 See *Programme of the Communist Party of the Soviet Union* (Moscow, 1961), part II, section V, p. 106, for reference to 'the moulding of the New Man'; and *The Programme of the Communist Party of the Soviet Union. A New Edition* (Moscow, 1986), part II, section V, p. 55. (Both these documents represent the official English translation of the respective programmes.) The term 'New Man' did not occur in the 1986 programme but did occur in the final resolution of the 27th Communist Party congress: see, *Pravda*, 6 March 1986, p. 3.

21 G. L. Smirnov et al. (eds), *Voprosy teorii i praktiki partiinoi propagandy* (Moscow, 1971), p. 209.

22 The text of the 1917 law on the press is reprinted in *Dekrety Sovetskoi vlasti*, vol. 1 (Moscow, 1957). The text of the law of 1931 is extensively quoted in Robert Conquest (ed.), *The Politics of Ideas in the USSR* (Bodley Head, London, 1967), pp. 43–4.

23 *Pravda*, 24 August 1986, p. 2.
24 Ibid., 8 February 1986, p. 2.
25 See Yurii Borin and Mikhail Fedotov, 'The right to information', *Zhurnalist*, November 1986, pp. 24–25.
26 For example, the writer Vasil' Bykov has described the way in which manuscripts were sometimes 'ground down, softened up and turned to dust. And if you tried to object to such interference, the book would simply not get published': *LG*, 14 May 1986, p. 2. Another writer, Robert Rozhdestvenskii, complained that the greater the talent revealed in a manuscript the longer the delay in publication: ibid., 2 July 1986, p. 8.
27 This was stated in an article by the radio and television journalist Vladimir Tsvetov in *LG*, 13 August 1986, p. 14.
28 *LG*, 2 July 1986, p. 2.
29 See *Vedomosti Verkhovnogo Soveta SSSR*, 37 (10 September 1986), pp. 729–30.
30 According to one textbook of the 1970s: 'The party's ideological work embraces all spheres of the spiritual life of Soviet society and is directed towards the development and dissemination of Marxist–Leninist theory and the formation of a new man': see K. M. Shchegolev et al (eds), *Partiinoye stroitel'stvo* (Moscow, 1978), p. 248.
31 See *BSE*, 3rd edn, vol. 1 (Moscow, 1970), p. 323 for the origins and functions of this Academy. As to its upgrading, see *Partiinaya zhizn'*, 7 (1978), p. 3.
32 *Partiinaya zhizn'*, 7 (1978).
33 See A. I. Yakovlev, *Effektivnost' ideologicheskoi raboty* (Moscow, 1984), p. 62. The Ministry of Higher and Secondary Special Education was subsumed in 1988 under a new State Committee for National Education.
34 The decision to re-organize was announced in *Pravda*, 1 October 1988, p. 1, which mentioned a new 'Ideological Commission'. For a description of the Central Committee departments in the past, see Jerry F. Hough and Merle Fainsod, *How the Soviet Union is Governed* (Harvard University Press, Cambridge, Mass., 1979), pp. 419–24. Soviet publications had not, in recent years, given any detailed lists of, or information about, these departments; the only partial exception was the Chief Political Administration of the Soviet Army and Navy whose origins are described in *BSE*, 3rd edn, vol. 6 (Moscow,1971), p. 573. This administration is officially given the status of a Central Committee Department under article 68 of the party statutes: see *Ustav Kommunisticheskoi partii Sovetskogo Soyuza* (Moscow, 1986). Information about other Central Committee departments had to be culled from passing references in the Soviet press. For example, the departments of Propaganda, Science and Education and Culture are all mentioned in *Pravda*, 8 August 1987, p. 4.
35 See *BSE*, 1st edn, vol. 60 (Moscow, 1934), p. 552. The department's present name was apparently first used in *Pravda*, 12 June 1966, p. 3. Its name immediately before this was 'The Department of Propaganda and Agitation' – a designation which is still used to refer to the corresponding departments which function at local levels.
36 See A. I. Yakovlev, *Effektivnost' ideologicheskoi raboty* pp. 63–4.

37 The sector for 'party study' is referred to in *PS*, 10 (1979), p. 114; and the sector for newspapers is mentioned in *Pravda*, 29 November 1973, p. 3.
38 The department was identified in *Pravda*, 19 September 1978, p. 1; and Leonid Zamyatin was identified as its head in ibid., 10 January 1979, p. 1.
39 I have been told this by Soviet journalists.
40 *LG*, 23 May 1984, p. 11.
41 *Pechat' SSSR v 1986 godu* (Moscow, 1987), p. 116. The size of the adult population over the age of 18 is calculated, here and later, from the size of the electorate, which in 1987 comprised 184,425,691 registered voters: see *Pravda*, 27 June 1987, p. 4.
42 See (in English) M. Semichayevsky, *Organisation of Party Educational Work in the USSR* (Moscow, 1974), pp. 14–15.
43 Its origins are briefly outlined in Stephen White, *Political Culture and Soviet Politics* (Macmillan, London, 1979), pp. 70–2. For a Soviet account of the same subject, see Fyodor Krotov, *Shkola ideinoi zakalki. Ocherki istorii marksistskoi-leninskogo obrazovaniya v KPSS* (Moscow, 1978), ch. 1.
44 See Krotov, *Shkola ideinoi zakalki*, p. 145.
45 The changes (now superseded by more recent reforms) were outlined in *PS* 6 (1981), pp. 3–7.
46 See the Communist Party resolution of 31 August 1971 'On the improvement of the economic education of the working people', published in *Voprosy ideologicheskoi raboty KPSS. Sbornik dokumentov (1965-1973gg.)*, 2nd edn (Moscow, 1973), pp. 311ff, esp. p. 314.
47 See as to the origins and functions of people's universities, *BSE*, 3rd edn, vol. 17 (Moscow, 1974), pp. 282–3.
48 One form of adult political education in the past were the 'schools of communist labour' inaugurated in the early 1960s, but abolished under the 1987 reforms of the political education system described later in this chapter.
49 Its origins are described in *BSE*, 2nd edn, vol. 9 (Moscow, 1951), p. 328.
50 See *Spravochnik sekretarya pervichnoi partiinoi organizatsii* (Moscow, 1977), pp. 253–65; ibid. (1980), pp. 265–76.
51 See M. A. Morozov (ed.), *Spravochnik propagandista* (Moscow, 1980), pp. 82ff.
52 See A. L. Unger, 'Soviet mass political work in residential areas', *Soviet Studies*, 22:4 (April 1971), pp. 556–61.
53 See E. M. Tyazhel'nikov (ed.), *Za vysokoye kachestvo i deistvennosti ideologicheskoi raboty. Materialy vsesoyuznogo seminara-soveshchaniya ideologicheskikh rabotnikov. Moskva, 20–5 aprelya 1981g.* (Moscow, 1981), p. 78. This remark was made by Mikhail Zimyanin, a secretary of the Communist Party Central Committee.
54 See *Spravochnik sekretarya pervichnoi partiinoi organizatsii* (1980), pp. 279–80.
55 The following account of the 1987 reforms is based, except where otherwise stated, on the Communist Party Central Committee resolution 'On the restructuring [*perestroika*] of the system of political and economic study by the working people' published in *PO*, 10 (1987), pp. 9–21.
56 See the party resolution 'On the organization of the political and economic education of the working people in the academic year 1986–7', published in *Pravda*, 14 August 1986, p. 1.

57 The draft was published in *PO*, 5 (1987) and was discussed in later issues of that journal during that year and also in other Soviet newspapers and journals.
58 *PO*, 10 (1987), pp. 4 and 16.
59 Ibid., 1 (1988), p. 9.
60 *Pravda*, 25 February 1976, p. 8.
61 See *The Programme of the Communist Party of the Soviet Union* (Moscow, 1986), section V, p. 56.
62 V. I. Stepakov, *Partiinoi propagande - nauchnye osnovy* (Moscow, 1967), p. 59.
63 See, as to the number of years involved, *Voprosy teorii i metodov ideologicheskoi raboty*, 2 (Moscow, 1973), p. 192.
64 This syllabus is set out in *Programma shkoly osnov marksizma-leninizma* (Moscow, 1970).
65 See *Spravochnik sekretarya pervichnoi partiinoi organizatsii* (1977), p. 356.
66 *PS*, 8 (1978), p. 80. This particular article seemed to be referring to 'the political and economic education of cadres', i.e. officials, but its whole tenor underlined the basically political purpose of 'economic' education.
67 *Ekonomicheskaya gazeta*, 21 (1976).
68 *Programma nachal'noi politicheskoi shkoly* (Moscow, 1973).
69 *Spravochnik sekretarya pervichnoi partiinoi organizatsii* (1980), p. 259.
70 *Ekonomicheskaya gazeta*, 21 (1976).
71 See, e.g., *Spravochnik sekretarya pervichnoi partiinoi organizatsii* (1980), p. 259; also, B. Ts. Badmayev, *Elementy psikhologii i pedagogiki v partiinoi propagande* (Moscow, 1973), pp. 134ff.
72 *PO*, 10 (1987), p. 4.
73 See the resolution of 1971 on economic education above published in *Voprosy ideologicheskoi raboty KPSS* (1973), pp. 311ff, esp. pp. 314, 316.
74 *PO*, 10 (1987), p. 5.
75 See the party resolution of 8 August 1971 'On the Marxist–Leninist study and economic education of senior cadres in the Tashkent city party organization' published in *Voprosy ideologischeskoi raboty KPSS* (1973), pp. 365ff, esp. pp. 370–1.
76 See, for a more detailed account of these moves and counter-moves, Aryeh L. Unger, *The Totalitarian Party: Party and People in Nazi Germany and Soviet Russia* (Cambridge University Press, 1974), pp. 146–50.
77 See the party resolution 'On the enhancement of the role of oral political agitation in the fulfilment of the decisions of the 25th congress of the CPSU', published in *Pravda*, 25 February 1977, p. 1. This resolution condemned the 'incorrect opinion' that the importance of oral agitation had been diminished by the rise of the mass media. The resolution dealt not only with the old-style agitators but with rapporteurs and *politinformatory* as well.
78 See Krotov, *Shkola ideinoi zakalki*, p. 142. The Soviet adult population (electorate) in March 1954 numbered 120,750,816 voters; see *Keesing's Contemporary Archives* (1954), p. 13495.
79 See, respectively, Krotov, *Shkola ideinoi zakalki*, p. 143; *Partiinaya zhizn'*, 10 (1965), p. 73 (quoted in Conquest, *The Politics of Ideas in the USSR*, p. 105);

Kommunist, 14 (1964), p. 3 (quoted in Ellen Propper Mickiewicz, *Soviet Political Schools*, New Haven, Conn., 1967, p. 10).

80 This is approximately calculated from the size of the Soviet electorate in 1966 which was given as 144,000,973: See *Pravda*, 15 June 1966, p. 1.

81 See *Spravochnik sekretarya pervichnoi partiinoi organizatsii* (1977), p. 356 and ibid. (1980), p. 353.

82 *Pravda*, 11 August 1981, p. 2; for earlier policy see *Spravochnik sekretarya pervichnoi partiinoi organizatsii* (1980), p. 257.

83 The size of the Soviet electorate at this time was 184,425,691 registered voters: see *Pravda*, 27 June 1987, p. 4.

84 *Spravochnik sekretarya pervichnoi partiinoi organizatsii* (1977), p. 355; *Voprosy teorii i praktiki ideologicheskoi raboty*, 17 (Moscow, 1985), p. 6, which gives an estimate of 'over 300,000 rapporteurs'.

85 *Agitator*, 15 (1973), p. 12; *Voprosy teorii i praktiki ideologicheskoi raboty* 17 (1985), p. 6.

86 See, respectively, M. A. Morozov (ed.), *Spravochnik propagandista* (Moscow, 1971), p. 115; also *Spravochnik sekretarya pervichnoi partiinoi organizatsii* (1977), p. 355; *Voprosy teorii i praktiki ideologicheskoi raboty*, 17 (1985), p. 6.

87 M. A. Morozov (ed.), *Spravochnik propagandista* (Moscow, 1973), p. 82; *Partiinaya zhizn'*, 21 (1987), p. 20.

88 *Pravda*, 30 July 1977, p. 2.

89 *Pravda*, 29 November 1977, p. 2. The author, however, also quoted examples of lectures which did appeal to the audience.

90 *Spravochnik sekretarya pervichnoi partiinoi organizatsii* (1980), p. 273.

91 See, for an account of the functions of comrades' courts, Unger, *The Totalitarian Party*, chs. 3 and 5, *passim*.

92 *Voprosy teorii i metodov ideologicheskoi raboty*, 4, (Moscow, 1975), p. 15.

93 See the party resolution 'On the tasks of party propaganda in contemporary conditions', published in *Pravda*, 10 January 1960, which stated that party propaganda should reach 'every Soviet person'. See also ibid., 12 December 1984, p. 2, where it is said that the party's objectives must 'be brought to the awareness of every member of society'.

94 Yakovlev, *Effektivnost' ideologicheskoi raboty*, p. 68.

95 See the party resolution 'On the further improvement of ideological and political-educational work', published in *Pravda*, 6 May 1979.

96 *Pravda*, 24 February 1981, p. 8.

97 Speech by Boris Ponomarev, then a secretary of the party Central Committee, reported in *Pravda*, 12 July 1978, p. 4. As noted in ch. 1, the Soviet authorities do now admit that they may have made mistakes in foreign policy.

98 V. M. Gorokhov and V. D. Pel't, (eds), *Masterstvo zhurnalista* (Moscow, 1977), p. 217.

99 *Spravochnik sekretarya pervichnoi partiinoi organizatsii* (1980), pp. 308–9.

100 *Pravda*, 27 December 1973, p. 3 (V. Sudakov).

101 Ibid., 5 September 1977, p. 4 (S. Vtorushin).

102 *Izvestia*, 17 October 1986, p. 3.

48 HOW TO PERSUADE?

103 *Zhurnalist*, November 1986, p. 25.
104 *LG*, 11 March 1987, p. 12. The same article also reported an accusation that one quarter of the library's stock of books was excluded from the catalogue used by the public.
105 Ya. Shafir, *Rabochaya gazeta i eë chitatel'* (Moscow, 1926), pp. 195, 216.
106 Quoted in *Lenin and Stalin on Propaganda* (Lawrence & Wishart, London, 1942), p. 30.
107 Ivan Maisky, *Memoirs of a Soviet Ambassador: The War, 1939–45*, tr. Andrew Rothstein (Hutchinson, London, 1967), pp. 206–7.
108 See *XXII s"yezd KPSS i voprosy ideologicheskoi raboty* (Moscow, 1962), p. 174.
109 *Zhurnalist*, 10 (1972), p. 2.
110 See *Sotsiologicheskie issledovaniya*, 1 (1975), p. 16, reporting a speech made in December 1974 by V. N. Yagodkin, a secretary of the Moscow city party.
111 *Pravda*, 28 November 1978, p. 2.
112 Speech reported in E. M. Tyazhel'nikov (ed.), *Delo vsei partii. Materialy Vsesoyuznogo soveshchaniya ideologicheskikh rabotnikov. Moskva, 16–17 oktyabrya 1979* (Moscow, 1980), p. 33.
113 Harold D. Lasswell, Ralph D. Casey and Bruce Lannes Smith, *Propaganda and Promotional Activities* (University of Minnesota Press, Minneapolis, 1935), which cited between 4,000 and 5,000 references; see also the same authors' *Propaganda, Communication and Public Opinion* (Princeton University Press, Princeton, 1946).
114 See F. Teer and J. D. Spence, *Political Opinion Polls* (Hutchinson, London, 1973), ch. 1.
115 This definition was formulated by Harold D. Lasswell and was first put forward in *Propaganda, Communication and Public Opinion*, p. 121.
116 See, among many other sources, Joseph Klapper, *The Effects of Mass Communication* (Free Press, New York, 1960); W. Phillips Davison, *International Political Communication* (Praeger, New York, 1965), esp. ch. 3.
117 V. M. Yakushev, *Gnoseologicheskie i psikhologicheskie osnovy propagandy i agitatsii.* Avtoreferat (i.e. published abstract of unpublished dissertation) (Lvov, 1967), p. 3.
118 *Psikhologicheskii zhurnal*, 5 (1980), p. 21 (E. V. Shorokhova).
119 See in particular, Ellen Mickiewicz, 'Policy issues in the Soviet media system', in Erik P. Hoffman, (ed.), *The Soviet Union in the 1980s* (Academy of Political Science, New York, 1984), pp. 113ff. See also Ellen Mickiewicz, 'Political communication and the Soviet media system', in Joseph L. Nogee (ed.), *Soviet Politics: Russia After Brezhnev* (Praeger, New York, 1985), pp. 34ff.

3
Persuasion, Public Opinion and Ideology

The strength of Bolshevik agitation lies in its truth, in its content and not in any particular methods, forms, external qualities or distinctive features. These methods and forms play a not inconsiderable role ... but it is a subordinate, not a primary role.

L. Perchik, *Agitatsiya* (1937 p. 39)

... it is essential to study the practice of propaganda work from the point of view of its content. In other words, the old truth that the decisive thing in propaganda is its content is now becoming particularly relevant.

G. L. Smirnov, Assistant Head of the CPSU Propaganda Department, *Sovetskii chelovek* (1971, p. 334)

As socialist society continues to develop, the role of planning grows immeasurably. This also applies in full measure to ideological work.

P. Ukrainets, in a book on propaganda work, *Partiinoye rukovodstvo ideino-vospitatel'nym protsessom* (1982, p. 137)

Introduction

The last chapter discussed at some length the outward features of traditional Soviet propaganda. This chapter will look a little more closely at the thinking which lay behind it and at the interconnections between the Soviet approach to propaganda and public opinion, on the one hand, and the official ideology, Marxism–Leninism, on the other. We shall also, more briefly, consider some of the historical or 'sociological' factors which must have helped to shape Soviet official attitudes in this field. A good deal is said about propaganda and (to a lesser extent) public opinion, both in the statements of Soviet leaders and also in more specialized literature in the USSR. However, since this chapter involves a number of different strands, and since it does not follow an invariably chronological sequence, it may be useful at the outset to restate the most basic question which concerns us in this book. This is: did the Soviet authorities ever evolve anything which could properly be called a psychological 'blueprint' for mass persuasion or indoctrination? The weight of the evidence indicates that they did not. It is of course perfectly true, and has often been pointed out, that Soviet communism has been concerned to 'form' public opinion. But it is also true – although seldom pointed out – that Soviet propagandists have traditionally been very little concerned with psychology, even for the purposes of cynical mass manipulation. In this respect there was a marked contrast between the Bolshevik approach to propaganda and that of the Nazis.

Soviet literature on propaganda and public opinion has almost invariably discussed these subjects in the context of ideology. This fact itself provides at least some clue to Soviet preoccupations. The major part of this chapter will therefore examine the 'ideological dimension' of Soviet propaganda. It will do so from a number of angles – both historical (that is, in relation to the ideas of Marx and Engels, Lenin and Stalin), and contemporary (that is, in relation to Soviet thinking in the Brezhnev era and after). Lastly, bringing the subject back to the specific question of methods of persuasion, we shall examine what Soviet propaganda specialists have themselves had to say about this. First, however, something should be said about the *non-*ideological, or sociological, factors which must have helped to shape Soviet thinking.

Propaganda in the context of Soviet society

Soviet ideology is highly complex and controversial. Indeed, many observers refuse to accept it at face value. To this we shall return later on. But no one, of course, imagines that Soviet policy – with regard to propaganda or anything else – is shaped solely by considerations of abstract ideology. No purely abstract theory can operate in a vacuum. Ideas have to be applied to specific situations in specific societies; and they are necessarily mediated through people. As a result, the ideas may be developed or they may get distorted or oversimplified or they may, sometimes, become atrophied. Indeed, ideas can sometimes continue to wield influence even when they are seen not to be working. All this has to be kept in mind when trying to assess the role of Marxism–Leninism in Soviet policy-making. So far as propaganda is concerned, it is obvious that Soviet thinking has partly been shaped by factors which have nothing directly to do with ideology.

One important factor, naturally enough, has to do with the historical conditions when the Bolsheviks in Russia won and retained power. Much of Soviet history has been riven by conflicts and crises, some – although by no means all – of which were the result of the Bolsheviks' own actions. The Bolshevik revolution of 1917 came in the middle of a world war. It was followed by civil war, economic breakdown and foreign intervention. The late 1920s and early 1930s saw crash programmes of industrialization and collectivization; these were accompanied or followed by massive social upheavals and gross abuses of power by Stalin which the Soviet leadership has now publicly condemned. The 1940s brought the Nazi invasion, whose appalling effects necessitated many years of economic and social recuperation. In these circumstances, the Soviet leaders resorted to coercive methods, sometimes on a horrendous scale, which have had a long-lasting effect on Soviet society. The consequences for propaganda were plain: it increasingly became an adjunct to force – and in no way a substitute for force.

A second important factor which affected the style of Soviet communication had to do with the sort of people who rose to power, both at the top and at lower levels.[1] All the Soviet top leaders – and in particular Lenin, Stalin, Khrushchev and Gorbachev – have made a very personal mark on the style of Soviet communication. The fact, for instance, that Gorbachev has been much more effective than his predecessors in handling the Western media has gained for the Soviet Union a considerably more respectful hearing on the world scene. But that is, to a considerable extent, due to Gorbachev's personal calibre. At lower levels, the problem of recruiting propaganda 'cadres' (that is, of getting people qualified for the job) has been frequently mentioned by the Soviet authorities. It cannot have failed to affect the quality of the propaganda message.[2]

One could dwell at far greater length on these two factors – of history and of the quality of leadership. They are dealt with only briefly here, not because they are of minor importance but because they seem so self-evident. A third, and closely related, factor which must have influenced the nature of Soviet propaganda was the well-known phenomenon of bureaucratization. This subject, discussed for many years by Western Sovietologists and more recently discussed in depth by Soviet writers themselves,[3] is an immense one which goes far beyond the scope of this book. Yet it cannot be doubted that 'bureaucratism' (to use the favourite Soviet term) has had a profound effect on the whole style of Soviet communication. Some of the most familiar features of the Soviet media in the past – the depersonalized style, the use of clichés and coded language, the secrecy and the importance attached to protocol – are all attributes commonly associated with bureaucratic hierarchy. Concern with protocol has for many decades been apparent in the Soviet media. Indeed, the

Soviet newspaper practice of listing party leaders in precise hierarchical order was at one time an important source of clues for Western Kremlinogists. One minor indication of the importance attached to protocol is the fact that misprints in Soviet newspapers are exceedingly rare and seem to be regarded as serious lapses. One of the few misprints in *Pravda* during the Brezhnev era occurred in an item in July 1978 which inadvertently referred to opponents of the regime in Chile as 'neo-fascist' instead of 'non-fascist'. Most readers might have failed to spot the mistake, had *Pravda* not deemed it necessary to publish a correction the following day – which is what makes the story worth telling.[4]

It need hardly be pointed out that these traditions – of coercive policies often implemented by bureaucratically-minded officials – all militated against any great reliance on psychology. Indeed, bureaucracy is notoriously hard to reconcile with good journalism. And the traditional Soviet media system was not primarily geared to audience psychology (as we shall see in more detail in later chapters). Like much else in the Soviet system, its output was heavily influenced by the law of plan-fulfilment. It is noteworthy that in 1986 the head of a well-known Moscow publishing house complained about what he called 'the clumsy and artificially protracted system of planning' in the publishing field; he said that publishers might have to wait four or five years before discovering how their books had sold.[5]

The link between propaganda and organization in Soviet thinking

All that has just been said may help to explain two basic guidelines of Soviet propaganda which become so well-established that they deserve to be specially singled out. The first is that correctness of content (that is, conformity to party policy) is what matters above all in propaganda. Soviet communicators have always attached basic importance to this, as the quotations at the beginning of this chapter show. (The idea of public disagreement or 'socialist pluralism' is therefore very much a novelty.)

A second basic guideline is that successful propaganda and efficient organization are inseparably interconnected. This notion can be traced back at least to the 1930s. In the Brezhnev era, it was emphasized by Soviet writers again and again. Thus, Viktor Afanasyev, then Editor of *Pravda*, wrote in 1977: 'The effectiveness of information work, of ideological activity as a whole depends on who plans, organizes and controls it; and this is the prerogative of the party.'[6] Afanasyev did go on to list a number of other preconditions for effectiveness (such as correctness of content, competent cadres). But the importance attached to organization was unmistakable. According to another Soviet authority, Mikhail Nenashev, in 1976: 'Practice shows that after a correct political line has been drawn up, organizational work decides everything, including the fate of the political line itself.'[7] In exactly the same vein, yet another Soviet propaganda specialist, Pavla Ukrainets, writing in 1982, insisted that: 'Efforts to influence people's minds and behaviour in an unplanned, unsystematic way do not produce the desired results, although such work takes up far more time and energy than work which is planned and goal-directed. This has long since been proved.[8]

Much of the vast Soviet literature on propaganda has consisted of party officials describing what they have done to improve its organization. One reason for this approach has been the avowed wish of the authorities to ensure that the official message reaches literally everyone (a point which we noted in the last chapter). It is, of course, in striking contrast with the Western politicians' concentration on marginal voters. It should also be noted here that, according to traditional Soviet thinking, the link between propaganda and organization works both ways. In other words, not only must propaganda be efficiently planned: propaganda itself is of importance in organizing public activity. This co-ordinating (or 'mobilizing') function of propaganda frequently became an instrument, not necessarily for influencing public opinion but simply for transmitting party directives from the top level to the population at large.

This assumption that if communist propaganda is highly organized, *therefore* it must be highly effective seems to have become deeply rooted in Soviet thinking; and it also seems to have been implicitly accepted by some Western observers of the Soviet scene. One of the purposes of this book is to examine its validity. The origins of this Soviet belief probably stem more from the specific conditions of Soviet development (particularly the Stalinist 'five-year-plan' mentality in the 1930s) than from Marxism–Leninism as such. It is obvious in any case that 'propaganda', in the sense of the handing down of directives from above, has no necessary connection with persuasion or indoctrination. As a persuasive method, it is not based on anything but the most primitive psychological theory.

Propaganda through psychological manipulation: the Nazi example

Throughout its history, the Soviet Communist Party has had much to say about propaganda, its content, how it should be organized and, not least, the need for it to be under party control. At the same time, as we shall seek to show, the Soviet authorities have said very little about the connection betwen propaganda and psychology. In particular, so we shall argue, it is a basic misconception for non-communist observers to suppose that the Soviet leadership has ever been greatly preoccupied with psychological manipulation. (One or two apparent exceptions to this will be dealt with later in this book as they arise.) And in order to bring into relief the kind of psychological manipulation which the present argument has in mind it may be useful to look briefly at the propaganda of Nazi Germany – with which Soviet propaganda has often been compared. The points of resemblance between the two doctrines – such as one-party control of the media and the attempt to form a monolithic public opinion – have been highlighted in the West many times. The contrasts between the two propaganda doctrines have tended to be minimized or ignored. One such contrast relates to the exploitation of psychology. And what does clearly emerge from the writings of Hitler and Goebbels (apart from a very open cynicism) is a constant preoccupation with the likely impact of a propaganda message on the feelings and prejudices of the target audience.

According to Hitler's *Mein Kampf*: 'The great majority of a nation is so feminine in its character and outlook that its thought and conduct are ruled by sentiment rather than by sober reasoning.'[9] On the evidence of Goebbels (as minuted in his secret wartime conferences) Nazi propaganda stratagems were all planned with carefully calculated psychological considerations in mind. Thus, during the German invasion of France in May 1940, the Nazis set up a 'black' clandestine radio broadcasting in French and purporting to be run by French communists. But Goebbels noted a complaint that the programmes were 'too doctrinaire and dull', whereupon he at once indicated concern and asked to see the scripts. Psychological considerations (as well as a truly Machiavellian amoralism) also shaped Goebbels's strategy for distracting world attention from the Jewish holocaust. He suggested launching a propaganda campaign against alleged British atrocities. In December 1942 he was minuted to the effect that: 'The Minister regards a general hullabaloo about atrocities as our best chance of getting away from the embarrassing subject of the Jews. Things must be so arranged that each party accuses every other of committing atrocities. This general hullabaloo will then eventually result in this subject disappearing from the agenda.' Explaining his philosophy in more general terms, Goebbels observed in 1940 that 'It is . . . a mistake to conduct propaganda in such a way that will stand up to the critical examination of intellectuals' because 'the most primitive arguments are the most effective and meet with the greatest agreement among the masses. Intellectuals always yield to the stronger, and this will be the ordinary man in the street.'[10]

It might seem plausible to argue that because the Nazi and Soviet propaganda systems both aimed at the formation of a monolithic public

Plate 2.   'The Ten Commandments of the Proletarian', by an unknown artist.

Plate 1.   Lenin speaking at the unveiling of a memorial to Karl Marx and Friedrich Engels in Moscow, November 1918.

Plate 3.   *'Forward, to the defence of the Urals', by Alexander Apsit.*

Plate 4.   The 'Red Star' propaganda ship, 1920.

ВОПРОС ОБ ЭЛЕКТРОФИКАЦИИ ПОСТАВЛЕН В ПОРЯДОК ДНЯ СЕЗДА
„МЫ ПРИ КРУПНОМ ПЕРЕЛОМЕ: НА ТРИБУНЕ ВСЕРОССИЙСКИХ
СЕЗДОВ БУДУТ ПОЯВЛЯТЬСЯ НЕ ТОЛЬКО ПОЛИТИКИ, НО И
ИНЖЕНЕРЫ.
ИЗ РЕЧИ ТОВ. ЛЕНИНА НА 8 СЕЗДЕ

1) МЫ ЗАЖГЛИ НАД
МИРОМ ИСТИНУ ЭТУ.

2) ЭТА ИСТИНА РАЗНЕС
ЛАСЬ ПО ВСЕМУ СВЕТУ

3) ТЕПЕРЬ НАМ НУЖ:
НЫ ОГНИ ЭТИ

4) ПУСТЬ ЭТОТ ОГОНЬ
РОССИЮ ОСВЕТИТ!
РОСТА № 742.

Plate 5. *'We kindled this truth above the world'. A Rosta window by Vladimir Mayakovsky, 1920.*

Plate 7. *Leon Trotsky, by an unknown photographer, 1920s.*

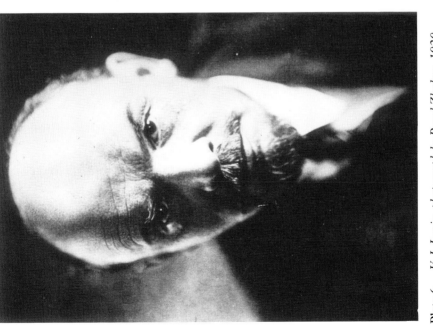

Plate 6. *V. I. Lenin, photograph by Pavel Zhukov, 1920.*

Plate 8.   *The meeting of instructors for the liquidation of illiteracy, Moscow, 1925.*

Plate 9.   *The Five-Year Plan in four years, poster by Viktor Deni, 1930.*

Plate 10.   *'Peasant woman, join the collective farm!', poster by M. M. Cheremnykh, 1930.*

Plate 11. *'The pipe of peace'. The Soviet Foreign Minister Maxim Litvinov offers the pipe of peace to Western diplomats who hurriedly paste up on the wall the sign 'No Smoking'. Poster by M. M. Cheremnykh, 1930s.*

opinion, both must therefore have relied on essentially similar psychological techniques. But this does not follow. Indeed the above quotations from Hitler and Goebbels have been deliberately selected because it would be impossible to match them by any known statement on the Soviet side. Nor is the difference merely one of style or rhetoric. It is tied to fundamental differences of philosophy, which in turn are of considerable practical importance where propaganda method is concerned.

Soviet ideology comprises a complex body of closely interrelated ideas – which do not make good material for demagogic uses. And the characteristic weaknesses of Soviet communication, noted in the last chapter, do not suggest any overriding Soviet concern with psychological manipulation. In any case, Soviet communicators have repeatedly disclaimed any intention to 'manipulate' their audience (whilst often accusing the capitalist media of trying to do precisely that). Furthermore, Soviet literature on this subject more or less clearly denies that it is even possible to consider propaganda method apart from the content of the message being propagated. For example, an authoritative textbook published in Moscow in the 1970s attacked Western sociologists for allegedly trying to discern 'a universal phenomenon of propaganda identically suitable for all socio-economic formations'. And the same book insisted that 'it is impossible to understand the nature, character and social functions of propaganda without an analysis of the character of Marxist–Leninist ideology'.[11] The rest of this chapter will examine the problem of propaganda method – as well as the related question of Soviet public opinion theory – in the context of the official ideology. This is of some importance since – whatever view one may take of the role of Soviet ideology – it does throw light on the framework of assumptions within which Soviet propaganda is supposed to operate.

The evolution of communist propaganda doctrine: the influence of Marxism

The relationship between the ideas of Marx and Engels on the one hand and those of Lenin on the other has been the subject of much debate. The purpose of what immediately follows is merely to argue one point which sometimes gets less attention than it deserves. Neither Marx nor Engels, (nor, indeed, Lenin) provided any blueprint in their writings for mass indoctrination: nor did their writings include any systematically expounded set of views on psychology comparable to their theories of, say, philosophy or economics.

The ideas of Marx and Engels did, however, have implications for psychology as well as for persuasion and public opinion; and they appear to have influenced Soviet doctrine in at least three ways. The first of these stems from the fundamentally important Marxist doctrine of materialism, which holds that ideas - although they can exert an influence on events as part of society's superstructure – are nevertheless themselves determined in the last resort by the social environment, the 'base' of society, in which the economic system is ultimately decisive.[12] This is what apparently explains the tendency in Marxist thinking to ignore or de-emphasize the role of psychological factors as an independent influence on society's development. For insofar as purely psychological factors are recognized as having such a role, this will tend to diminish the importance of the economic 'base' of society on which Marxism lays such stress.

A second influence in this area which stems from Marxism is the key importance which Marxism attributes to the notion of struggle. (This is itself linked with the theory of dialectics, which treats struggle, or 'contradictions', as an essential and ultimately creative force in nature and society.) 'Struggle' has certainly been a prominent theme in the communist message for many decades. A third way in which Marx influenced the communist approach to propaganda stems from Marx's belief that he had evolved a science. Therefore an appeal to reason was one of the foundations of his message.

Marx and Engels, however, did not develop any systematic doctrine of propaganda, although they did maintain that human nature would change – or that Man would change himself – as a result of changes in the environment. Furthermore, they based their prediction of revolution on the march of events: capitalism would, they believed, of itself create a class of people – the proletarians – who would have a compelling interest in the overthrow of the system and who would eventually become the majority of the population.[13] This, of itself, represented a theory of public opinion. But it was not one in which propaganda was to be the prime moving force.

Lenin on propaganda

The emergence of a communist propaganda theory as something distinct in its own right is generally attributed to Lenin who, at the turn of the century, was preoccupied with the strategy of the revolutionary movement in Russia. Lenin made important additions to earlier Marxist ideas – including, above all, the insistence on the need for the movement to be led by a disciplined 'vanguard' party of professional revolutionaries. The point needs, however, to be made that Lenin never produced any blueprint or recipe for mass indoctrination; nor were his ideas basically

переработка

concerned with psychological manipulation.

Lenin's writings contain only scattered references to mass psychology. Indeed, as a modern Soviet writer has observed, 'Lenin was interested in the phenomena of social psychology only as a revolutionary; and for the sake of the tasks of the revolution'.[14] He is on record as emphasizing the importance of understanding the psychology of every social stratum (when assessing the timing of a revolution);[15] and of the need for the party to know the moods of the masses.[16] He stressed, too, the need to mobilize mass emotions against the injustices of the old order. And, like Marx and Engels, he was committed to the belief that human psychology and behaviour could be fundamentally changed for the better – holding that in a future communist society 'people will *become accustomed* to observing the elementary conditions of social life *without force* and *without subordination*' (emphasis in original).[17] However, this radical change in attitudes (one corollary of which was to be the gradual withering away of the state) was foreseen as the primary result not of coercion or indoctrination from above but of changes in the environment. This was implicit in Lenin's observation that 'we see around us millions of times how readily people become accustomed to observing the necessary rules of social life if there is no exploitation, if there is nothing that causes indignation, that calls forth protest and revolt and has to be *suppressed*' (emphasis in original).[18]

Where propaganda was concerned, Lenin's starting-point was not so much with psychological methods, but rather with the *necessity* for propaganda, if socialist consciousness was to become widespread. Two basic propositions to which Lenin repeatedly returned were, first, that 'without revolutionary theory there can be no revolutionary movement' and, secondly, that working-class political consciousness could not arise spontaneously but could only come 'from without'.[19] Working-class involvement in industrial conflicts in the pursuit of purely economic grievances would not of itself – according to Lenin – generate an understanding by the masses of the socialist theory which a workers' party would need in order to come to power. Such a theory, he insisted, could only be formulated and imparted by intellectuals from the middle class. Lenin approvingly quoted the German Social Democrat Karl Kautsky who had written that: 'The contemporary socialist movement can come into being only on the basis of a profound scientific knowledge . . . The bearer of this science is not the proletariat but the *bourgeois intelligentsia*' (emphasis in original).[20]

In 1920, when Bolsheviks were in power, Lenin observed that 'We must re-educate the masses; and only propaganda and agitation can re-educate them';[21] but here again Lenin's focus was on the necessity for propaganda rather than on psychological methods. It was obvious, needless to say, that socialist ideas stood no chance of spreading rapidly amongst the largely uneducated working class, especially under the kind of authoritarian regime that existed in Tsarist Russia. Hence the importance of the original distinction (first put forward by the Russian Marxist Plekhanov, not by Lenin) between 'propaganda', that is, the presentation of complex ideas to a small group of politically-conscious people, and 'agitation', the presentation of a few simple ideas to large groups of people. (Today, as noted in the previous chapter, this distinction has lost much of its earlier importance.)

So far as the general strategy of propaganda and agitation was concerned, Lenin said little about psychology but did repeatedly make use of two concepts on which subsequent Soviet leaders have heavily relied. One concept was 'organization'; the other was 'education'. As far back as 1901, Lenin, in a much-quoted article, called for the creation of a socialist newspaper to cater for the whole of Russia; he observed that 'a paper is not only a collective propagandist and a collective agitator, it is also a collective organizer'.[22] (By this he evidently meant it should be a co-ordinator of the political activity of like-minded people.) At a later stage – in a remark typical of his general line of thinking – he wrote that 'organization increases strength tenfold'.[23] a point of obvious importance both for the winning and retention of revolutionary power. At the same time, Lenin constantly wrote about the importance of political 'education'; and argued, in an unfinished article in 1905, that 'there is and always will be a certain element of pedagogy' in the party's work.[24]

Lenin's view of the role of propaganda and agitation in the context of overall political strategy was perhaps best encapsulated in another article of his, written in 1905, where he set out the tasks of the revolutionary movement in the following order:

> Suppose that a small number of people are waging a struggle against a hideous evil of which the mass of slumbering people are unaware, or towards which they are indifferent. What is the main task of those waging the struggle? [It is] (1) to awaken as many of the slumberers as possible; (2) to enlighten them about the tasks and conditions of the struggle; (3) to organize them into a force capable of achieving victory; (4) to teach them how to make correct use of the fruits of victory.
> Naturally, (1) must precede (2)–(4), which without (1) are impossible.[25]

Here, in the most succinct fashion, Lenin focuses on propaganda as a *necessary* precondition for the achievement of other things. Implicit in this passage is the notion that the Bolshevik message was merely drawing attention to an objective reality; and also that the target audience would be sympathetic, once the message had been properly explained and understood. Therefore the question of psychological manipulation did not really arise. Even though Lenin did seek to appeal to emotions as well as reason, he never sought to exploit psychology in the manner of a demagogue who tailors the message according to what he thinks the audience wants to hear. Far from it: it was Lenin, above all others, who laid it down that in the sphere of ideology there could be no compromise.[26] There were times indeed (as in the case of his opposition to Russia's continuation in the war against Germany in 1917) when he found himself in a minority even within his own party.

Lenin's doctrine of propaganda did, however, contain one further important ingredient. He did not believe that propaganda was in itself all-powerful. Direct personal experience – so Lenin often said – played an indispensible part in political conversion. 'Surely there is no need to prove to Social Democrats that there can be no political education except through political struggle and political action', he wrote in 1899.[27] More than 20 years later, after the Bolshevik revolution had taken place, Lenin wrote that in order to produce mass support for an uprising 'propaganda and agitation are not enough. For this purpose the masses need their own political experience.'[28] And during the Russian civil war, he continued to cite personal experience as one factor which helped to persuade the peasant population that Bolshevik rule was preferable to that of the White armies.[29]

Lenin on public opinion: the question of majority support

This emphasis on the crucial persuasive role of personal experience leads us to another important question – the nature of Lenin's views about public opinion. If the experience of the masses is essential to the success of the revolution, then it might seem to follow that a socialist revolution cannot come about, or at any rate permanently survive, except on the basis of popular support. There are, in fact, pronouncements by Lenin which might seem to support this interpretation. On the eve of the 1917 revolution he indicated that an uprising should not be attempted without, among other things, 'the sympathy of the majority of the people, as proved by objective facts.'[30] And he maintained shortly before that, in September 1917, that such sympathy did in fact exist.[31] After the revolution had succeeded, Lenin also observed that 'socialism cannot be implemented by a minority, by the Party. It can be implemented only by tens of millions who have learned to do it themselves.'[32]

But it is precisely over this crucial issue of majority support that Lenin's pronouncements become opaque, if not inconsistent; and it may be that his views changed with time. For it is also true that on the eve of the 1917 uprising, he expressly rejected the argument that the Bolsheviks should be influenced by voting results at an election: 'For the Bolsheviks to await a "formal" majority is naive,' he is on record as saying. 'No revolution will wait for *this*' (emphasis in original).[33] In the elections to the Constituent Assembly – the first to be held after the revolution – the Bolsheviks failed to obtain a majority and almost at once, in January 1918, they dissolved the Assembly.

Lenin, in a well-known polemic against the German Social Democratic leader Karl Kautsky, explicitly rejected the suggestion that the proletariat – the backbone of support for the revolution – should seek power by winning an election based on universal suffrage. Lenin's strategy appeared to be: 'Act first, persuade later.' Therefore: 'The proletariat must first overthrow the bourgeoisie and win *for itself* state power, and then use that state power . . . for the purpose of winning the sympathy of the majority of the working people' (emphasis in original).[34] Exactly *how* that sympathy is to be won takes us back once again to the central theme of this book. But how in any case is this passage to be reconciled with Lenin's earlier claims that the Bolsheviks in 1917 did in fact enjoy the sympathy of the majority? A modern Soviet author draws attention to the apparent discrepancy but then dismisses it. According to him, 'the very concept of a popular majority is not uncommonly used in different senses' and he suggests that in one case Lenin was referring to the working class plus the peasantry who sympathized with it; whilst in the second quotation Lenin referred to the formation of a 'stable majority'.[35] Furthermore – in a passage which provides a highly significant insight into later Soviet attitudes towards public opinion – this author argues that majorities in a revolutionary situation cannot be measured by a mere counting of heads. He maintains that the revolutionary movement is made up of such heterogeneous elements that:

> in a vote on the basis of formal equality, the advantage will almost certainly be on the side, not of those who most clearly and consistently express the common progressive line of development of the majority, but on the side of those who are numerically preponderant, but who have doubts, who vacillate and who display irresolution and timidity in the face of drastic impending changes . . . Therefore the basic question in a revolution – the question of power – cannot be settled by voting alone.[36]

This attitude towards public opinion – which holds on the one hand that majorities are important, but on the other hand that they cannot be ascertained by mere voting results – naturally makes it difficult to pin down the Leninist view. Lenin's own statements also indicate a shift in his attitude over the need for majority support. He argued, after the revolution, that the proletariat because of its key position in the capitalist economy and because of the fact that 'it expresses economically and politically the real interests of the overwhelming majority of the working people under capitalism' wielded a totally disproportionate power:

> Therefore, the proletariat, even when it constitutes a minority of the population . . . is capable of overthrowing the bourgeoisie, and, after that, of winning to its side numerous allies from a mass of semi-proletarians and petty bourgeoisie who . . . only by their subsequent experience become convinced that the proletarian dictatorship is inevitable, proper and legitimate.[37]

This assertion that the taking of power by a minority might, under certain conditions, be feasible and justified, represented a view not found in the writings of Marx and Engels. It does not necessarily follow, however, that Lenin was indifferent to what the mass of people wanted, or that he believed that Bolshevik rule could survive in the long run without popular consent. Even in his new formulation, personal experience was to be the ultimate guarantee of popular support. However, that experience was to be acquired *after*, not before, the revolution.

Lenin's thinking about this may well have been governed by a totally different and more practical consideration. He had expected the Bolshevik revolution to trigger off a series of revolutions in other, more advanced, European countries; and had apparently counted on them helping to bale Russia out of her economic difficulties and in this way helping to consolidate popular support for the new regime in Russia itself.[38] This, possibly, was Lenin's strategic miscalculation. Foreign revolution and support for the Soviet regime did not, of course, materialize. In May 1918 Lenin admitted that: 'We can count on the politically-conscious workers alone; the remaining mass, the bourgeoisie and petty proprietors are against us.'[39]

In December 1921, one of Lenin's colleagues, Anatolii Lunacharskii, the Commissar for Education, put the problem of persuasion and public opinion in an unusually frank way. He did so when defending censorship:

> we were not in the least afraid of having to censor even artistic literature; for beneath its flag, beneath its artistic exterior, we might be injecting a poison into the as yet naive and unenlightened soul of the vast masses, who – because of the all too numerous ordeals of the journey – are daily on the verge of staggering; and of pushing aside the hand which is leading them through the desert to the Promised Land.[40]

It is unusual for Soviet leaders to invoke biblical analogies. This one –

the image of 'the desert and the Promised Land' – casts a useful light on
Soviet political theory because of the clue which it gives to the leadership's
self-justification: it serves to reconcile liberationist aims with the use of
sometimes extreme dictatorial methods. (This passage from Lunarcharskii
was approvingly quoted by a Soviet author in the 1970s.)[41] Even here,
however, the assumption is clear that *in the end* the masses will, having
reached the Promised Land, be won over to the system through personal
experience.

Stalin on propaganda and persuasion

Propaganda during the Stalin era is discussed at greater length in chapter
4. Something should, however, be said at this stage about Stalin's
pronouncements on the theory of propaganda. The first point to be noted
– which is not without irony – is that of all Soviet leaders it was Stalin
who insisted most strongly that the masses *must* learn from their own
experience; and that persuasion was an absolutely essential requirement if
the Communist Party was successfully to exercise its leading role. The
party, so he wrote in 1926, 'must heed the voice of the masses'.[42] The
party's authority and the 'iron discipline' within the working class were
based 'not upon fear or upon the party's "unlimited" rights, but upon the
working class's trust in the party'. Persuasion, he said, was 'the basic
method of the party's influence on the masses' and force was justified only
'in regard to a minority after the majority had been successfully convinced'.[43]
In the same context, Stalin was even prepared to recognize the possibility
of a rift between the party and the masses. What he said deserves to be
quoted at greater length:

> What happens if the party itself begins in one way or another to
> oppose itself to a class . . . violating the foundations of 'mutual trust'?
> Are such cases, *in general*, possible? Yes, they are. They are possible:
> 1 *If* the party starts to build its authority among the masses not on
>   its own work or on the trust of the masses, but on its 'unlimited'
>   rights;
> 2 *If* the party's policy is obviously incorrect, but it is unwilling to
>   re-examine and correct its error;
> 3 *If* the policy is correct as a whole but the masses are not yet
>   ready to adopt it; and the party is unwilling or unable to wait so
>   as to give the masses the opportunity to become convinced from
>   their own experience of the correctness of the party's policy . . .
> Is it possible to impose party leadership upon a class by force? No,

it is not. In any case, *such* leadership cannot be of any lengthy duration [emphasis throughout in original].[44]

Statements of this kind are of course totally at odds with Stalin's record of coercion and terror. They are, indeed, at odds with other things which Stalin said. At other times, he had used military analogies and referred to the party as 'the general staff of the proletariat',[45] implying that the party had the right to issue orders and not just guidance. The most important thing here, however, is not that Stalin was insincere, but that he put forward a (not entirely unrealistic) theory of persuasion and public opinion which continued to be proclaimed during the Stalin era but which was not followed in practice.

A second way in which Stalin contributed to Soviet propaganda doctrine was of much greater practical importance. Both Marx and Lenin had believed in the possibility of radically changing human attitudes – but, as we have seen, they saw this as resulting primarily through changes in the environment. In the 1920s, when the term 'New Soviet Man' apparently originated,[46] the focus of Soviet attention was still to a large extent on the role of the environment in changing attitudes. After the start of crash programmes of collectivization and industrialization, Soviet official thinking underwent a gradual but drastic shift of emphasis. From then on, it was not just the environment but education (as well as propaganda) which came to be treated as crucial in changing human nature.[47] One of the most forceful statements of this new view came from the Soviet educationalist Anton Makarenko (1888–1939), who won great official commendation for his work in rehabilitating juvenile delinquents. As Makarenko put it:

I profess infinite, reckless and unhesitating belief in the unlimited power of educational work, particularly under the social conditions pertaining in the Soviet Union. I do not know a single case where a genuinely valuable character was formed without a healthy educational background or, on the contrary, where a perverted character came about in spite of correct educational work.[48]

Stress on the importance of education was perfectly in tune with earlier Marxist doctrine; and indeed the expansion of Soviet education brought solid gains. But the suggestion (as in the passage just quoted) that education or upbringing had an almost decisive role appears to go beyond anything which Lenin ever maintained; and it had obvious implications for propaganda. It was in Stalin's time that the belief in the potential of mass indoctrination from above really gained ground; but that is the subject of the next chapter.

Stalin on the unanimity of public opinion

Another of Stalin's contributions to Soviet theory relates to the doctrine of public opinion. In his time, this term was never used systematically in the USSR; indeed no article on public opinion appeared in the authoritative *Large Soviet Encyclopedia* until 1974, in the course of its third edition.[49] (Only much later did the term become officially enshrined in the 1977 Soviet Constitution, article 9 of which defined socialist democracy as meaning, among other things, 'constant responsiveness to public opinion.)'[50]

Lenin, as we have already noted, was reluctant to concede that public opinion could be ascertained by a mere counting of heads. Furthermore, both Marxism and Leninism do have one important implication for public opinion theory – namely, that ideologies and attitudes ultimately reflect the interests of one or other class.[51] This could be, and has been, interpreted as a denial that any fundamental cleavage of public opinion is possible except as the result of class conflict. It was this line of reasoning which Stalin adopted when the third Soviet Constitution came into force in 1936. By that time, according to Stalin, the remnants of the exploiter classes no longer existed in the USSR; and there remained only two friendly social classes, namely the workers and the peasants, together with the intelligentsia. This was said to mean not only that the foundations of socialism had been created, but also that the basis now existed for what Stalin termed 'the moral-political unity of Soviet society'.[52] This was the inception of the celebrated (and non-empirical) doctrine of the 'unanimity' of Soviet public opinion – a doctrine which was to some degree modified during and after the 1960s, as we shall see in a later chapter, and which was eventually superseded by Gorbachev's concept of 'socialist pluralism'.

To sum up what has just been said: classical Marxism implicitly assumed that public opinion would in the end automatically come to support revolution. Lenin rejected this and was finally prepared to envisage the revolutionary seizure of power by a minority who would later convert the majority to its side. Stalin disposed of the whole problem of public opinion by effectively declaring it to be unanimous.

It can also be seen that the belief in the crucial role of mass indoctrination owed nothing to classical Marxism; it was also, arguably, a distortion of the views of Lenin, who insisted that propaganda was necessary but denied that it was all-powerful. Reliance on mass indoctrination (or the 'unlimited power' of education) began under Stalin, although he himself – in theory – continued to stress the need for non-coercive persuasion and warned against the dangers of the party trying to impose its policies against the will of the majority.

It can therefore be seen that Marxist–Leninist ideology did have a direct bearing on the subjects of both propaganda and public opinion. However, with regard to the purely psychological aspects of indoctrination there is little to be found even in the pronouncements of Stalin.

The Brezhnev era and after: propaganda and the 'ideology of stagnation'

So much, then, for the early origin and development of Soviet thinking. We now move forward, and turn to the situation in the period immediately before Gorbachev came to power. Here again, ideology had a direct influence on the official approach to propaganda and public opinion. During most of the post-Stalin era, as will be seen in later chapters, there was a much greater official interest in persuasion; this was largely because Stalinist methods of mass coercion had been abandoned. During the Brezhnev era, a sizeable literature appeared in the USSR on the subjects of propaganda and, to a rather lesser extent, public opinion. Almost all of it, however, had an ideological orientation. It was concerned to emphasize the importance of the 'leading role' of the Communist Party; and it had much more to say about the supposed aims and functions of propaganda in the context of party policy than about methods of persuasion as such. This 'ideological' aspect of the Soviet approach to persuasion, precisely because it gained such prominence, cannot be ignored.

The question may naturally be asked as to exactly *why* ideology became such a major Soviet preoccupation. Many observers in the outside world found the question a baffling one. Whilst some were inclined to dismiss ideology as a mere ritual, others tended to regard it in purely negative terms – as something dogmatic, mythological and anti-empirical, the antithesis of 'common sense' and an irrelevance if not an actual hindrance to the efficient everyday running of society. Political propaganda by the leadership might in itself have been understandable to an outsider. But outside observers found it a good deal harder to understand the specific emphasis on ideology, particularly since it was so often formulated in opaque language and was hardly calculated to have a mass appeal. How, it might be asked, could ideology be relevant to the achievement of the leadership's policy goals? How, indeed, did it strengthen the system's power-base?

In many respects, the Gorbachev leadership – having set out to reformulate the ideology in a less dogmatic and more pluralistic way – accepted the validity of the above questions. It repeatedly said that the ideology of the Brezhnev era was 'stagnant'. Yegor Ligachev, the member of the Politburo then responsible for ideology went so far as to say, at a conference in 1986 that 'we have very few [Marxist–Leninist] philosophical works which are intelligible or interesting to people.'[53] At the same conference, Leonid Abalkin, one of Gorbachev's leading economic advisers, cast a fresh light on the way that much of this 'ideological' literature came to be written. The authors concerned had, he said, devised a sort of 'theoretical' justification for separating theory from real life. They had argued, according to Abalkin, that 'the theoretical sciences ought to concern themselves with the global laws of social development; and ought to construct a kind of ideal model of socialist society, which stands above all negative phenomena, difficulties and contradictions', even when the latter developed on a fairly large scale. 'A whole generation' of social scientists, Abalkin said, had been reared on this kind of 'theoretical ratiocination'. And in one of the most forceful condemnations of traditional Soviet attitudes which any senior Soviet official had ever made up to that time, he said that this gap between theory and reality had led to 'hypocrisy, double-faced morality and double-faced psychology'.[54]

Quite clearly, then there *was* a problem about accepting the official ideology at face value. Equally clearly, the ideology was failing to fulfil the function that it was intended to fulfil; this explains why Gorbachev set out to reform it. But this still leaves the question: what *were* the intended functions of the ideology? To this, there is no short, clear answer; nor does our argument hinge on trying to provide one. (The main point for our purposes is simply the fact that ideology, for whatever reason, *has* been central to Soviet thinking.) All the same, one can suggest two likely purposes which Soviet ideology has in theory been intended to fulfil. The first has to do with the creation of mass motivation, common purpose and cohesion in Soviet society. The second has to do with resisting or containing those influences in society which the Soviet authorities see as hostile. Other explanations could be added. But the two just mentioned do, on examination, have a certain inner logic.

Let us take, first, the question of common purpose. It should perhaps be pointed out that the Soviet system – in total contrast to right-wing authoritarian regimes – has never been based on the notion of control by a ruling elite over a purely passive citizenry. The Soviet system derives its entire *raison d'être* from a programme of far-reaching social and economic transformation; and the system cannot achieve these goals merely by neutralizing opposition or protecting itself from overthrow. The attainment of the stated goals ultimately depends on the fulfilment of a further vital precondition – namely affirmative public action in pursuit of the goals. This, in turn, ultimately depends on the existence of conscious, motivated commitment to the goals at grass-roots level. Only then, according to Soviet theory, will the wheels of society go round in the way intended. Nor is this mere rhetoric. A number of Soviet achievements – above all in the Second World War – would have been impossible without a high degree of grass-roots effort. It should also be noted that Soviet leaders, from Lenin onwards, have seen the expansion of education (in the general, as distinct from the political, sense) as a strategically essential precondition for the realization of their policies. Soviet accomplishments in this field have, whatever the unsolved problems, been impressive. (This represents an important, and sometimes little-noticed contrast with the Nazis who never set themselves any comparable educational aims.) And all this ties in with another long-proclaimed objective of the Soviet political system: the goal of popular 'participation' in its management. It was Lenin who said that in the long run the workers themselves should carry out the day-to-day tasks of public administration.[55] And this (as opposed to the idea of a competitive party system) has in effect been the real kernel of the Soviet concept of democracy: indeed, the preamble to the 1977 Constitution of the USSR equates 'true democracy' with, among other things, 'the ever more active participation of the working people in the running of the state'.[56]

This itself takes us closer to the intended role of mass ideological commitment. For clearly enough 'participation', in the sense just described, cannot effectively function in the absence of positive, intelligent, motivated behaviour at the grass roots. This itself presupposes a minimum level of mass education for the job. It also presupposes the existence of a common social purpose which is both widely understood and widely supported by the mass of citizens. And it is precisely here that ideology becomes relevant – because it is supposed to provide and validate the common purpose – the attainment of a communist future – which unifies and motivates society.

The Soviet emphasis on ideology can, of course, be explained in other ways. It has sometimes been explained by outside observers as being due to the leadership's need to 'legitimate' the system. It is certainly true, as already noted, that Soviet ideologues have laid enormous stress on the importance of the Communist Party's 'leading role'. Nevertheless, the undoubted desire of the Soviet Communist Party to maintain and justify its rule can hardly provide the full explanation for the vast propaganda effort – if only because the enormous scale of that effort appears to go far beyond what such 'self-justification' would require. If any real sense is to be made of the party's enormous political and economic education network, this can only be done by postulating not just the aim of securing popular acquiescence in the system, but the further aim of securing active popular involvement in the operation of the system. The question for the moment is not whether or how far past Soviet leaders actually believed in this latter aim. It is simply that, without such an aim, a great deal of the propaganda effort would be pointless.

Such an interpretation of the intended function of Soviet ideology can be corroborated by Soviet statements. Indeed, it is in the light of the concept of mass dedication to a common cause that most of the Soviet discussion of 'participation', democracy, ideology and propaganda can most easily be understood. This was evidently the reason for the repeated Soviet insistence that the formation of appropriate public attitudes is not merely desirable but crucial from the regime's point of view. Mikhail Suslov, then a senior member of the Politburo, reiterated a well-known dictum when he said in 1979 that 'The formation of a New Man is not only the result but also a most important condition for the building of a new society'.[57] Brezhnev expressed the same idea in an even more forceful way when he said in 1980 that 'A gap between material and spiritual development must not be allowed; it would threaten many misfortunes'.[58] There is, therefore, a sense in which the Soviet system – precisely because it presupposes the changing of human attitudes – is actually *more* dependent on public consent than is the government of a Western-type democracy. It is in this context that the ideology has to be seen. It was Suslov who, not long before his death, said that one of the main purposes of 'ideological work' was 'to inculcate the desire and the ability to build communism'.[59] This succinctly explains the aim of the gigantic propaganda apparatus. The notion of ideology as the source of a unifying social goal was also implicit in Lunacharskii's metaphor of 'the desert and the Promised Land'.

It should immediately be pointed out, however, that – certainly in the Brezhnev era – the Soviet concept of 'participation' did not, even in the long run, envisage the emergence of a liberal, or still less a pluralist society. Rather, it appeared to envisage the development of a collectivist, self-regulating society, guided for the foreseeable future by the Communist Party, but increasingly relying on the 'consciousness' of its citizens. In this type of society, the need for discipline would remain, but the need for externally imposed coercion would gradually diminish – and come to be replaced by individual self-discipline, voluntarily accepted out of an awareness of the public good. This would seem, indeed, to be the meaning of a passage in the 1986 Soviet Communist Party Programme (substantially similar in this respect to the earlier programme of 1961), which speaks of the ultimate goal of what it terms 'communist public self-government' but also speaks of the need in a future communist society for 'a high level of consciousness, social activity, discipline and self-discipline of members of society, in which observance of the uniform, generally accepted rules of communist conduct will become an inner need and habit for every person'.[60]

It would be a mistake to assume that offical concern with 'participation' and 'ideological work' in the Brezhnev era was totally devoid of meaning. The then Soviet leadership must have been well aware of the need to involve the public in implementing its policies – since the policies clearly could not be achieved on the basis of public passivity. And even if most of the decisions in Soviet society were (or are) taken at higher levels, the need still remained for people at lower levels to implement those decisions in an intelligent way. Nevertheless, the whole official approach to 'participation' and 'ideological work' at that time was, even in the regime's own terms, seriously flawed. Members of the Soviet public could have little interest in 'participating', when this meant merely helping to implement, rather than influence, major decisions. Gorbachev's policy of encouraging greater debate and holding multi-candidate elections was, of course, intended to make participation more real. Furthermore – and this is a crucial point in the context of this book – even if the Brezhnev leadership really did acknowledge the need to win support from public opinion at home, it in no way necessarily followed that propaganda or 'ideological work' was the most promising way of getting that support. Yet Brezhnev himself seemed to regard propaganda as one of the prime moving forces in shaping attitudes. As he himself said in a speech at the party congress in 1971:

> The moral and political make-up of Soviet people is moulded by the entire socialist way of our life, by the entire course of affairs in society and, *above all*, by purposeful, persevering ideological and educational work by the Party, by all its organizations [emphasis added].[61]

This again suggests that the leadership saw ideology as a purpose-giving, unifying, motivating social force. Its importance in Soviet thinking has evidently been considerable. After all, *if* the goals of the system really did enjoy the kind of well-motivated grass-roots support which the leaders intended, then many of the Soviet Union's social and political problems would vanish. It is worth recalling that some years ago an article in *Pravda* more or less directly repudiated the notion that the fulfilment of the system's goals was something which for ever receded into the future. It should not be supposed, in the words of the article, 'that the socialist ideal can be likened to the rim of the horizon, which always lies ahead'.[62]

At the same time, I am not arguing that this belief in the motivating power of ideology is in itself a complete (or totally convincing) explanation of the Soviet leadership's traditional thinking. A second important reason for the scale of the propaganda effort was the supposed need to *contain* the spread of attitudes which the leaders saw as unacceptable. It was closely interwoven with the deeply ingrained Soviet notion of persuasion as a form of struggle; and with the belief (exaggerated or not) that if the propaganda effort were relaxed then other forces would gain the upper hand. During the Second World War, when anti-religious propaganda was halted, there was a resurgence of religion in the USSR.[63] And the slackening of this propaganda in the immediate post-war years was said to have created a situation 'which religious organizations were not slow to exploit'.[64] The upsurge of opposition in Poland in the 1970s and the subsequent rise of Solidarity was partly blamed, in the Soviet press at the time, on the 'ideological complacency' of the Gierek leadership through whose fault, so it was said, 'the very concept of the struggle of ideas, of ideology, was removed from the agenda.'[65] On the same general theme, a Soviet journal in the 1970s made the following unusually frank comment: 'Practice ... has shown that under conditions of fierce ideological struggle, any departure from Marxist–Leninist principles *inexorably leads to anti-communism*' (emphasis added).[66] How far that is true may be debatable. But it does shed a light on the mentality of Soviet conservatives. They would no doubt support their argument by quoting the case-histories of all those Soviet dissidents who began as advocates of reform from within, but ended up as out-and-out opponents of the system.

It would be a mistake to construe this Soviet attitude as an admission that anti-regime sentiments inside the USSR are necessarily widespread. Rather, it seems to stem from an assumption that *any* potential threat will spread if it is not checked. Richard Kosolapov, then Editor-in-Chief of the theoretical journal *Kommunist*, had this to say in 1983, when arguing the need to combat such well-known problems as speculation and parasitism:

> Who does not know that in the absence of proper concern for a healthy social climate, where educational work in a socialist collectivist spirit is allowed to flag, the influences opposed to [*antipody*] communist morality will spontaneously increase? ...
>
> Such elements are especially dangerous, because wherever they manage to form a nest then, like moths, they eat away at the fabric of socialist social relationships.[67]

We have been suggesting, then, that two reasons for the heavy reliance on ideology are, first, to promote mass commitment to the system's aims; and secondly to contain (or 'struggle' against) other influences which, it is thought, might gain in strength unless constantly checked. Whether these represent complete or satisfactory explanations is not crucial to our theme. At all events, it is extremely difficult to dismiss the Soviet preoccupation with ideology as a mere ritual, if only because of all the time and effort which goes into formulating and teaching the ideology. In particular, as any Soviet textbook on the subject shows, ideological considerations have played a major part in the Soviet approach to propaganda method. It is to this aspect of the matter that we now turn.

The influence of ideology on propaganda method

The first thing to be noted under this heading concerns the Marxist–Leninist claim to the status of a science. This in itself has had implications for propaganda method. In the Brezhnev era, one Soviet ideological specialist summarized the functions of propaganda as follows: 'First, it serves to disseminate a scientific world outlook ... Secondly, it provides a real, objective knowledge of the world. Thirdly, it helps the working class to attain self-knowledge, that is, a correct awareness of its own interests.'[68]

According to this doctrine, then, the question of psychological manipulation does not really arise: the essential strategy of propaganda is to show the masses by patient explanation where their 'objective' interests lie. Hence part of the reason why (as in the quotations at the beginning of this chapter) Soviet communicators lay such great emphasis on the importance of content. Some, apparently for this reason, have been known to express doubts about reliance on psychological techniques, although, as we shall see in due course, Soviet thinking on this point changed in emphasis from the 1960s. Soviet propaganda specialists would, however, be unlikely to disagree with the proposition that the impact of their message ultimately stands or falls by its essential content. Here in particular the concept of 'interests' and of how they are to be ascertained and by whom is of crucial importance. (How for example does one persuade Polish Catholic workers that the existing regime in Poland is in their 'interests'?) From a theoretical point of view, the whole subject of 'interests' is still an under-explored area of study in the Soviet Union. One difficulty with this concept, apart from all else, is its vagueness.[69]

Soviet propaganda, according to its own exponents, performs not a manipulative but an essentially explanatory (as well as an organizing) function. And this leads us to a second way in which the ideology has influenced propaganda methods – namely the stress on propaganda as a form of education. 'Persuasion' (*ubezhdenie*) has been said to be of fundamental importance in the Communist Party's approach to its own population,[70] and there is no reason to doubt this. But 'persuasion' in its Soviet connotation has not, in the past, had the overtones of dialogue, negotiation or compromise with which the word is sometimes associated. (Compromise in the realm of ideology was held to be inadmissible.) Persuasion, according to the Soviet concept, has always been an essentially pedagogical activity; and this is reflected in the common Soviet expression 'ideological-educational work'. In the 1960s the the head of the Communist Party's Propaganda Department made this point very specifically. 'Pedagogy', he said, meant:

> the science of instructing and educating people, the science of the all-round moulding of the personality and of the collective. And propaganda? This is a powerful instrument for the ideological enlightenment of the working people, for their communist education. This means that to conduct propaganda activity successfully without relying on pedagogy is utterly impossible.[71]

This concept of persuasion was apparently that of a relationship between a teacher (the party) and a pupil (the masses). It all savoured very much of the 'schoolmaster state'. This 'didactic' approach to persuasion (which should not be confused with either the liberal idea of dialogue or the Nazi method of manipulation) provides one of the major keys to traditional Soviet propaganda theory. It explains, for one thing, the criteria by which the media selected or rejected their material. There was a ban in principle not only on what was politically unacceptable but on anything not considered to have a socially educative value. Some years ago (to take a minor example) the Moscow newspaper *Komsomol'skaya pravda* published an apparently innocuous report about whales who had died whilst hurling themselves on to the shores of Australia. This earned a rebuke from *Pravda*. A Soviet book entitled *Problems of Information in the Press* quoted this case and added the comment:

> Journalists, especially in the information department, must always think about the purpose of the material being published. Why is it being printed? What does it give to the reader? What does it teach? What example does it inspire? A paragraph which performs no social, educative or didactic function is a sop which must have no place in the Soviet press.[72]

This belief that nothing should be published which did not set a 'positive' example was of course, one of the reasons invoked to justify censorship; it may indeed have a measure of popular backing. Some years ago, *Pravda* published a complaint from a reader who apparently opposed the portrayal of negative items on television on the grounds that 'If there are no such negative phenomena in our lives, then they will start to appear after these programmes. But if they do not exist, then there is all the more reason not to play on the viewer's nerves.' Another letter protested about television plays which portrayed children who disobeyed their parents; this, the letter argued, could lead to imitation.[73] This did not of course reflect the *Pravda* view. But it did offer a glimpse of the way the Soviet mind sometimes works.

The pedagogical flavour of Soviet persuasion can also be discerned from the way political study sessions were traditionally conducted. Great importance was attached to discussion; but the more or less avowed purpose was to preclude genuine debate and steer the discussion to a pre-ordained conclusion. Marxism was to be taught rather as one might teach an elementary natural science or a foreign language where there are either right or wrong answers. The following advice from a Soviet book of 1978 on how to teach philosophy to students made this abundantly clear:

> After different opinions have been expressed on the subject under discussion, the teacher must direct the audience towards the proof of the untenability and invalidity of those points of view which do not correspond to the truth ... In the course of this critical examination it is very important to point out methodological errors made by one or other of those who have spoken. After a critical examination of incomplete, inaccurate or erroneous answers and statements by students, it is essential to provide a sufficiently complete and thorough validation of the right solution to the question.[74]

Such advice merely underlined one inherent difficulty of traditional Soviet propaganda method. Since it discouraged the expression of unorthodox points of view, it naturally made it harder for party speakers to gauge what impact they were making on the audience. The Gorbachev leadership, as we have already seen, insisted that there was not necessarily only one correct point of view. And Gorbachev himself seemed to repudiate the 'schoolmaster state' idea. In 1987, when addressing the Komsomol, he deplored the fact that 'We have tormented our young people with sermons.'[75]

But this in turn takes us to a third – and paradoxical – way in which the Soviet approach to propaganda has been influenced by ideology. For whilst it excluded or severely circumscribed debate, it did (and does) nevertheless lay great stress on a rationalistic appeal. Indeed Marxism–Leninism (in contrast to all religions and most other ideologies) does *not* ask to be accepted even partly on trust: it appears to claim that it can be validated solely through an appeal to the intellect. And whilst it is true that Soviet persuaders always have attached importance to the appeal to emotions (which is one reason why the Communist Party insists on its right to guide the arts), nevertheless Soviet doctrine has always emphasized the primacy of reason over the emotions. This has been a continuing theme in official literature. In the words of a pamphlet published in Moscow in the 1930s: 'Bolshevik agitation is the political *education* of the masses:

therefore it influences in the first place the awareness of the masses, their reason' (emphasis in original).[76] A Soviet book which appeared in 1977 likewise stated that the appeal to reason was the 'basic method of influencing people's awareness'.[77] A handbook for propagandists published in 1970 devoted an entire chapter to the laws of logic; and it went, in some detail, into such problems as induction, deduction, the law of identity and the law of the excluded middle.[78] This in turn reflected a deeply rooted assumption about human nature. According to a Soviet writer in the late 1960s: 'Marxist psychology proceeds from the premise that in the last resort reason always prevails over the emotions.'[79] This is of course the diametrical opposite of the propaganda doctrine of the Nazis.

What concerns us here is not the intellectual validity of Soviet ideology, but its intended intellectual appeal, which has left deep traces on its propaganda method. The study of Marxism–Leninism – which, as we saw in the last chapter, has been greatly expanded in recent years – makes a heavy demand on the critical faculties of the audience; it requires perseverance as well as intellectual effort. This cannot fail to have an influence on propaganda method, and it partly explains the vast network of political education courses (which had no counterpart in Nazi Germany).

A fourth way in which ideology affected the Soviet approach to propaganda has already been mentioned: it concerns the official belief in the 'malleability' of human nature. If human attitudes are so susceptible to change (as claimed for example by Makarenko, see p. 63 above), then it must follow that the potential of propaganda is correspondingly greater. A Soviet textbook of the 1970s explicitly made this point: 'All mental functions . . . can be changed, depending on the peculiarities of the social environment. Guided by this, the propagandist, when he arranges his work, takes account not only of what a man is at a particular time . . . but of the powers and capacities within him which can and must be developed.'[80]

This faith in human capacity for psychological change went hand in hand with the doctrine of the creation of a New Man – a term which figured prominently in the Communist Party Programme of 1961, although it was not used in the subsequent party programme of 1986. But regardless of terminology, the belief in the 'malleability' of human nature remained very much a part of orthodox Soviet thinking. It is noteworthy that on one occasion in the late 1970s, a Leningrad psychiatrist did publicly query this doctrine in a letter to the Moscow *Literaturnaya gazeta* in which he expressed doubts as to whether human beings would ever be free of such vices as 'envy, love of power, egoism, brutality, selfishness and many others' and went on to ask: 'What grounds do we have for counting on a radical change in human psychology?' An article in the newspaper replied by saying that even to ask such a question raised 'objections in principle'. Human vices and virtues, the article said, remained permanent 'only at the highest level of abstraction'. For example, the psychology of the slave and the slave-owner had vanished not because 'people had become better' but because slavery had disappeared. It was only 'social conditions' which produced the human failings to which the letter-writer referred.[81]

Finally, when discussing the relationship between ideology and propaganda, something needs to be said, if only briefly, on the subject of ethical motivation. Here again, the contrasts between Communism and Nazism need to be spelled out. The existence of an ethical motivation in the Marxist idea has been acknowledged even by some of Marxism's most uncompromising critics. As Sir Karl Popper, for example, has written:

Marx's condemnation of capitalism is fundamentally a moral condemnation. . . . The system is condemned, because by forcing the exploiter to enslave the exploited it robs both of their freedom. Marx did not combat wealth, nor did he praise poverty. He hated capitalism, not for its accumulation of wealth, but for its oligarchical character; he hated it because in this system wealth means political power in the sense of power over other men. Labour power is made a commodity; that means that men must sell themselves on the market. Marx hated the system because it resembled slavery.[82]

It is here, most clearly, that attempted comparisons between communism and Nazism break down. Nazism did not originate from any comparable moral protest. Nor, with its doctrinaire commitment to inequality, nationalism and racism, was it ever capable of offering any genuinely universal appeal.

At the same time, it would be one-sided to discuss the ethical motivation of communism without acknowledging the existence of a real, and evidently widespread, cynicism in Soviet society. Yet here again, there is a contrast with Nazism which needs to be brought into relief. In Nazi thinking (as exemplified in the writings of Hitler and Goebbels quoted earlier), cynicism was *a point of departure*. It has yet to be claimed that Hitler betrayed the early hopes of the Nazi movement; or that the Nazi road to hell was paved, even in part, with good intentions. In the Soviet case, by contrast, cynicism, where it exists, is in large measure a by-product, arising from a *discrepancy* between proclaimed ideals and reality. It is this discrepancy (whether inevitable or not) which to a great extent accounts for the extreme bitterness of some Russian dissidents as well as disillusioned foreign ex-communists. But certainly since the 1970s, there have been signs that the Soviet authorities acknowledged this discrepancy and saw it as one of the great weaknesses in the system. Already in 1979, for example, a party secretary in the once notoriously corrupt Soviet republic of Georgia warned in a speech that:

The ability to demonstrate in a convincing way the superiority of the Soviet way of life and its moral values requires not only great skill but also inner conviction and sincerity with regard to facts, events and people ... Where a gap arises between words and deeds, between an idea and its practical realization, this leads to a deformation of public awareness; and the gates are thrown open to phenomena which are the antithesis of socialism.[83]

This gap between the supposed and the real was seized upon by Gorbachev barely a month after he became leader. Addressing a meeting of the party Central Committee in April 1985, he criticized the 'inability to talk to people in the language of truth' and added: 'It sometimes happens that a man hears one thing, but sees something else in life. The question is a serious one, not only from the educational, but from the political point of view.'[84] It is a theme which has since been taken up by the Soviet leadership many times. And it has implications not just for Soviet propaganda but for propaganda in general. For a political message – if manifestly at odds with the audience's own knowledge – can artificially widen the gap between the ideal and the real, and so make cynicism even more prevalent.

Traditional Soviet guidelines for propagandists

We have so far been concerned with the evolution, nature and functions of propaganda in the Soviet system. From this we now turn to the traditional directives or practical advice which Soviet propaganda workers were given. (In more recent years these guidelines have shown a somewhat greater concern with psychology, but such concern was little in evidence in the past.) The traditional guidelines may indeed seem somewhat pedestrian: they were presented in systematic form in textbooks published in and after the 1960s,[85] but can be traced back far earlier. The most important of them are the following:

1   Party-mindedness
2   Truthfulness
3   A 'link with life'
4   Clarity, intelligibility, cogency
5   A 'concrete-historical' approach
6   A differentiated approach to different audiences
7   The maintenance of 'close links with the masses'

The first two of these guidelines – 'party-mindedness' and truthfulness – represent the core of the traditional Soviet propaganda philosophy as publicly explained; and they have to be taken together, since all Soviet literature treats them not as opposites, but as mutually complementary. The value of truthfulness acquired a totally new importance in connection with the *glasnost'* of the later 1980s. But it should be mentioned first of all that the importance of truthfulness has been constantly emphasized during almost the entire period of Soviet rule. Soviet literature frequently quotes Lenin's dictum in 1921 that 'We must condemn most resolutely those who regard politics as a series of cheap little tricks, frequently bordering on deception ... You can't fool a class.'[86] According to the *Large Soviet Encyclopedia* in 1929, 'Truthfulness is the main reason for the influence of Bolshevik agitation on the working masses.'[87] Or again, according to the Head of the Propaganda Department in 1967, 'one of the most important Leninist requirements of party propaganda is its *truthfulness*' (emphasis in original).[88] (It may be noted that in another context Lenin advised foreign communist parties 'to resort to various stratagems, artifices and illegal methods, to evasions and concealment of the truth' in order to gain influence within trade unions,[89] but this advice may have related to underground work rather than overt propaganda.)

The principle of 'party-mindedness' (that is, devotion to the cause of communism – in Russian, *partiinost'*) is self-explanatory and indeed tautological. It is presented in Soviet writings as a necessary correlative to truthfulness. Thus, it has been said in the past that 'Party-mindedness and objectivity in communist journalism are inseparable'.[90] According to one textbook, 'The truthfulness of communist propaganda is determined by the truth of Marxist–Leninist ideology.'[91] What this appeared to be claiming was that the Soviet political message is 'objective' (that is, it corresponds to objective truth) but that it is not, and cannot be, impartial because, in the nature of things, there cannot be a neutral attitude towards political facts – which in any case have to be selected in accordance with some set of ideological criteria. On one occasion Soviet media specialists took the trouble to publish a comparative content analysis of the coverage of the 1967 Arab–Israeli war in, respectively, *The Times*, the British communist *Morning Star* and *Izvestia*. The factual discrepancies were not very great; but the Soviet authors made the comment that 'Even if one were to allow that every individual fact in the bourgeois press was properly established, nevertheless the general picture is distorted because of the way the facts are selected.'[92] According to Soviet propaganda specialists, it was either unrealistic or hypocritical for their opponents to claim that they did not engage in propaganda. Both sides, it was argued, did so – with the sole difference that Soviet communicators honestly admitted what they were doing. The nature of 'objectivity' can, needless to say, give rise to an open-ended philosophical debate; Soviet political literature on this subject, however, rarely dealt with the rather obvious objection that audiences in the West have access to competing points of view.

The proclamation of *glasnost'* in the late 1980s naturally highlighted the issue of truthfulness as never before; and it challenged, even if it did not entirely eradicate, the earlier thinking. In April 1985, as already mentioned, Gorbachev criticized 'the inability to speak to people in the language of truth'. This gradually unleashed a flood of criticism about past misrepresentation in the media. In 1986, for example, a well-known Soviet television correspondent even described how in past years he had sent politically-slanted reports from abroad. He now quoted the dictum of Leo Tolstoy that 'It is not enough to avoid direct lying; one must try to avoid lying negatively – by maintaining silence.'[93] Yegor Ligachev, when addressing a conference in October 1986, observed that, with regard to the social sciences 'There are, of course, problems with curricula, with textbooks, with method. But all the same the essence of the matter is the deficit of complete truth.'[94] It was in this context that the history of the Stalin era was re-opened.

It should be mentioned, however, that even before the Gorbachev era, the question of truthfulness was the subject of some – admittedly low-key – debate in Soviet writings. Thus in 1967, the Head of the party's Propaganda Department warned about the possible 'boomerang' effect of statements by party lecturers which conflicted with the personal experience of the audience.[95] On the other hand, the Soviet authorities also let it be understood that care should be taken when divulging facts which might be exploited by anti-communists or by the foreign media. Indeed, in 1968, one Soviet author even protested against this attitude. According to him:

> Some propagandists think that we should not give full or truthful information about shortcomings in the development of our economy since this will be used against us by the imperialist bourgeoisie, which strives in every way to inflate these shortcomings ... But we must not proceed from this premise. Lenin repeatedly emphasized that the party's policy was built on truth ... This strengthens the energy of the masses in rectifying shortcomings.[96]

This was, in effect, an early statement of the case for *glasnost'*. But it was not universally endorsed. Thus a Soviet textbook for the training of journalists published in 1980, which included a section on 'Truthfulness and Objectivity', also noted that: 'The mass information media, when reporting on events ... in cases where there are grounds for fearing that the information may be used by the class enemy, must find an appropriate mode of expression.'[97]

This, then, was part of the conservative case against *glasnost'*. As recently as 1984, only a few weeks before Gorbachev came to power, it seemed to find some support from the Editor of *Pravda*, Viktor Afanasyev, who warned that:

> Unfortunately . . . we journalists sometimes relish . . . shortcomings, we 'unload' them without discrimination on to the pages of our publications and on to the airwaves. And we often do not reflect that all this is 'bread' for our opponents, for the denigration of Soviet reality.
>
> We cannot travel along this path. Our criticism must be positive and it must outline ways of surmounting shortcomings and difficulties.[98]

The emphasis here was markedly different from that of Gorbachev. But as regards the more traditional Soviet approach to 'truthfulness' and 'party-mindedness', it may fairly be said that no Soviet citizen could have been in any doubt as to its avowedly propagandist nature. Thus, the traditional Soviet propaganda doctrine appeared to hold that facts cited should be accurate; but at the same time that the facts should be carefully selected so as to further the policies of the Communist Party. Indeed, as one Soviet book in the 1970s had stated:

> A fact is the core, the foundation of news. Facts correctly chosen acquire the most important political resonance . . . We have never denied the party-mindedness, the bias of information. Very often an item of news appears in the Soviet press as a fact which is commented upon. But our press seeks to give an objective evaluation of the fact reported, to explain its significance to the masses.[99]

Apart from 'party-mindedness' and 'truthfulness', the remaining guidelines listed above stemmed largely from the party's 'didactic' approach and call for little comment. The insistence on a 'link with life' refers to the Marxist–Leninist doctrine of 'the unity between theory and practice'. The insistence on clarity etc. is self-explanatory. The 'concrete' approach means that propaganda and information should, for the party's purposes, be directly addressed to specific tasks, situations and audiences.[100] Related to this is the traditional idea of a 'differentiated approach' when presenting material to different audiences; it is exemplified by the old distinction between propaganda (for the few) and agitation (for the many); and also by the great variety of different study courses in the political education network.

The emphasis on links between the party and the masses is not, strictly speaking, a propaganda guideline since it has a much wider application in Soviet thinking. As already noted, in 1920 Lenin had spoken of the importance of understanding the psychology of every social stratum and of knowing the moods of the masses.[101] The doctrine of 'links with the masses' is reflected in the immense importance which the Communist Party has always attached to the oral propaganda system involving, as it does, face-to-face communication. One long-standing principle of this system is that lecturers or speakers are expected to answer all questions – even so-called 'sharp' (that is, difficult or awkward) questions – which may be put by members of the audience. 'The agitator must not leave unanswered a single question that has been put to him,' according to a Soviet handbook of the 1930s, although it was deemed permissible in cases of difficulty to put off giving the answer until another occasion.[102]

It is possible that a large proportion of audience questions to speakers relate to personal problems (such as housing). But this is not the invariable rule – as shown by the following examples from published Soviet sources in the 1970s and early 1980s, before Gorbachev came to power:

> Why does the bourgeoisie allow workers' parties and 'freedom of communist propaganda'? Some propagandists were said to be at a loss to answer; but the 'decisive factor' was said to be that the bourgeoisie was no longer in a position to deny certain rights and freedoms to the working class.[103]

> Why at elections is only one candidate put forward? 'In the course of discussion [according to a speaker's handbook] such a question may arise and one has to be ready for it.' Audiences, so it was said, should be told that Soviet law imposed no limits on the number of candidates on the ballot paper; but even in bourgeois states there was only one candidate per party and in the Soviet Union there was only one party. Moreover, deputies to Soviets were accountable to their voters and could have their mandates revoked.[104]

> What about the Soviet defence budget? At one meeting a member of the audience said to the speaker: 'You have talked about the growing military budget of the US and NATO. You've explained all the peaceful benefits which these resources could give. But surely we spend a great deal too – and also to the detriment of our peaceful needs?' The speaker at first agreed, but after an intervention by an elderly man in the audience, he went on to say: 'We know that imperialism has not changed its aggressive nature. Therefore, we do everything to guarantee the security of what we have created.'[105]

Such question-and-answer sessions (whether convincing to the audience or not) have been the main traditional Soviet method of feedback. It has also been the practice of the authorities at higher levels to collate and analyse the questions.[106] How far these agitators' question-and-answer sessions provided effective feedback in the absence of an atmosphere of complete frankness is a subject to which we shall return in a later chapter. Another difficulty mentioned in the past in the Soviet press was that 'sometimes lecturers and rapporteurs evade questions on the grounds that they have nothing to do with the subject, that they are supposedly based on rumours for unseemly purposes.' Such an attitude was said to be wrong.[107]

Other traditional methods of influence

The above guidelines are essentially concerned with how to present the political message. But beyond that, Soviet communicators have also relied on two other methods of influence, which go beyond mere advice on presentation. For one thing, they have always publicly insisted that the sincerity and personal example of the persuader are essential if he is to get his message accepted.[108] (This principle suddenly acquired a new importance in connection with the campaigns against corruption in recent years.)

A second traditional method of Soviet propaganda has been its emphasis on what may be termed the 'active involvement' of the audience. This is yet another facet of the principle of 'participation' which is seen not only as an ultimate goal of communism and as an essential means of building communism, but also as one means of inculcating communist political attitudes. Lenin, as noted earlier, had mentioned participation as an essential requirement for political education. The idea has been repeated in Soviet literature on many occasions since.[109] As one writer put it in the 1970s: 'Just as one cannot learn to swim without going into the water, so one cannot become a communist, master communist ideas or develop communist convictions within oneself without taking part in the practical struggle for communism.'[110]

Even as far back as the 1920s, pupils in the political study system were expected to take part in practical activities (such as the preparation of election campaigns or even the organization of work connected with agriculture) as part of their educational process.[111] In the Brezhnev era literature on the political study system laid considerable stress on the value of pupils' preparing papers on particular subjects for discussion in class. Furthermore, even the delivery of speeches by propaganda workers at meetings has been held to have an educative influence on the speakers themselves, since as one author argued: 'In the process of disseminating political knowledge, an individual has occasion to come closely into contact with other people, to answer their questions and to vindicate his own point of view. All this directly leads to the formation of an ideological fighter for the party.'[112]

Practice, in other words, was deemed essential to the learning process, another illustration of the way in which Soviet ideas of persuasion have been modelled on those of teaching. How this method actually operated will be discussed in chapter 6.

Public opinion as a weapon of persuasion

We noted earlier that the term 'public opinion' was not systematically used in the USSR until the 1960s, when empirical opinion research began on a regular basis. Nevertheless, even under Stalin, the concept of 'public opinion' did play a certain part in Soviet thinking; but in a sense quite different from the one commonly understood in the West.

In liberal democracies, public opinion is commonly thought of as a force which acts as a counterweight to the government. In Soviet thinking, by contrast, public opinion was implicitly regarded as a force which should be used *by* the authorities as a lever against what they saw as deviant behaviour. This was evidently the idea behind the creation in the early years after 1917 of the so-called 'comrades' courts' as an informal sanction against anti-social behaviour or breaches of labour discipline at work-places.[113] The Programme of the Soviet Communist Party adopted in 1919 recommended the 'social censure' of law-breakers as a desirable substitute, wherever possible, for criminal punishment.[114] The Soviet educationalist Anton Makarenko emphasized that the teacher's authority over children who broke the rules depended, to a crucial extent, on the teacher's ability to get the pupil peer-group on to the side of authority; and he attached great importance to what he termed 'the powerful force of public opinion as a regulating and disciplining educational factor'.[115] This approach gained a strong hold in Soviet educational theory. Already in Stalin's time, teachers were advised to use this kind of pupil 'public opinion' as a sanction against individual pupil misconduct. And this principle appears to have continued in Soviet schools in more recent times.[116]

In the Soviet Communist Party Programme of 1961, this whole concept of public opinion as a sanction was given a new prominence:

> The general public, public opinion and extensive criticism and self-criticism must play a big role in combating survivals of the past and manifestations of individualism and selfishness. Comradely censure of anti-social behaviour will gradually become the principal means of doing away with manifestations of bourgeois views, customs and habits.[117]

Viewed in this context, 'public opinion' is just one more manifestation of collectivism; it becomes a form of group influence or group pressure against recalcitrant individuals. During the Brezhnev era, this idea was pursued as vigorously as under Khrushchev. A resolution adopted by the Soviet Communist Party congress of 1971 declared that: 'Public opinion [at places of work] must be more resolutely directed towards the struggle against violations of labour discipline, acquisitiveness, parasitism, thefts, bribe-taking and drunkenness'.[118] The same message was frequently repeated in the Soviet press.

Soviet theoreticians, so it would appear, placed heavy reliance on this particular notion of public opinion, in their blueprint for a future 'self-regulating' communist society. As society moved towards that goal, public opinion was envisaged as one of the substitutes for legally imposed coercion. It has been said that 'moral condemnation in the conditions of a communist society will be an extremely severe [form of] punishment for a wrongdoer.'[119]

A Soviet author writing in 1964 shed further light on official thinking about this subject. He noted that 'when we talk about the unanimity of members of our society we refer not to everybody without exception' but only to 'the absolute majority of Soviet people'.[120] That is to say, 'unanimity' should not be interpreted literally. Then, in a chapter on 'The Influence of Soviet Public Opinion on the Individual', he had, in particular, this to say:

> The collective opinion . . . consists in the unity of opinions of the majority of people. This unity or unanimity creates a sense of confidence amongst supporters of public opinion; and a sense of confusion amongst its opponents. It is natural that some of the opponents of the general opinion will reach a spiritual turning-point and come over to the side of the majority.[121]

It would be misleading to suggest that this concept of group pressure represented the sum total of Soviet public opinion theory even in the Brezhnev era. In fact, as we shall see in due course, Soviet doctrine since the 1960s has recognized a role for public opinion in influencing the authorities. Nevertheless, the above quotations do illuminate an important part of Soviet doctrine in two ways. First, if public opinion is gradually to replace coercion, one can understand the strategic importance which the party attaches to shaping public opinion. Only when this has finally been done will the system go 'into orbit' and become, as it were, self-sustaining. Secondly, these passages help to explain the importance which the Soviet authorities once attached to unanimity. If society's opinion is intended as a social sanction, then obviously, the closer it comes to unanimity the better. It need not be doubted that a strongly held, spontaneous public opinion can be highly intolerant of non-conformity, and therefore a powerful social sanction in any society. The real question, of course, is how far such a public opinion can be created from above.

Conclusion: a method of persuasion?

It remains, in this chapter, to bring the discussion back to this book's central theme – namely the question of exactly *how* the persuader's message is to be made convincing and effective. What light does Soviet ideological literature throw on this question? And how far do any of the successive Soviet leaders appear to have been concerned with the psychological problems which propaganda involves?

Neither classical Marxism, so we have argued, nor the writings of Lenin, were concerned with the psychological strategy of mass indoctrination. Classical Marxism had practically nothing to say about propaganda. Lenin's ideas about propaganda were not primarily motivated by an interest in psychology. They focused on the need for a propaganda strategy in a *pre-revolutionary* situation. That involved mobilizing a part of the population against the old order at the particular moment of revolution; it was quite distinct from the much more ambitious goal of ensuring permanent mass support *after* power had been won. That was a problem to which Lenin did not address his mind in great detail. He never maintained, however, that propaganda was all-powerful, but stressed the role of direct personal experience as a crucial factor in shaping public opinion. Stalin paid ostentatious lip-service to this idea, but did not adhere to it in practice.

One of the central themes of this chapter has been that although the 'moulding' of public opinion has always been a major Communist Party objective (especially during and since the Stalin era), nevertheless Soviet propaganda (in contrast to that of the Nazis) has never been greatly interested in control through psychological manipulation. In order to understand Soviet thinking, it becomes relevant to examine the role of Soviet ideology. There are, we have suggested, a number of ways in which that ideology has coloured Soviet attitudes towards persuasion. For example, the emphasis on philosophical 'materialism' can lead to the down-grading of psychology; the belief in the malleability of human nature can lead to an exaggerated belief in the power of propaganda; the emphasis on 'science' entails a rationalistic approach; the concept of 'struggle' implies confrontation, that is, pressure on those who refuse to be persuaded. Not the least important is the apparent concept of persuasion as an essentially educational – or 'pedagogical' – activity.

All of this, however, relates more to the nature and functions of propaganda than to its methods. The central question of *how* to make persuasion effective was, only too often, skirted round in Soviet literature. When 'method' was in fact discussed – as in the propaganda directives listed earlier – much of the practical advice offered was somewhat elementary or even pedestrian (for instance with regard to truthfulness, clarity, sincerity, etc.) It was in stark contrast with the sort of 'black arts' propounded by Goebbels. So far as Soviet propaganda did evolve any genuinely distinctive methods – apart of course, from the monopolistic control of the media – such methods seemed to amount to the following:

1   Didactic, repetitive explanation of the party's message with the aim of ensuring so far as possible that the message reaches everybody. This was by far the most important part of Soviet propaganda method, involving as it does a stress on correctness of content and efficiency of organization. As well as this however, two further methods should be mentioned namely,
2   'Active involvement' of individuals – through giving them tasks of political or social importance – on the supposition that the fulfilment of these assignments will generate an increased sense of political commitment on the part of those concerned; and
3   The mobilization of group influence (or public opinion in the sense described in the last section) against deviant attitudes or behaviour.

These methods, whatever else they may achieve, certainly represent a powerful system of *pressures*. And in that sense they could have been taken as evidence that the authorities in the Soviet Union were interested specifically in the psychology of indoctrination. Whether such methods generate the kind of uncoerced support which the party claimed to want, is a separate question to which we shall return in chapter 6. A degree of uncoerced support for the system does of course exist: the question is how far it is the result of planned propaganda measures from above.

But it still remains to ask how far Soviet propaganda has traditionally depended on the social sciences – such as psychology, opinion surveys and communication research of the kind that has been so influential in mass persuasion in the West. This will be the subject of the next two chapters. And in order to explain the background we have, first of all, to go back to the Stalin era.

Notes

1   See on this point Alec Nove, 'Was Stalin really necessary?', *Encounter*, 103 (April 1962), p. 89. Nove points out how Stalin's 'revolution from above' meant that 'toughness in executing unpopular orders became the highest

qualification for Party office', as a result of which 'the emergence of Stalin and of Stalin-type bullying officials, of the sergeant-major species, was accompanied by the decline in importance of the cosmopolitan journalist-intellectual type of party leader who had played so prominent a role earlier.'

2 In 1986 the party secretary of Moscow University gave one specific example of the 'cadre' problem: namely that nearly two-thirds of the faculty heads and professors of the university concerned with the social sciences were above pensionable age, and had until the recent past successfully resisted attempts to retire them. Retirements were now being expedited; but the effect of the previous policy had been to hamper 'boldness and resolve in putting forward new ideas'. See V. I. Zubarev et al. (eds), *XXVII s"yezd KPSS i zadachi kafedr obshchestvennykh nauk* (Moscow, 1987), p. 156 (V. N. Gorokhov).

3 All Soviet leaders, including Stalin, castigated bureaucracy, but did not admit that it stemmed from the system as such: see, e.g., the article on Bureaucratism in *BSE* 2nd edn, vol. 6 (Moscow, 1951), pp. 473–4, which explained it as a temporary survival of capitalism. For a more recent and very different interpretation see Viktor Legler in *Novyi Mir*, 12 (1987), pp. 242–5, where bureaucracy is blamed for, among other things, 'corruption . . . silence and falsehood in propaganda and mass information' and 'the violation of the constitutional rights of citizens'.

4 The paper had quoted a Chilean communist leader as saying that 'unity of all neo-fascist Chileans is a guarantee of the overthrow of the Junta': *Pravda*, 28 July 1978, p. 5. For the correction see ibid., 29 July 1978, p. 6.

5 *LG*, 30 April 1986, p. 3 (D. Yevdokimov, Editor-in-Chief of the Moskovskii Rabochii Publishing House).

6 V. Afanasyev, in G. L. Smirnov et al. (eds), *Problemy kompleksnogo osush-chestvleniya zadach kommunisticheskogo vospitaniya v svete reshenii XXV s"yezda KPSS* (Moscow, 1978), p. 302.

7 M. F. Nenashev, *Ratsional'naya organizatsiya ideologicheskoi raboty* (Moscow, 1976), p. 22.

8 Pavla Ukrainets, *Partiinoye rukovodstvo ideino-vospital'nym protsessom* (Minsk, 1982), p. 135.

9 Adolf Hitler *Mein Kampf,* tr. James Murphy (Hurst & Blackett, London, 1939), p. 161.

10 See Willi A. Boelcke (ed.), *The Secret Conferences of Dr Goebbels, October 1939–March 1943*, tr. Ewald Osers (Weidenfeld & Nicolson, London, 1967), pp. 48, 309, 293. These quotations come from minutes compiled at the time by officials of the German Ministry of Foreign Affairs or the Ministry for Popular Enlightenment and Propaganda: see ibid., pp. x–xi.

11 P. K. Kurochkin et al. (eds), *Kommunisticheskaya propaganda. Voprosy teorii i metodiki* (Moscow, 1974), p. 9.

12 See, e.g., Karl Marx's 'Preface to "A Contribution to the Critique of Political Economy"' (1859) for his much-quoted statement: 'The mode of production of material life conditions the social, political and intellectual life process in general. It is not the consciousness of men that determines their being, but,

on the contrary, their social being that determines their consciousness.' Many years later, in 1890, Engels, in a letter to J. Bloch, qualified this statement by saying: 'According to the materialist conception of history, the *ultimately* determining element in history is the production and reproduction of real life. More than this neither Marx nor I have ever asserted ... The economic situation is the basis, but the various elements of the superstructure ... also exercise their influence on the course of the historical struggles and in many cases preponderate in determining their *form*. There is an interaction of all these elements, in which ... the economic movement finally asserts itself as necessary.' Engels also added in this letter: 'Marx and I are ourselves partly to blame for the fact that the younger people sometimes lay more stress on the economic side than is due to it.' See *Karl Marx and Frederick Engels, Selected Works* (Lawrence & Wishart, London, 1970), pp. 181, 682–3.

13 See, e.g., Frederick Engels, Anti-Dühring (Lawrence & Wishart, London, n.d.) p. 308, where the author states: 'By more and more transforming the great majority of the population into proletarians, the capitalist mode of production brings into being the force which, under penalty of its own destruction, is compelled to carry out this revolution.'

14 B. F. Porshnev, *Sotsial'naya psikhologiya i istoriya*, 2nd revised edn, (Moscow, 1979), p. 63.

15 V. I. Lenin, *Polnoye sobranie sochinenii* (*Complete Works*, 5th Russian edn, Moscow; hereafter *PSS*), vol. 41, p. 192.

16 Ibid., vol. 44, p. 497.

17 V. I. Lenin, *The State and Revolution* (Lawrence & Wishart, London, n.d.), p. 63; *PSS*, vol. 33, p. 83.

18 Lenin, *The State and Revolution*, p. 68; *PSS*, vol. 33, p. 90.

19 Lenin, *PSS*, vol. 2, p. 463; ibid., vol. 6, pp. 24, 30, 79.

20 Ibid., vol. 6, p. 39.

21 Ibid., vol. 41, p. 408. It was also in 1920, at the 9th party congress, that Lenin first used the expression 'communist education' (*kommunisticheskoye vospitaniye*), which later became a stock phrase: see *Voprosy teorii i metodov ideologicheskoi raboty*, 12 (Moscow, 1980), p. 24, quoting *PSS*, vol. 40, p. 277.

22 *PSS*, vol. 5, p. 11.

23 V. I. Lenin, *Collected Works* (English edn, Moscow, 1960–70), vol. 19, pp. 406; (hereafter *CW*); *PSS*, vol. 24, p. 34.

24 *PSS*, vol. 10, p. 357.

25 Ibid., vol. 11, pp. 319–20.

26 In 1902 Lenin had written that 'the *only* choice is either bourgeois or socialist ideology. There is no middle course (for mankind has not created a "third" ideology, and, moreover, in a society torn by class antagonisms, there can never be a non-class or above class ideology). Hence, to belittle the socialist ideology *in any way, to turn aside from it in the slightest degree* means to strengthen bourgeois ideology' [emphasis in original]. See *CW*, vol. 5, pp. 384–5, *PSS*, vol. 6, p. 39. This has been the text most heavily relied on by the Soviet authorities to support the proposition that compromise in the sphere of ideology is inadmissible.

27 *CW*, vol. 4, p. 288; *PSS*, vol. 4, p. 312.
28 *PSS*, vol. 41, p. 78.
29 *PSS*, vol. 40, p. 17.
30 *CW*, vol. 26, pp. 212–13; *PSS*, vol. 34, p. 415.
31 *PSS*, vol. 34, p. 300.
32 *CW*, vol. 27, p. 135; *PSS*, vol. 36, p. 53.
33 *PSS*, vol. 34, p. 241.
34 *CW*, vol. 30, p. 263; *PSS*, vol. 40, p. 12. Lenin wrote this in December 1919.
35 Yu. A. Krasin, *Revolyutsionnyi protsess sovremennosti* (Moscow, 1981), pp. 103–4.
36 Ibid., pp. 107–8.
37 *CW*, vol. 30, p. 274; *PSS*, vol. 40, p. 23.
38 See, on this point, Neil Harding, *Lenin's Political Thought*, vol. 2, (Macmillan, London, 1981), p. 188. I must acknowledge my debt to both volumes of this work (of which the first appeared in 1977) when exploring Lenin's attitude to propaganda and public opinion.
39 *CW*, vol. 27, p. 402; *PSS*, vol. 36, p. 369.
40 A. V. Lunacharskii, *Sobranie sochinenii*, vol. 7 (Moscow, 1967), p. 241. His article first appeared in the journal *Pechat'i revolyutsiya*, (May–July, 1921).
41 Georgii Kunitsyn, *V. I. Lenin o partiinosti i svobode pechati* (Moscow, 1971), p. 237.
42 I. Stalin, *Sochineniya* vol. 8 (Moscow, 1953), p. 43. These and the following passages from Stalin all date from January 1926.
43 Ibid., pp. 46, 52, 53.
44 Ibid., pp. 48–9.
45 Ibid., vol. 6, p. 172. Stalin said this in April 1924.
46 For an early use of this term, see a speech on 28 October 1928 by Mikhail Kalinin in the course of which he said: 'It seems to me that now, more than ever before, we are confronted with the task of the formation of a *New Man*' (emphasis in original). This speech is reprinted in M. I. Kalinin, *O kommunisticheskom vospitanii i obuchenii* (Moscow, 1948), p. 23. I have been unable to ascertain when or by whom the term 'New Man' was first used.
47 This is one of the major themes explored in Raymond Bauer, *The New Man in Soviet Psychology* (Harvard University Press, Cambridge, Mass., 1952). Besides stressing the key role of education, the Soviet authorities from the 1930s onwards also emphasized the individual's own responsibility for 'self-training', see ibid., p. 149.
48 A. S. Makarenko, *A Book for Parents* (English edn, Moscow, 1954) p. 77 quoted in James Bowen, *Soviet Education: Anton Makarenko and the Years of Experiment* (University of Wisconsin Press, Madison, 1965), p. 181. Makarenko himself, as Bowen points out, also strongly believed in the key educational role of the family.
49 *BSE*, 3rd edn, vol. 18 (Moscow, 1974), pp. 242–3.
50 *Konstitutsiya (Osnovnoi Zakon) Soyuza Sovetskikh Sotsialisticheskikh Respublik* (Moscow, 1977), art. 9.
51 See, for example, Lenin's dictum in 1913 that 'People always were and always

will be the stupid victims of deceit and self-deceit in politics until they learn to discover the *interests* of some class behind all moral, religious, political and social phrases, declarations and promises' (emphasis in original) in his article of 1913, 'The three sources and three component parts of Marxism': *PSS*, vol. 23, p. 47.

52 See Robert H. McNeal (ed.), I. V. Stalin, *Sochineniya*, vol. 1 (Hoover Institute on War, Revolution and Peace, Stanford University, California, 1967), pp. 346, 367. See also *Istoryia Vsesoyuznoi Kommunisticheskoi partii (bol'shevikov). Kratkii Kurs* (Moscow, 1942), p. 329. This book, first published in 1938, was the standard textbook of party history in Stalin's lifetime.

53 Zubarev et al., *XXVII s''yezd KPSS i zadachi kafedr obshchestvennykh nauk*, p. 21.

54 Ibid., pp. 99–100.

55 The development of, and changes in, Lenin's thinking on this subject are described in Harding, *Lenin's Political Thought*, vol. 2, ch. 8.

56 *Konstitutsiya* (1977).

57 M. Suslov in E. M. Tyazhel'nikov (ed.), *Delo vsei partii. Materialy Vsesoyuznogo soveshchaniya ideologicheskikh rabotnikov, Moskva 16–17 oktyabrya 1979g.* (Moscow, 1980), p. 28.

58 *Pravda*, 1 April 1980, p. 1.

59 M Suslov in E. M. Tyazhel'nikov (ed.), *Za vysokoye kachestvo i deistvennost' ideologicheskoi raboty. Materialy Vsesoyuznogo seminara – soveshchaniya ideologicheskikh rabotnikov. Moskva, 20–25 aprelya 1981g.* (Moscow, 1981), p. 9.

60 *Pravda*, March 1986 p. 4. For the official English text see *The Programme of the Communist Party of the Soviet Union. A New Edition* (Moscow, 1986), part II, section I, p. 26

61 *Pravda*, 31 March 1971; also (in English) *Report of the CPSU Central Committee to the 24th Congress of the Communist Party of the Soviet Union, delivered by Leonid Brezhnev on 30 March 1971* (Moscow, 1971), p. 97.

62 *Pravda*, 25 November 1983, p. 2 (V. Pechenev).

63 For example, the number of Orthodox churches is reported to have risen from 4,225 in midsummer 1941 to 16,000 four years later: see Robert Conquest (ed.), *Religion in the USSR* (Bodley Head, London, 1968), ch. 2, esp. pp. 34, 37.

64 B. N. Konovalov, *K massovomu ateizmu* (Moscow, 1974), p. 124.

65 *LG*, 6 May 1981, p. 14 (Feliks Kuznetsov).

66 *PS*, 8 (1973), pp. 36–7 (T. Yarkina).

67 *Pravda*, 4 March 1983, p. 3.

68 G. L. Smirnov et al. (eds), *Voprosy teorii i praktiki partiinoi propagandy* (Moscow, 1971), p. 9.

69 The difficulties of defining 'interests' are discussed in Mary McAuley, *Politics and the Soviet Union* (Penguin Books, Harmondsworth, 1977), pp. 307ff. The more recent Soviet concept of 'socialist pluralism' does, of course, make it possible to admit the existence of, and empirically explore, conflicts of interests and values within Soviet society.

70 See, among many other Soviet authors, S. N. Mostovoi, *Leninskie printsipy ideino-vospitatel'noi raboty* (Moscow, 1972), p. 271, where it is said: 'Persuasion is the basic means by which the party seeks to ensure that Marxist–Leninist ideas enter the awareness of the working people . . . But the power of this influence is itself due to the fact that the party's ideology, Marxism–Leninism, corresponds in every way to the vital interests of the working people.' 'Not to command but to persuade' was said to be an essential prerequisite for the party's success: ibid., p. 272.

71 V. I. Stepakov, *Partiinoi propagande - nauchnye osnovy* (Moscow, 1967), pp. 184–5.

72 S. Gurevich (ed.), *Problemy informatsii v pechati* (Moscow, 1971), pp. 135–6.

73 *Pravda*, 10 July 1978, p. 3.

74 G. Vdovichenko (ed.), *Prepodavanie filosofii i kommunisticheskoye vospitaniye studentov* (Kiev, 1978), pp. 46–7.

75 *Pravda*, 17 April 1987, p. 2.

76 L. Perchik *Agitatsiya* (Moscow, 1937), p. 12.

77 *Voprosy teorii i metodov ideologicheskoi raboty*, 7 (Moscow, 1977), pp. 12–13 (A. K. Uledov).

78 A. Vishnyakov (ed.), *Metodika partiinogo obrazovaniya*, 2nd edn, (Moscow, 1970), pp. 103ff.

79 *Voprosy teorii i praktiki massovykh form propagandy*, 1 (Moscow, 1968), p. 290.

80 Vishnyakov, *Metodika partiinogo obrazovaniya*, p. 131.

81 *LG*, 15 August 1979, p. 10 (I. B. Mikhailovskaya and L. I. Spiridonov).

82 K. R. Popper, *The Open Society and its Enemies* vol. 2, 5th revised edn (Routledge & Kegan Paul, London, 1966), p. 199.

83 G. Enukidze in Tyazhel'nikov, *Delo vsei partii*, pp. 159–60.

84 *Pravda*, 24 April 1985, p. 2.

85 Both the traditional and the more modern guidelines for propaganda can, in particular, be found in A. G. Efimov and P. V. Pozdnyakov, *Nauchnye osnovy partiinoi propagandy* (Moscow, 1966); V. I. Stepakov, *Partiinoi propagande - nauchnye osnovy* (Moscow, 1967); and P. Kurochkin et al. (eds), *Kommunisticheskaya propaganda: voprosy teorii i metodiki* (Moscow, 1974).

86 *PSS*, vol. 43, pp. 58, 59.

87 *BSE*, 1st edn, vol. 1 (Moscow 1926), p. 419 (article on 'Agitation').

88 Stepakov, *Partiinoi propagande - nauchnye osnovy*, p. 77.

89 *PSS*, vol. 41, p. 38. In the official English translation, the words 'concealment of the truth' are slightly glossed over and are rendered by the term 'subterfuge': see *CW*, vol. 31, p. 55.

90 See Gurevich, *Problemy informatsii v pechati*, p. 23.

91 See Kurochkin, *Kommunisticheskaya propaganda*, p. 46.

92 See Gurevich, *Problemy informatsii v pechati*, pp. 17–18.

93 *LG*, 13 August 1986, p. 14 (Vladimir Tsvetov).

94 See Zubarev et al., *XXVII s"yezd KPSS i zadachi obshchestvennykh nauk*, p. 30; *Pravda*, 2 October 1986, p. 2. Ligachev denied, however, that truth should be equated merely with negative criticism.

95   Stepakov, *Partiinoi propagande - nauchnye osnovy*, p. 258.
96   B. A. Chagin, *Sub''yektivnyi faktor. Struktura i zakonomernosti* (Moscow, 1968), p. 206.
97   E. P. Prokhorov et al., *Vvedenie v teoriyu zhurnalistiki* (Moscow, 1980), pp. 97–101, esp. p. 100.
98   Speech reported in B. Stukalin et al. (eds.), *Sovershenstvovanie razvitogo sotsializma i ideologicheskaya rabota partii v svete reshenii iyun'skogo (1983 g.) plenuma TsK KPSS. Materialy Vsesoyuznoi nauchno-prakticheskoi konferentsii. Moskva, 10–11 dekabrya 1984g.* (Moscow, 1985), p. 77.
99   See Gurevich, *Problemy informatsii v pechati*, p. 127.
100 '*When, where, who* and *how* to inform – that, in short, is the essence of the requirement of concreteness in the political information process': see Viktor Afanasyev in *Problemy nauchnogo kommunizma*, 8 (Moscow, 1974), p. 96.
101 *PSS*, vol. 41, p. 192 and ibid., vol. 44, p. 297.
102 Perchik, *Agitatsiya*, p. 98 For a more recent restatement of this principle see Afanasyev in *Problemy nauchnogo kommunizma*, 8 (1974), p. 95.
103 *PS*, 4 (1970), p. 18 (G. Smirnov).
104 *Sobesednik. Ezhemesyachnik voprosov i otvetov*, 2 (1980), pp. 37–8.
105 *Pravda*, 4 February 1981, p. 2.
106 See ch. 5, p. 156, *post.*
107 *Pravda*, 4 February 1981, p. 2.
108 Thus according to Perchik, *Agitatsiya*, p. 82: 'The power of example is enormous and the agitator must demonstrate it to perfection.' According to Stepakov, *Partiinoi propagande -nauchnye osnovy*, p. 88: 'the most effective way of influencing people is through personal example, the organic combination of word and deed.'
109 *Partiinoye stroitel'stvo. Posobie dlya slushatelei vysshikh partiinykh shkol* 4th rev. edn (Moscow, 1978), p. 261.
110 P. F. Kolonitskii, *Ateizm i formirovanie kommunisticheskoi lichnosti* (Moscow, 1975), p. 146.
111 M. F. Nenashev, N. I. Mekhontsev, N. N. Mikhailov, *Prakticheskie zadaniya v rabote propagandista* (Moscow, 1978), p. 4.
112 B. Ts. Badmayev, *Elementy psikhologii i pedagogiki v partiinoi propagande* (Moscow, 1973), p. 142.
113 As to the early creation of 'comrades' courts', see A. D. Boikov, V. I. Kriger and N. A. Noskova, *Tovarishcheskii sud* (Moscow, 1980), p. 3. See also the article on this subject in *BSE*, 3rd edn, vol. 26 (Moscow, 1977), p. 20.
114 See the (second) 'Programme of the Communist Party of Russia', adopted at the 8th party congress held from 18 to 23 March 1919, para. 74, reprinted in E. H. Carr (ed.), *Bukharin and Preobrazhensky, The ABC of Communism* (Penguin Books, Harmondsworth, 1969).
115 A. S. Makarenko, *Sochineniya*, 2nd edn, (Moscow, 1958), vol. 4, p. 489, quoted in M. P. Pavlova, *Pedagogicheskaya sistema A. S. Makarenko* (Moscow, 1972), p. 92.
116 For example, a 1946 Soviet textbook for schoolteachers stated: 'If a healthy

public opinion [in the school] is developed, the collective is able to force its own offenders to admit ugly pranks and delinquencies, to confess them, and to correct their behaviour': see George S. Counts and Nucia P. Lodge, *'I Want to Be Like Stalin'* (John Day Co., New York, 1947), p. 93. This book is a translation of a Soviet textbook on *Pedagogy*, by B. P. Yesipov and N. K. Goncharov, published in Moscow in 1946. As to more recent times, see Urie Bronfenbrenner, *Two Worlds of Childhood: USA and USSR* (Allen & Unwin, London, 1971), esp. pp. 51–69.

117 *Programme of the Communist Party of the Soviet Union* (Moscow, 1961), part II, section V, sub-section 1, p. 110.

118 Quoted in *KPSS o formirovanii novogo cheloveka. Sbornik dokumentov i materialov (1965–1976)* (Moscow, 1976), p. 44.

119 *LG*, 15 August 1979, p. 10 (I. B. Mikhailovskaya and L. I. Spiridonova).

120 B. A. Erunov, *Sila obshchestvennogo mneniya* (Leningrad, 1964), p. 26.

121 Ibid., pp. 48–9.

4
Propaganda, Psychology and Stalinism

Paraphrasing Comrade Stalin's words about writers ('writers are the engineers of human souls'), one may say that the Bolshevik agitator must be the architect of human souls. In our epoch, when the main and basic task is the liquidation of the survivals of capitalism in the economy and in people's awareness, Bolshevik agitation is a powerful battering-ram which breaks down the hostile fortresses of the old traditions and practices.

L. Perchik, *Agitatsiva* (1937, p. 70)

During the decades of Stalin's rule, mass propaganda (or indoctrination) was drastically intensified and came to occupy a place of central importance in the entire Soviet system. On this point no one, whether communist or non-communist, is likely to disagree. Indeed the Stalinist era abounds in events which themselves had a propaganda aspect. Stalin's campaigns against his political rivals such as Trotsky and Bukharin in the 1920s; his decision at the end of that decade to collectivize agriculture and industrialize the country; the 'mobilization' from the 1930s of literature and the arts; the show trials, soon afterwards, of former Soviet leaders; and above all the deliberately fostered personality cult of Stalin himself – these are only a few instances of policies which of necessity involved attempts to shape public opinion.

This is not the place to narrate the history of Stalin's propaganda campaigns. Their effect on millions of ordinary Russians was probably enormous but it is is not possible to make any totally reliable assessment of the domestic *impact* of propaganda in the Stalin era. The main, and indeed obvious, reason for this is that public opinion surveys which evolved in the West during the same time never developed in Russia. This takes us to the central theme of the present chapter and also to one of the major paradoxes of Soviet propaganda itself – namely that at the very moment when the Soviet leadership's emphasis on indoctrination reached its peak, the climate of intellectual intimidation made empirical opinion research impossible. However, this is not quite the whole story. What is less well known is that the suppression of opinion surveys and communication research under Stalin was not a mere oversight, but an act of deliberate, avowed policy. During the period up to the early 1930s, communication research (comparable to the research then taking place in the West, although in a rather primitive form) *was* carried out in Russia; and it enjoyed official encouragement. But then, in the 1930s, in the aftermath of collectivization, industrialization and the purges, official Soviet policy underwent a gradual but near-total change. Public opinion surveys as well as social psychology (the branch of psychology most directly relevant to propaganda) were branded as heretical and were effectively proscribed. It therefore became quite impossible for Soviet communicators to accumulate the kind of propaganda expertise built up in the West at this period and later. Amidst all the obscurity which surrounds so much that occurred in Russia under Stalin, this fact is something which can be documented with some precision. The circumstances in which this happened are the topic to which we now turn.

Soviet communication research in the 1920s

When the Bolsheviks came to power in Russia in 1917, their scope for positive, proselytizing propaganda was severely circumscribed. Widespread illiteracy, as well as severe shortages of paper and distribution difficulties in the aftermath of war, were alone enough to restrict the influence of the press.[1] Radio (except as a transmitter of morse code signals) had not yet come into being. Regular radio broadcasting began only in 1924.[2] There was, furthermore, an acute shortage of speakers able to carry the Bolshevik message to the population at large. In 1922, so a Soviet author has said, party propagandists and agitators were still heavily outnumbered by preachers of the Russian Orthodox Church.[3] In the face of all these handicaps, the Soviet leaders had a strong motive for trying to ensure that the limited resources at their disposal were put to the best possible use. This probably explains the strong desire of the Bolsheviks in those early years to find out exactly what impact their message was having on the still largely uneducated peasant population. This could be done only by means of empirical research – particularly in relation to those who read books and newspapers. As one Soviet author of the 1920s observed: 'It is not only the publishers and editors who are interested in the study of the reader. In the last resort, the study of the reader must provide an answer to the question of how the entire system of our agitation and propaganda ... is perceived.'[4]

On one occasion, Lenin personally wrote to the editor of the newspaper *Bednota* (which was intended for the peasants) asking to be informed at least one every two months about how many letters the paper was getting and what light they shed on the morale and preoccupations of the peasants.[5] Nor was this an isolated case. There is evidence during this early period not only of a concerted effort to conduct empirical research into attitudes but also of a definite interest in the psychological (as distinct from the organizational) aspects of propaganda. It has been said that in Russia between 1918 and 1928, as many as 872 books, pamphlets and articles were published which touched in some way on readers' psychology.[6] In January 1921, a directive from the Political Department of the Armed Forces enjoined the staff of army libraries to 'study the psychology of the reader'.[7] Also in 1921, the People's Commissariat for Enlightenment (*Narkompros*) set up a special commission, one of whose tasks was to carry out systematic research into this subject.[8] In 1925 the *Agitprop* department set up a special 'institute for the study of readers' interests' to direct and co-ordinate research throughout the country.[9] At about this time, research was begun into the newly emerging audience for radio.[10] Furthermore, at least in the late 1920s, *Agitprop* was reported to be interested in the question of how to make greater use of psychology for its work.[11]

In the USSR in later years, the story of this early communication research was mentioned only very rarely. It would no doubt be a mistake to exaggerate its importance. Much of it was primitive and it seems to have achieved little in the way of practical results, which is one reason why it lost its impetus. What is, however, absolutely clear is that this research was getting active encouragement from above; and it therefore throws light on the Soviet leadership's approach to propaganda at that time. Amongst all the writers of that period who were associated with this research, three in particular deserve special mention. They were, first, Nikolai Rubakin (1862–1946) whose lifelong interest was in the popularization of public libraries; secondly Ya. A. Shafir, a one-time Comintern official who later worked in *Agitprop* and was said to have been interested in the theories of Freud[12]; and thirdly, V. A. Kuz'michev, of whom no biographical details appear to be known, but who in 1929 published a rare, if not unique, Soviet book on the subject of public opinion.

Rubakin, whose work is still remembered with respect in the Soviet Union, was a somewhat unusual phenomenon: he was a Russian who lived abroad for much of his life both before and after the revolution and who was at times openly critical of Bolshevik policies, but who nevertheless managed to remain on friendly terms with prominent Bolsheviks.[13] He had been a committed opponent of Tsarism even in the 1880s and 1890s; and already before the revolution had got to know Lenin's wife Krupskaya. His lifelong and passionate interest was in books and the best way of popularizing them. This led him to study the psychology of readers, a subject about which he wrote prolifically. (In his later life he also became interested in cinema and radio.) Rubakin's writings, given their obvious relevance to the promotion of mass education and mass literacy, had attracted a favourable mention from Lenin already on the eve of the First World War.[14] This helps to explain why Rubakin was treated with respect by the Soviet authorities, in spite of his less than orthodox views, and also why he gained an entry into all three editions of the *Large Soviet Encyclopedia*.[15]

Rubakin was the inventor of a subject which he termed 'bibliopsychology' and once defined as 'the scientific study of all psychological phenomena connected with the creation, circulation and utilization of the printed, written or spoken word'.[16] Clearly, his subject was that of communication research. His central concern was with the impact of the printed word upon the reader, and his general thesis was that, regardless of the author's intention, the reader puts his own meaning into what he reads. (For example: 'The book of peace and love – the Gospel – leads to the Inquisition.')[17] This thesis, which may have been one-sided if not idiosyncratic, was in any case hardly a Marxist view. Furthermore, Rubakin had other disagreements with the Bolsheviks. He opposed censorship in principle, as running counter to his belief that the information in books should be available to all. In addition, although he was a convinced socialist, his sympathies seem to have been more in the direction of peace research than polemics. Indeed he once earned a rebuke from Lenin for expressing the view that 'polemics is one of the best ways of darkening the truth.'[18]

Rubakin's career is a separate story and is only peripheral to our theme. What is, however, relevant is that during the early 1920s the Soviet authorities showed a definite interest in Rubakin's theories, which they thought might assist them in understanding the psychology of propaganda. Evidence of this Soviet interest can be seen in a letter written to Rubakin in early 1923 by Vyacheslav Karpinskii (a close friend of Lenin, who had shared his exile in Switzerland and who later joined the *Pravda* editorial board). Karpinskii's letter was apparently in response to a manuscript on bibliopsychology which Rubakin had sent. It is noteworthy that Karpinskii's letter specifically reproached Rubakin for having declared himself opposed to 'the cultivation of hatred, revenge, enmity and so on', which Karpinskii maintained was tantamount to being 'an opponent of civil war and revolution'. Nevertheless, despite a vehement disagreement with Rubakin's general philosophy, Karpinskii went on to express a friendly and most positive interest in Rubakin's theories pertaining to propaganda. His letter continued:

What most interests me is, of course, the practice of bibliopsychology. And most of all, that part of it which deals with the question of *scientific methods of agitation and propaganda*, in other words: *what can purely scientific knowledge reveal for making the spoken and written word (regardless of content) as persuasive as possible in a given context?* . . . Arming our agitators and propagandists with the sharp, precise and never-changing weapon of professional scientific methods – that is the crux of the matter. In this way we shall increase our strength a hundredfold and take gigantic strides forward [emphasis in original].[19]

There is therefore no doubt that the Soviet authorities at this time were interested not just in the content and organization of propaganda but, specifically, in its psychological methods. Such a statement by a leading Soviet personality is, indeed, most unusual. Karpinskii went on to suggest various practical uses to which the findings of bibliopsychology might be put: they might, he said, be useful when conducting questionnaire surveys of newspaper readers; and also, in connection with the possible setting up of a school for agitators and propagandists, 'for the purpose of training scientifically-minded workers in the profession, which at present we lack'. A 'purely scientific institute' was needed in order to analyse the data assembled. Karpinskii went on to suggest that a 'Bibliopsychology Institute' should be established in Russia with Rubakin at its head. Karpinskii did, at the same time, make it clear that his own interest was in getting results and not in the pursuit of abstract knowledge for its own sake: 'Soviet Russia,' he said 'can entrust the leadership of such an institute, particularly as regards its practical work, only to people who have decisively and irrevocably come over to our side of the barricade. It cannot be otherwise in a matter of such primary importance as the education of the masses.'[20]

In the event, Rubakin's ideas about propaganda made little or no impact on Soviet thinking. A book which he wrote about readers' psychology was published in Moscow in 1929, but its theories were criticized as non-Marxist.[21] A further manuscript by Rubakin, dated 1936, was deposited in the Lenin Library in Moscow but remains unpublished. Its title is: 'Propagandology. The theory and practice of disseminating knowledge, ideas, attitudes and action with the minimum expenditure of effort, time and resources'.[22] This clearly shows the author's concern with methods of persuasion. It only remains to add that Rubakin received a Soviet state pension in 1930 and that from then on he lived and pursued his writing in Switzerland where, during the Second World War, he helped Russians who had escaped from Nazi captivity. In 1948, two years after his death, his remains were taken to Russia, where they are now buried. In the Soviet Union today, he is officially honoured almost entirely because of his interest in libraries. In the words of one modern Soviet author: 'Despite his erroneous standpoint over questions of theory, N. A. Rubakin remained an outstanding popularizer of books and made a contribution to the education of the popular masses.'[23]

The two other authors mentioned earlier – Shafir and Kuz'michev – were less well known than Rubakin, but their approaches to the psychology of propaganda were more closely in line with orthodox Bolshevik thinking. Shafir had, in 1921, headed a section of the Executive Committee of the Communist International in Moscow but was later moved to work in *Agitprop*, where his personal interest in readers' psychology first arose.[24] In 1925, the daily newspaper *Rabochaya Gazeta* pioneered one of the first major readership surveys in Russia; Shafir, although not involved in the original project, subsequently analysed the results and wrote a book about them. It is true that the survey suffered from certain defects. It was quite clearly not based on a representative sample because there was no attempt to select the respondents by social group: the newspaper simply printed the questionnaire, which the readers were invited to fill in and return. The replies were said to have been overwhelmingly friendly, which suggests that it was mainly the pro-Bolshevik sympathizers (possibly unrepresentative of the public as a whole) who responded. Another difficulty about interpreting the results is that no overall statistical picture was ever published. Shafir in his book simply summarized results in percentages on a region-by-region basis. Nevertheless there is no reason to doubt the bona fides of the investigation. A total of 7,483 readers' replies were received from all over the country; and the survey provides an unusual glimpse of the atmosphere in Russia at that time.

The ten-point questionnaire seems to have been drawn up with considerable thought. Two of the questions were open-ended and asked respondents why they read this newspaper, and whether they had any criticisms or suggestions. Other questions asked the respondents who they were, where they worked, whether they were members of the Communist Party, how long they had read the newspaper, which parts of it they read first of all, what they thought of certain regular features (such as technical articles) and whether they had any comments or suggestions as to print or layout. One question, in particular, was phrased much more pointedly than would be likely in a Soviet questionnaire in later years. It asked: 'Did you read to the end the reports by [the then party leaders] comrades Molotov, Rykov, Dzerzhinski and others which were published as supplements? Is it worth our while to go on providing such supplements? If you did not read to the end, why not?'[25]

Whatever the methodological faults of the survey may have been, the results do have a flavour of authenticity – because they tally in significant ways with the findings of much more recent Soviet surveys carried out in, and after, the 1960s. Shafir discovered a high degree of interest in international affairs amongst all groups of readers.[26] Indeed some readers specifically asked for more information about Russiam émigrés.[27] Interest in the economic sections of the paper was found to be 'very low' (attracting less than 5 per cent of readers).[28] Barely more than 5 per cent of those who replied showed any interest in official 'reports and speeches'. Shafir – in a comment which may be topical even today – gave it as his view that speeches printed verbatim 'frighten the reader by their incredible length' and that 'by their appearance alone they represent a threat to the reader's time and make him apprehensive that he will have to expend a great deal of effort and energy but will get nothing in return for his exertions.'[29]

Another – still topical – question touched on in this survey was that of misconduct by Communist Party officials. Shafir deduced that some of the readers who asked for more press coverage of 'party ethics' in fact wanted the paper 'to expose the unethical behaviour of certain party members'.[30] He quoted a number of readers' complaints on this score, such as the following:

'I think that some party members have become very bureaucratic and forget our party statutes and think more of themselves than of the country's social life ... I propose that there should be wide press coverage of party comrades who cling to the party and abuse their positions. There is a mass of injustices in regard to non-party people.'
'If a party member beats up a non-party man he gets no punishment and I don't like this.'
'If a non-party man is ill he goes to the grave, but a healthy member of the party goes to a health resort.'
'I don't want to slander the party ... but I don't want to hide the fact that there are many misdemeanours.'[31]

The reasons why, in Shafir's view, empirical research was important are also illuminating – particularly as they came from an *Agitprop* official and may therefore reflect the views of the authorities. Indeed, many of his reasons are as relevant to Soviet society now as they were then. In his opening chapter, Shafir contrasted what he saw as the fundamentally different goals of Bolshevik and non-Bolshevik journalism:

The bourgeois mass newspaper talked to the reader about facts which usually required no comment. Murder, robbery, rape, railway accidents and every kind of sensation in general make up a significant part of the content of a bourgeois newspaper . . . But the building of socialism amidst capitalist encirclement necessitates the discussion of an endless number of the most difficult problems of a social-political nature, which it is sometimes difficult even for a trained reader to understand . . . It is therefore quite natural that journalists should be faced with the problem of verifying to what extent the reader correctly grasps all that the press offers him.

One particular argument for empirical research, put forward by Shafir, had to do with the disappearance of the old, commercially-run newspapers:

Our press organs do not depend on their readers . . . Competition between press organs has to a considerable extent been eliminated. There is nothing to be ashamed of here. Under the dictatorship of the proletariat, competiton between press organs which express one and the same interests and views and which pursue one and the same political line would be the greatest absurdity. But the disappearance of competition – which was previously a method by which the press adapted to its readers (usually to their prejudices and weaknesses) – does make it necessary for us to devise other ways and methods of maintaining links with the reader.[32]

Shafir did not believe that current tastes should be made 'the supreme yardstick of value'.[33] But he did insist that tastes had to be investigated as they actually were. He therefore advocated 'not guesswork, but study'.[34] And, as he also observed: 'It is obvious that the elucidation of the motives for choice will, to considerable extent, help us to influence that choice.'[35] In a second book, which appeared in 1927, Shafir referred to the study of the reader as 'a social-psychological task'. It was, he said, a matter of 'extreme urgency', partly because 'Those who work in the press feel that a not altogether normal relationship has arisen between the present-day press and the reader. It is, in many ways, dangerous for the press to be cut off from its readers.'[36] Feedback, in other words, was presented as a sheer practical necessity. And in several respects, Shafir's thinking paralleled that of communication research students in the West. Persuasive efforts, he warned, might prove counter-productive since 'it is quite possible that an article may have an influence . . . directly opposite to what was intended . . . by the author.'[37] He touched on the problem of selective attention, saying that it was difficult to imagine anyone who was 'equally interested in an entire newspaper from beginning to end'. Therefore, one should differentiate between different groups and try to discover a reader's 'predominant interest'.[38]

Soviet propagandists have always paid lip-service to the importance of 'links with the masses', as we noted in chapter 3. What is noteworthy about this particular author is his obvious concern with achieving an intellectually rigorous approach to this problem: indeed, he specifically urged the abandonment of 'old, primitive methods' in favour of 'methods that are relatively more precise and well-tested'.[39] Among the techniques which he discussed were: observation, experiment, questionnnaires and the analysis of statistical information about readers' choices from libraries.[40] However, as we shall see in a moment, Shafir was far from satisfied with the results obtained to date.

V. A. Kuz'michev, the third Soviet propaganda specialist mentioned above, was also preoccupied with the study of propaganda's *impact*. Although an avowed Marxist, he was prepared to see if anything could be learned from Western, including US, experience in this area. In his book on *Printed Agitation and Propaganda* which appeared in Moscow in 1930,[41] Kuz'michev devoted several pages to an examination of US advertising methods (including US advice on 'how to sell a car'), and expressed a cautious interest. 'Not all of this is acceptable to us. But one must examine the way in which the practical Yankee carefully utilizes every element in the reader's psyche'.[42] One of his general conclusions was that 'one has to put oneself in the position of the reader';[43] and in order to make this easier, he (like Shafir) recommended a whole battery of techniques – including meetings and talks with readers, written questionnaires and also 'psychological tests', which sometimes took the form of 'knowledge and comprehension' tests. One test, conducted apparently in Baku in 1928, set out to discover how far the commonest terms in the official vocabulary were actually understood. It transpired that only 57 per cent of those interviewed could correctly define the word 'proletariat', whilst only 48 per cent understood the word 'imperialism', and a mere 26 per cent understood the term 'anti-religious'.[44] In another test also conducted in Baku, a small sample of 135 people were asked to identify the then party leaders. Less than one-third were able to answer the question 'Who is Stalin?'[45] (This itself indicates the relatively relaxed atmosphere in the Soviet Union in the late 1920s. Only a short time afterwards, such a question would have been unthinkable.)

An interest in Western expertise was also apparent in Kuz'michev's book mentioned above on *The Organization of Public Opinion*,[46] which appeared in 1929; he expressly acknowledged his debt to Walter Lippman, whose book on 'Public Opinion' had appeared in the United States some years earlier. In a section (rare for a Soviet author) dealing with the nature of public opinion, Kuz'michev said it was the product of 'a struggle of private opinions and their interaction' and was 'a process of the continuing, but not always visible, circulation of opinions'.[47] The dogma of 'unanimity' still lay in the future. The press, Kuz'michev observed, was one of the organizers of this opinion; and most of his book was concerned with how it could carry out this function more effectively.

Kuz'michev, like Shafir, was at pains to point out that a message could sometimes be interpreted by the public in a sense which had not been intended; he was concerned, in other words, with the danger of a breakdown of communication between the propagandist and his audience. To illustrate the kind of danger he had in mind, he gave a somewhat graphic, real-life example. It concerned the way the Soviet press had allegedly mishandled the reporting of a series of earthquakes which had erupted in the Crimea between June and October 1927. These disasters (not unnaturally) produced an enormous demand by the local inhabitants for information; and 'every new tremor had led to a feverish leap in the retail sales of newspapers'. The first question to which everyone wanted an answer, according to Kuz'michev, was 'What was the trouble, why did the earthquake occur and would it continue?' However, he went on, this was precisely the question which the media never properly dealt with. (Exactly how they could have done so is not entirely clear.) But Kuz'michev drew particular attention to the disturbing political consequences of this failure. Because of the lack of official information, the situation got out of hand. Distrust of the press increased 'to the point of morbidity', according to Kuz'michev. Furthermore, 'the influence of the church increased to an unprecedented degree' and 'the mosques were often crowded 24 hours a day.' (At this time there was a large Moslem population of Tartars in the Crimea, who were deported to Central Asia during the Second World War.) People then began to say, 'Under the Tsar, no such calamity . . . occurred.' Meanwhile, 'anti-Soviet elements . . . intensified their pressure and agitation.' The overall result, according to this author, was that 'a geological disaster became a political issue.'[48]

This whole episode, Kuz'michev went on, 'provides us with the richest material for studying and checking our methods of mass agitation'. One of the main mistakes, in his view, was the failure of the press to take due account of 'the mood of their readers'. This was by no means the last occasion in Soviet history when an official failure to provide information led to the proliferation of uncontrollable rumours. But this unusual historical account (probably long forgotten even in Russia itself) does have a direct bearing on the theme of this book. In 1927, Russia was a much more closed and more isolated society than she now is: there were no Russian-language broadcasts from the West to which Soviet citizens could turn. Yet even the near-total official monopoly of the media was insufficient to prevent the demonstration of an autonomous public opinion.

In Russia during the 1920s, there was a sizeable volume of literature bearing on communication research. Much of it appears to have been of merely transitory interest and to have made no great impact on official thinking; therefore a full inquiry into this literature is outside the scope of this book. It should be mentioned, however, that one quite common form of opinion survey in the 1920s as well as the early 1930s had to do with religious belief (this at a time of sustained anti-religious propaganda and, indeed, pressure). Questionnaires or surveys on religious attitudes sometimes unearthed surprising information – showing for instance that among some of the smaller non-Russian peoples on the Volga, a decline in Christianity in the aftermath of the 1917 revolution had led to a revival of earlier pagan cults. In the case of some surveys, lack of proper control led to obviously freak results. For example, in Moscow in 1929 a questionnaire on religious belief (to be filled in anonymously) was sent by post to 11,000 people at their home addresses. First results seemed highly satisfactory to the authorities: they showed that 88.8 per cent of those who filled in the questionnaire described themselves as unbelievers. However, as Soviet authors themselves later pointed out, only 3,000 replies (that is, less than 30 per cent of the total number of questionnaire forms sent out) were ever received or processed.[49]

Another area of inquiry in Russia at that time (with a potential relevance to propaganda) was that of social psychology. Writing in 1930, one of the leading Soviet psychologists of the time, K. N. Kornilov, said that 'extensive' research was being conducted by his institute at an important enterprise in Moscow on what he termed 'class and collective psychology'. (The latter term referred to 'the study of . . . behaviour, arising under the influence of the mutual relations of people'.) It was, Kornilov added, 'too early . . . to speak of any concrete results'. However, as he also observed, the subjects of 'class and collective psychology' were of obvious concern to Marxist thinking.[50]

Discussion and research of the various kinds described above were entirely in character with the relatively free intellectual climate in the USSR in the 1920s. Stalin himself, as we noted in chapter 3, was making apparently liberal-minded statements at this time about the importance of persuasion. And although openly anti-communist ideas were already banned, this did not prevent genuine debates from taking place in a number of socially important areas – for example, in relation to the arts and in relation to the country's economic future, which had not as yet been finally decided by the Soviet leadership. Sociological inquiry (even though embryonic) also enjoyed a considerable measure of freedom: Shafir's readership survey is one case in point.

Of all the social sciences studied in Russia in the 1920s, few were in a greater state of flux than psychology. For this there were two basic reasons. The first stemmed from the West where, then as now, psychologists were divided into contending schools of thought and could offer no unanimously accepted body of doctrine. The second reason was that during the early years of Soviet rule, the party leadership had itself developed no absolutely definitive standpoint towards psychology. As to this, something should now briefly be said.

Psychology, as was pointed out in chapter 2, was never a major concern in the Marxist classics. The writings of Marx, Engels and Lenin – which dealt monographically and systematically with economics and philosophy – gave no similar treatment to psychology. It is, indeed, noteworthy that although Lenin delighted in polemics with numerous opponents whom he attacked by name, nevertheless the very full index to his *Collected Works* contains not a single reference to Freud. Lenin's only recorded mention of Freud was in a conversation in 1920 when Lenin voiced scepticism about Freud's theories of sex.[51] However, the record of this conversation was not made public until 1925.[52] And in any case, Lenin's negative views did not prevent a relatively free and sometimes sympathetic discussion of Freud's theories in Soviet literature during much of the 1920s. Indeed, some party theoreticians were at one time interested in trying to evolve a synthesis between the ideas of Freud and those of Marx.[53]

During this period, there was a considerable Soviet interest in ideas from abroad. Soviet psychologists, as one of their number later wrote, had 'an excellent knowledge of foreign psychology . . . they were in personal contact with many Western scholars . . . they published their own works abroad and took part in international congresses and conferences.'[54] Western psychological literature (including the writings of Freud) was freely accessible in Russia. Furthermore, the article on 'Behaviourism' in the first edition of the *Large Soviet Encyclopedia* was written by J. B. Watson, the founder of this school in the United States[55]; it was a rare example of a non-Marxist contributing to a major Soviet publication. All this reflected not just a passive toleration by the authorities; it was due to a very real desire on their part to study the expertise of social scientists both in Russia and abroad and utilize it selectively, in order to further the (as yet not wholly defined) social goals of the regime.

However, throughout most of the 1920s in Russia, the very status of psychology as an independent discipline in its own right was a matter of controversy. Some of the opposition came from non-Marxists claiming to rely on natural science. Among them were Vladimir Bekhterev (1857–1927), the founder of a school known as 'reflexology', later officially condemned; and the physiologist Ivan Pavlov (1849–1936), famous for his theory of the 'conditioned reflex', whose research got official support. Both Bekhterev and Pavlov were critical of 'subjectivist' psychology. So also were many of the party theoreticians. In their eyes, any theory which implied that 'mind' could exist independently of the brain was ruled out as a form of philosophical 'idealism', harmful because of its possible religious implications and totally incompatible with scientific materialism. As early as 1923, the Director of the Moscow Institute of Psychology, Konstantin Kornilov, had called for the rebuilding of psychology on Marxist (that is, materialist) foundations. Yet this merely stated the problem rather than solving it. A 'materialist' approach still left room for argument about the relative importance of heredity or biology as opposed to environment in shaping human nature (although by the late 1920s orthodox Soviet thinking placed a decisive stress on the primacy of environment).[56] Moreover, the 'materialist' approach had tended to produce a 'mechanistic' view of human beings, as essentially passive creatures, with no will or initiative of their own, who merely reacted to external stimuli. This mechanistic model was, shortly afterwards, decisively rejected.

During the whole of the 1920s, according to one leading historian of Soviet psychology, 'there was no psychological school which could be called a truly Marxist school.' And one of the reasons for this was that 'despite all the obviousness of the fact that psychology could not remain a "science of the soul" Soviet psychologists still had considerable difficulty in determining what psychology should deal with as a separate science.'[57] Clearly then, the Bolsheviks of that time regarded psychology with some ambivalence. However, the absence of any clear-cut party line made it easier for debate to continue.

When discussing the 1920s, it remains to note one final point. The debate about psychology in Russia at that time seems to have produced few practical recommendations. The authorities, according to at least one Soviet author, were disappointed. 'Never, perhaps, either before that time or since, was the belief in the inexhaustible potential of psychological research so great ... Unfortunately ... psychologists, from the best of motives, took upon themselves commitments which could not be fulfilled and performed the role of "oracles" when they could, in effect, be no more than modest consultants.' This is said to have undermined the credibility of Soviet psychology 'for many years' later on.[58]

In much the same way, Soviet propaganda and communication research at this time never achieved any breakthrough. Shafir complained in 1926 about the 'mainly raw, unprocessed material' which researchers had accumulated, and said that most of the interpretations to date were 'more than dubious'.[59] A more modern Soviet author has said that in the early 1930s 'the rapid accumulation of material obtained by empirical methods [about readers' attitudes] came into contradiction with the slow rate at which it was interpreted' and that therefore newspapers became 'convinced of the supposed fruitlessness' of this research.[60] This is hardly surprising – given the relative lack of knowledge even among Western experts at the time. It is, however, apparent that Soviet communication research never succeeded during the 1920s in producing any clear theoretical conclusions or practical recommendations. Subsequently, in the 1930s, when the authorities became actively hostile to this research, they were able with a certain plausibility to dismiss it as 'pseudo-scientific' and of no practical value.

Soviet communication research from the 1930s

Until the late 1920s, as we have noted, Soviet communication research, like other areas of intellectual activity, was able to function in an atmosphere of relative freedom. But henceforward this became increasingly difficult; indeed by the mid-1930s, it had become impossible. The reason lay not in some local difficulty but in the total transformation which at that time gripped the whole life of the USSR.

The first Soviet Five Year Plan for industrialization was submitted for Communist Party approval in 1929, with retrospective effect from the year before.[61] First news of the firm decision to embark on the all-out collectivization of agriculture was given to the Soviet public on 7 November of that year. Historians, both Soviet and non-Soviet, agree that this marked a watershed in the history of Bolshevik rule. (In Stalin's time, it was described as being 'equivalent in its consequences to the revolutionary upheaval of October 1917.')[62] Collectivization – which entailed the dispossession and eventual deportation of several million private peasants – was a policy which could not have been achieved without the use of force on a vast scale. For that reason alone, it had consequences which reverberated not just on the economy but throughout the whole of society. The food shortages which ensued, and the eventual famine, led the authorities to rely even further on coercion and on the suppression of news. It was a time which saw the increasing concentration of power in the hands of Stalin – and the rise of the Stalin personality cult. The atmosphere became increasingly pervaded by the notion of 'struggle'. The new policies were pushed through amidst a sustained campaign of class war – against 'rich' peasants, capitalist remnants and foreign agents. All this was done very much in the spirit of the maxim that 'Those who are not with us are against us'. That is not to say that Stalin totally lacked enthusiastic followers. Nevertheless – and this has a direct bearing on our subject – the new policies marked a radical shift on the part of the authorities *away* from reliance on persuasion. From now on, one of the constant themes of official policy was 'mobilization'. All activities, whether of workers or of intellectuals, were to be harnessed to the success of the Five Year Plan.

The impact of this great upheaval on propaganda was twofold; and, as we shall see, it was to a considerable degree double-edged. The first and most conspicuous result of the new policies was a drastic intensification of the official propaganda effort. This requires no explanation. But the second result – which is more easily overlooked and which takes us to one of the major paradoxes of Soviet propaganda – was the eventual demise during the Stalin era of all communication research, including attitude research, on which propaganda expertise (at least in the West) so heavily relies. In order to understand why this happened one has to look at another well-known aspect of Stalinism in the 1930s: the gradual but relentless imposition from above of intellectual uniformity throughout the whole of Soviet society.

The imposition of intellectual uniformity in Russia in the 1930s has been described many times; and it had far-reaching repercussions – on literature, the arts, law, economics, the study of history and virtually all the social sciences. It should be noted that policy disagreements between Stalin and his opponents were treated as issues not just of policy but of ideology. Therefore, ideological orthodoxy, as laid down from above, became mandatory for everybody; and the voicing of unorthodox ideas became positively dangerous because it was liable to attract accusations of deviationist or counter-revolutionary sympathies. Furthermore, the new policies were openly aimed at replacing the old, politically suspect, intelligentsia with a new, younger, generation of people committed to the Bolshevik cause. (A comparison with the Chinese Cultural Revolution of the mid-1960s is not, in this respect, out of place.) In the prevailing atmosphere of 'mobilization', all intellectuals were now subordinated to a new and more stringent version of 'party-mindedness' (or *partiinost'*, meaning an unreserved commitment to the goals of the Communist Party); and they were also required to gear their work to the solution of the party's current tasks (in accordance with the Marxist–Leninist doctrine of 'the unity of theory and practice').[63] The practical result was a steady increase in intellectual heresy-hunting. As one Western specialist has noted, discussions on philosophy virtually came to an end in the 1930s and were replaced by 'discussions' 'devoted to discovering and "rooting-out" deviations by individual authors'.[64] The resulting damage to the country's intellectual life, including the social sciences, in this period was recognized even by some Soviet authors of the Khrushchev and Brezhnev eras. (Indeed, one of the most conservative of the Soviet leaders, Mikhail Suslov, admitted on one occasion that the Stalin cult had 'seriously impeded and hampered the development of the social sciences'.)[65] The basic facts are therefore scarcely in dispute. What concerns us in the remainder of this chapter is the way in which this conformist atmosphere affected propaganda doctrine and communication research.

The fate of Soviet psychology has a direct bearing on this subject. Because of its relevance to the creation of a New Soviet Man, it was one of the first of the social sciences to come under tighter ideological supervision. From about 1931, its subject-matter was radically redefined. It was no longer centred on the science of 'behaviour' as in the 1920s, but was declared to consist of 'the science of the psyche, of consciousness as a property of the brain reflecting objective reality'.[66] This ended the debates of the previous decade: psychology was now recognized as a scientifically autonomous discipline, but in a manner deemed consistent with dialectical materialism. The new emphasis on 'consciousness' (itself a key concept in Marxism) was linked with another ideologically-motivated change. The emphasis in Soviet thought now shifted to the concept of people as active beings, capable of will and initiative; and not merely as passive beings who merely responded to external stimuli. (This partly reflected the campaign against the ideological deviations of 'mechanism' and 'idealism' of which Stalin accused his opponents.)[67] The change of emphasis also had an undoubted practical purpose: human initiative and will-power were to be the prime moving forces in the fulfilment of the Five Year Plans. (Indeed, in the absence of any foreign aid, the 'great leap forward' could hardly be achieved in any other way.) One further result of the new emphasis on 'consciousness' was an official rejection of both Freudianism (because of its emphasis on the unconscious mind) and of the doctrine of conditioned reflexes, as adequate bases for a psychological theory.[68] (Pavlov, though at all times respected because of his work as a physiologist, had little direct influence in this period on Soviet psychology as such.)

It would perhaps be wrong to portray Soviet psychology, even under Stalin, as being purely a deduction from ideological tenets. But in relation to communication research, the content of Soviet psychological doctrine was probably not what mattered most. A far more serious handicap was the mounting political pressure from above to which all the social scientists were at that time subjected. An article by a Soviet psychologist in 1932 conveyed this pressure obliquely – but very clearly:

One of the inescapable conclusions to be drawn from the Marxist–Leninist doctrine of the unity of theory and practice and of party vigilance in science is that every theoretical mistake, every error in the field of methodology is inescapably transferred into a political error. Similarly, in the present state of things, every such error not only weakens the front of socialist construction, but it arms our enemies.[69]

There could be little incentive for original social science research in the face of the argument that theoretical mistakes might help the enemy. This kind of argument was symptomatic of the heresy-hunting atmosphere which was steadily gaining ascendancy. The long-term effect on the quality of research can be gauged from the following statement, taken from a historical survey of Soviet psychology, published in 1947: 'The requirement of genuine party-mindedness in scientific work is a fundamental one for Soviet psychologists. Psychology is one of those sciences where academic 'objectivism' and the divorce between science and politics are especially inadmissible.'[70] The earlier relationship between political decision-making and the social sciences was therefore, by degrees, almost totally reversed. In the 1920s, the authorities had shown a genuine interest in consulting the social scientists, but from the 1930s, social scientists were increasingly expected to make their findings conform to official policies. This went hand in hand with a further restriction: foreign ideas of whatever kind became more and more suspect. To quote from this same book of 1947: 'There was a basic reversal in the thinking of Soviet psychologists with regard to psychological schools abroad. The desire to see in every "theory" springing up abroad some new kind of "latest word in science" . . . was resolutely condemned.'[71]

The same writer also noted that not only must 'bourgeois' psychological theories be rejected, but 'bourgeois' empirical data should be ignored as well, since, at best, they were derived from false theories.[72] Thus contact with Western thought was severed at precisely the time (in the mid-1930s) when American communication research was getting into its stride.

These intellectual restrictions were not, however, imposed all at once. In the short run, the launching of industrialization and collectivization actually led to a fresh upsurge of enthusiasm for research; and the negative official reaction to this is, in some ways, the most revealing part of the whole story. In January 1930 a large-scale 'Congress on Human Behaviour' assembled in Leningrad, attended by some 3,200 Soviet psychologists, education specialists and other social scientists.[73] It pledged its full commitment to the party goal of 'building a New Man'; this was the occasion when Freudianism was repudiated as a suitable doctrine for bringing this goal about.[74] But the Congress did lay great stress on the key importance of psychology in furthering the social transformation which had just begun. The Congress's final resolution urged, among other things, that a psychological basis should be provided for 'agitation-propaganda work in general', and that psychology should be a subject for 'mass popularization . . . in the sphere of anti-religious propaganda, in regard to the rationalization of all forms of man's social behaviour . . . in the organization of technical and mental work and in questions of teaching'.[75] Support for empirical research came in a letter to the Congress from Lenin's widow, Krupskaya. It was 'extremely important,' so she was quoted as saying, 'to study different strata of the population from the point of view of their class attributes, to study their world outlook and the dynamics of this world outlook, to study . . . the role of persuasion in human behaviour, the organization of the activity of a collective' and also 'to study readers, [cinema] viewers and pupils as representatives of particular social strata.'[76]

At this stage then, empirical research might have seemed fully in keeping with the leadership's policy goals. But it was precisely at this point that the specific issue of political opinion surveys came to a head. It arose in an episode now almost entirely forgotten which had to do with a survey technique known as the 'method of collisions'. This method was based on the use of multiple-choice questionnaires, and it got its name because interviewees were confronted with a set of conflicting views and were then invited to choose between them. The 'method of collisions' had gained a certain currency in the 1920s; an attempt was now made to apply it to the sensitive political issues of the day. One questionnaire form – which, somewhat remarkably, was issued by the Publishing House of the Academy of Communist Education in Moscow – sought to elicit attitudes towards industrialization and collectivization.[77] It set out, and invited comments on, three (apparently typical) attitudes towards current issues, as follows. First, the officially-approved attitude:

> We are creating large factories, state farms and collective farms. We are vanquishing the petty trader and the *kulak* [the rich peasant]. We are moving with rapid strides towards the time when there will be no classes. We are building socialism.

The questionnaire then set out a second, more sceptical, attitude towards the changes:

> We are building socialism but there is no point in hastening; otherwise we may harm ourselves through overstrain and ruin the revolution.

Finally, the questionnaire included an openly hostile view:

> What kind of socialism is this! There's not enough meat, there's not enough bread, there are no manufactured goods, there are queues at the co-operatives. Life has become very difficult. It is necessary to think not about socialism but about there being no queues.

A separate questionnaire, apparently distributed at the same time, dealt with the familiar subject of 'socialist competition' at work. It, too, listed different attitudes, including one which was obviously hostile to the regime: 'Competition has been devised in order to exploit the workers; one cannot demand that a worker should go all out to make sacrifices. If we want to produce more, we must either hire more workers or else raise the wages.'

Political attitude surveys in Russia, which provided an opportunity to express openly anti-communist views, were rare if not unique. Indeed, it is unclear whether these questionnaires were ever actually administered. But their sponsors justified them by the argument that 'depth research' of this kind would help to make propaganda more effective. This argument closely paralleled Western thinking. As one of the advocates of the 'method of collisions' put it: 'We often talk about the state . . . of our ideological work simply "off the top of our heads" [s potolka] . . . and in that situation blunders and mistakes of all kinds are absolutely inevitable.' Another supporter of the method argued that the empirical study of public opinion would make it easier to change that opinion: 'We have got, within the shortest possible time, to remould the ideology of the broadest masses . . . But this process will be all the more rapid, the better we know the ideology of the masses' (emphasis in original).

The very fact that opinion surveys were at one time seriously advocated – as an aid to Communist Party policy – is something which itself deserves to be placed on record. But the storm of official condemnation was not long in coming. The above questionnaires came into the hands of the local party authorities in the city of Syzran, in the Kuibyshev province – who then lodged a complaint about them at a higher level. In 1931, the whole concept of the 'method of collisions' was condemned in its totality in a violently polemical article, which was nevertheless remarkably frank. The article hinted in barely veiled terms, that such attitude surveys could serve the purpose of anti-communist propaganda, since:

It is well known . . . that it is precisely our avowed enemies and their agents within the party who strain every nerve to 'prove' that the unprecedently high degree of confidence which the masses are showing in the party by their active participation in the building of socialism is a deceptive appearance which supposedly conceals an anti-Bolshevik substance.

Somewhat disingenuously, the author insisted that the true test of public attitudes lay, not in answers to surveys, but in mass behaviour. (This was at a time when peasants were joining collective farms in large numbers as the result of massive coercion.) To adopt a 'scornful-negative attitude' towards mass behaviour, so he went on to argue, meant 'undermining confidence in the powerful creative enthusiasm which has seized hold of the working class and the peasantry in our country'. Proponents of the 'method of collisions' were accused of 'tailism' (which in Bolshevik terminology meant following the masses rather than leading them). All in all, the article said, 'The anti-Leninist nature of this method is quite apparent. It is no less apparent that this method plays directly into the hands of all those who crave for "freedom of the press" and "freedom in the choice of ideas".' In the meantime, the 'method of collisions' was formally banned by the Communist Party's Culture and Propaganda Department on the grounds that it 'is politically harmful, it runs counter to the basic principles of our propaganda, educational and agitation work.'

The ending of opinion surveys in Russia in the 1930s was therefore in no way an oversight; and the above article has been quoted at some length because it gives probably the fullest explanation of the ban ever to be made public. From that time onwards genuine attitude research became impossible.

But the subject of political opinion surveys did not immediately fade from public attention. Rather remarkably, it formed part of the plot of a Stalinist morality play which appeared in 1931. The play, entitled *Fear*, was written by the Soviet dramatist Alexander Afinogenov and was widely performed in theatres throughout the USSR. The plot centred on a certain Professor Borodin, director of the 'Institute of Physiological Stimuli', who had set out to discover the most important stimulus of people's behaviour. Through the use of deliberately biased samples, he came to the conclusion that 80 per cent of those investigated were ruled by the stimulus of fear. As the very end it turned out that the institute has been infiltrated by wreckers; these were duly unmasked and the Professor saw the error of his ways. But the most dramatic moment in the play came earlier, when the Professor was delivering a lecture explaining in detail what his findings meant. His message seemed to anticipate that of Solzhenitsyn by more than 30 years:

> The milkwoman is afraid that her cow will be confiscated, the peasant is afraid of compulsory collectivization, the Soviet worker is afraid of the endless purgings . . . the scientific worker is afraid that he will be accused of idealism, the technical worker is afraid that he will be accused of sabotage . . . Man becomes suspicious, shut in, dishonest, careless and unprincipled. Fear gives rise to absences from work, to the lateness of trains, to breakdowns in industry, to general poverty and hunger . . . The rabbit who has seen a boa constrictor is unable to move from the spot . . . All of us are rabbits . . . In view of this,

can we work creatively? Of course not![78]

It was most unusual for any Soviet author to put such persuasive words into the mouth of an opponent. But this particular author enjoyed official backing: he got an entry in the *Large Soviet Encyclopedia* in 1950;[79] that is, he survived the purges. The play was intended as a cautionary tale about what could happen if scientific research got into 'enemy' hands. Indeed, the Professor was immediately and vehemently refuted by a Bolshevik woman activist:

> You can't get away with it, Professor! . . . You too . . . will be exposed pitilessly, because you are defending, not the Soviet worker, but the bureaucrat – not the Party member, but the fellow who has wormed his way into the Party – not the technical worker but the sabotager – not the peasant, but the kulak. This fear . . . yes, it stalks behind those who deceive us, who wait for the return of the old order . . . When we break the resistance of the last oppressor on earth, then our children will look for the explanation of the word 'fear' in a dictionary.[80]

The play thus raised – but then neatly sidestepped – the question whether the Bolsheviks had public opinion on their side. But it is in any case obvious that in the atmosphere which the play itself depicted, opinion research was a practical impossibility.

The really remarkable thing is that the subject of opinion surveys continued, even for some years after this, to be officially mentioned. As late as 1936, the then Director of the Institute of Psychology in Moscow, Viktor Kolbanovskii, found it necessary to say: 'Such questionnaires as concern the subject's political views or probe the deep, intimate side of life must be categorically *banned* from use' (emphasis in original).

It was the most forthright official condemnation of opinion research which has survived on the record. And Kolbanovskii's explanation was itself illuminating. One reason why political questionnaires were ruled out was, he said, because experience had shown that: 'The use of . . . tests based on political material could not fail to lead to counter-revolutionary conclusions.'[81]

At this particular time, political pressures from above were reaching their height in Russia; and indeed, when Kolbanovskii died in 1970, an official obituary noted that he had taken over this Institute during 'a difficult time for Soviet psychology'.[82] It may be noted that the date of Kolbanovskii's pronouncement – August 1936 – was less than three months before the US presidential election in which public opinion polls in the United States at last became established on a scientific basis. Consequently, opinion research in Russia was cut short at almost the exact time when opinion research in the West was beginning to produce results. This was the moment, almost unnoticed, when the respective Soviet and American approaches to propaganda and communication finally parted company.

The suppression of opinion research in Russia was itself the by-product of the much more general process already mentioned: the suppression of the empirical social sciences as a whole. What to all intents and purposes finally sealed the fate of attitude surveys was a Communist Party resolution of 4 July 1936 which categorically forbade the use of psychological or intelligence tests under any circumstances. The ostensible purpose of this resolution was to ban the so-called discipline of 'pedology' – the branch of educational research which dealt with child development and which relied extensively on psychological tests of various kinds. But the consequences of the resolution went very much wider. From the early 1930s, the use of tests had, for a variety of reasons, come under increasing attack in the Soviet press. Some tests may have been incompetently carried out. It was alleged that they could give rise to elitist or even racist doctrines. But the main reason for the attacks was, quite obviously, a different one. The authorities were clearly afraid that these tests could – by undermining the doctrine of the malleability of human nature – give rise to defeatism about the feasibility of the regime's goals. If a pupil did badly in a test, it was not permissible to blame this on heredity. Nor, by the mid-1930s, was it permissible to lay the blame on a bad environment, because this could have been interpreted as a slur on the Soviet system. This seems to have been the true meaning of the 1936 resolution, which denounced pedology for resorting to 'senseless and harmful questionnaires, tests and so forth' which assumed 'the fatalistic determination of the destiny of children by biological and social factors, by the influence of heredity and by some kind of unchanging environment'. This was said to be in 'flagrant contradiction with Marxism and with the entire practice of socialist construction, which is successfully re-educating people in the spirit of socialism and liquidating the survivals of capitalism in the economy and in people's awareness'.[83] According to the prevailing orthodoxy of the 1930s, the key factors in transforming Soviet society were education, will-power and discipline, as well as individual responsibility. Research which cast doubt on these principles was not to be tolerated.

Empirical sociology of all kinds disappeared at about this time. The second half of the 1930s were, according to a post-Stalin Soviet writer, a time of 'serious difficulties' for Marxist sociology.[84] Another Soviet writer has referred to a period when 'even the word "sociology" was in effect banned' and when 'social research, like the study of the facts in general, was neglected'.[85]

Psychology – on which the authorities had placed such hopes in the 1920s – fared no better. Between 1934 and 1955 there were no Soviet journals exclusively devoted to the subject as such.[86] And although 'general psychology' (dealing with such topics as perception, attention, will and so on) continued to be studied, social psychology – which has the most direct bearing on propaganda and communication theory – ceased in the early 1930s to be studied at all. The exact circumstances in which it was discontinued have been little discussed. The only known Soviet monograph on this subject (an unpublished dissertation of 1968), explains the winding up of the study of social psychology in the 1930s as being due, among other things, to the influence of those who advocated 'materialism interpreted in the purely economic sense' and who feared 'the psychologization of the social sciences'.[87] In other words, social psychology was apparently seen by the authorities at that time as a potential challenge to the Soviet Marxist interpretation of society. Another Soviet author in the 1960s made the same point even more explicitly when he referred to 'the apprehension which constantly arose that social psychology tended, when investigating historical events, to supplant historical materialism'.[88] Yet another Soviet author in the 1960s blamed the disappearance of social psychology not only on the Stalin cult but on what he called the 'anti-psychologism' prevailing in Russia at that time.[89] In general he explained what happened in terms of both intellectual and political difficulties:

the difficulty of defining the methodological foundations of Marxist social psychology, the not entirely healthy atmosphere in which arguments were conducted, the pronouncements of dogmatists and vulgar sociologists who considered social psychology to be incompatible with Marxism . . . as well as other reasons – all this, taken together, led to the winding up of social psychological research.[90]

If such psychological research was being curtailed, then clearly it could have played little or no part in Stalinist propaganda methods. And this, by degrees, is what apparently happened. The study of readers' psychology, which had earlier attracted so much official encouragement, gradually came to an end in the early 1930s.[91] And – to judge by Soviet specialized literature of that period – psychological expertise came to have less and less direct influence on propaganda activities in general. For instance, a textbook of psychology written by Konstantin Kornilov and published in Moscow in 1935 did contain a passing reference to propaganda – noting that 'problems of the impact of a military or political poster on those who see them, problems of the impact of the cinema and the radio, the problem of rational advertising and advertisements – all this comes within the province of psychology.'[92] However, a later textbook on psychology, of which Kornilov was a co-author and which appeared in 1938, contained no similar remarks. In the intervening period, the whole of Soviet psychological doctrine had been thrown into disarray by the 1936 resolution which effectively banned empirical research. The preface to this later textbook described the 1936 resolution as a turning-point which involved 'the radical revision of the entire system of psychology'. Soviet scholars, the authors said, now faced the task of 'setting out on the road indicated by Comrade Stalin for the creation of an advanced science'. The authors were so obviously unsure of their ground that, as they frankly admitted, they preferred to leave 'a whole number of more or less large gaps' in the textbook, rather than include 'disputed or unverified propositions'.[93]

It was not only the intellectual community in the USSR which suffered through the suppression of the social sciences. Many issues of great practical importance were consequently neglected. The 1936 resolution was treated as a reason for banning 'psychotechnics' (the rough equivalent of industrial psychology) since it, too, relied on psychological testing. The study of sexual development of children was ended 'because of the rejection of all problems which were in any way linked with the name of Freud';[94] and the neglect of sex education has caused long-term social damage, as at least some Soviet specialists now recognize. Harm was caused in other areas as well. As late as 1969, a Soviet author complained that educational backwardness and juvenile delinquency 'were hardly studied at all over the past 30 years'.[95]

This, then, was the background against which the ending of Soviet communication research has to be understood. The reasons for its suppression were, as we have seen, various. Clearly, the Stalin cult was one factor which inhibited original thinking. Even more clearly, the policy of coercion made opinion surveys both irrelevant and impracticable. It also appears (and this has a direct relevance to the present) that there really *is* some degree of tension between Soviet Marxism–Leninism and the findings of social psychology. On the other hand, it may be doubted whether the upheavals in Russia in the 1930s (or indeed in China during the Cultural Revolution of the 1960s) are entirely amenable to rational explanation. The mass coercion applied by Stalin, as well as Mao Zedong, frequently led to arbitrary and senseless (as well as vicious) acts which went *beyond* what the official policy goals would have required. The appropriate term 'excessive excesses' is sometimes used to make this point.[96] The suppression of the study of child sexuality (for which no authority can be found even in the writings of Stalin) is a small but telling example.

It is not part of our argument to suggest that Soviet psychology was entirely moribund even at this time, or to deny that it made any progress.[97] The essential point is that psychology played virtually no part in Soviet propaganda doctrine; and that the connection between psychology and political beliefs was never studied. It is true that psychology continued to be written about and taught: indeed, from 1936 onwards it was authoritatively said to be concerned with the teaching and upbringing of children.[98] But its links with education were later said to be merely 'formal';[99] and in any case, an educational doctrine intended for teaching children was found hardly appropriate for propagandists addressing an adult population.[100] From the mid-1930s such 'method' as existed in Soviet propaganda (and education) theory was of a strictly 'practical' kind – with an emphasis on content, organization and the various 'do's and don'ts' already listed in chapter 3. Soviet educational policy from the 1930s was heavily influenced by the ideas of Anton Makarenko, who had won fame for his work in rehabilitating homeless and delinquent children in colonies run by the secret police, then known as the NKVD. Makarenko had stressed the importance of family upbringing, discipline, collectivism and the power of pupil 'public opinion' in curbing deviant behaviour. His writings had a humane as well as a strongly authoritarian emphasis and were by no means devoid of insights. However, his methods owed virtually nothing to professional psychology.[101]

As to the monitoring of public opinion at this time, the main methods were the traditional one of questions and answers at 'agitators'' meetings; and the compilation by the authorities of confidential reports on public opinion. (Some of these reports were discovered in Soviet archives captured during the Second World War by the Nazis, and were later published in the West.)[102] However, in the absence of an atmosphere in which people could express their views frankly, and in the absence of reliable methods of sampling opinion, such methods could have only a limited value.

It remains, when dealing with the suppression of the social sciences in Russia in the 1930s, to take note of one ironic fact. The curtailment of psychology, opinion surveys, and the social sciences in general all went hand in hand with an increasingly strident emphasis by the leadership on the need for a radical transformation – not only of society but of Man himself. Thus it was that the crash programme of industrialization was followed by a ban on the study of industrial psychology. Yet, at the same time, the power of education was deemed to be without limit – as shown by the then orthodox Soviet saying 'There are no bad pupils – there are [only] bad teachers'. (In the post-Stalin years, this maxim was said to have had a 'negative influence' on education).[103] Sidney and Beatrice Webb, who visited Russia in the early 1930s, reported seeing a slogan at the Moscow Sports Club which said: 'We are not only rebuilding human society on an economic basis: we are mending the human race on scientific principles.'[104] In the words quoted at the beginning of this chapter,

Bolshevik agitators were enjoined to be 'the architects of human souls'; and their work was described as 'a powerful battering-ram'. At this time – as the 'battering-ram' metaphor implies – will-power was to be the main agent of change. Nevertheless the paradox remains that at a moment when propaganda was seen as a crucial instrument for changing people and the environment, it was simultaneously forbidden to make any real investigation of people and the environment.

Stalin, Pavlov and 'mind control'

We argued in the last section that, in view of the curtailment of psychological research in the Stalin era, Stalinist propaganda method can have owed little to the findings of psychology. But we must now briefly turn to a piece of evidence which, at first sight, seems not to fit into this picture. This relates to the influence on Soviet thinking of the ideas of Ivan Pavlov. In the West, especially in the 1950s, fears were repeatedly voiced that the Russian, as well as the Chinese, communists really had devised techniques for 'mind-control', based, so it was thought, on Pavlov's discoveries. The fears originated with the disturbing and baffling spectacle of communist political show trials, where the accused readily made (often the most improbable) confessions of their own guilt. The fears were greatly strengthened by the reported communist success in indoctrinating American soldiers taken prisoner during the Korean war of 1950–3. And Western observers could also point to the fact that in 1950 the Soviet authorities had decreed that all psychological doctrine was to be re-orientated on the basis of Pavlov's theories. Meanwhile, this period saw the publication of George Orwell's *1984*, which powerfully dramatized the whole subject of 'brainwashing' and made a deep and lasting impression on the public imagination.[105] In the United States, the possibility that the communists had indeed made a breakthrough in 'mind control' was taken so seriously that the CIA for a number of years sponsored a whole series of secret (and probably illegal) experiments in an attempt to find out whether 'mind control' was scientifically feasible. In the end, the experiments apparently proved fruitless. They came to light only in 1977, as the result of disclosure by the United States authorities.[106]

Were these US fears, then, the result of pure fantasy or cold war myth? The answer is not entirely simple. The fears did rest, to some degree, on factual evidence. The real question is how the evidence ought to be interpreted. It is notoriously true that political prisoners in communist countries at that time were subjected to the most ruthless psychological as well as physical mistreatment. These methods of pressure were devastatingly effective in producing confessions, although it is doubtful whether many of the victims were 'brainwashed' in the sense of coming to accept the ideology of their captors. (On this specific point the evidence is less than clear. Some of Stalin's victims were, of course, veteran Bolsheviks whose communist party loyalty must have disorientated them when faced with rejection by the party.[107] However, most of the evidence of attempts at 'brainwashing' in the true sense comes from China rather than the USSR.)[108] But none of this is crucial to our theme. Techniques of pressure against prisoners can hardly be applicable in campaigns for the mass indoctrination of entire popoulations. Is there then, any evidence that Stalin used, or attempted to use, Pavlovian techniques for *this* purpose? Here again, the evidence is not entirely straightforward.

The general influence of Pavlov's ideas on Soviet thinking has been widely recognized.[109] Ivan Pavlov (1849–1936) had won international renown as a physiologist long before the Bolshevik revolution. He had been awarded the Nobel Prize for physiology in 1904 and his experiments on conditioned reflexes in dogs had made him famous even among laymen. Despite his well-known anti-Bolshevik views (at least in the early years of the new regime),[110] he had, almost from the first, enjoyed official Soviet encouragement in his research; this was reflected in a government decree of 1921 signed by Lenin personally, which created a special commission to ensure 'the most favourable conditions' for his work.[111] Up to this point, the facts are well established.

However – and this is something which is often overlooked – it appears that Pavlov found favour with the Soviet authorities for reasons which had little or no direct connection with indoctrination techniques. As at least one Western specialist has pointed out, Pavlov's ideas were attractive to the Bolsheviks for reasons of a general philosophical nature. Pavlov, like Lenin, was a materialist and a monist (in the sense of denying that mind could exist apart from matter); and he sought to reduce reality to *systems*. Furthermore, Pavlov was strongly environmentalist – in the sense of being optimistic about the possibility of improving an organism through environmental influence.[112]

However, during most of the thirties and forties, although always revered in Russia as a physiologist, Pavlov seems to have had very little influence on the development of Soviet psychology. In 1930, as already noted, the concept of conditioned reflexes was rejected (alongside Freudianism) as an adequate model for the New Soviet Man, on the grounds that the doctrine of reflexes reduced human beings to automatons.[113] This official attitude continued for many years. As late as 1947 a Soviet psychologist insisted that 'by itself, the doctrine of conditioned reflexes is inadequate even for an understanding of the physiological basis of human behaviour.'[114] Some years later, Soviet psychologists were all accused of having ignored Pavlov's doctrines up to 1950.[115] All this suggests that if the authorities were indeed interested in using Pavlov's methods for the purpose of mass indoctrination, then their interest arose only in the late 1940s, towards the end of Stalin's life. This indeed seems to be the case. And when trying to assess the scientific genuineness or otherwise of this Pavlovian revival, it is relevant, as we shall shortly see, to recall that these were the years when the spurious genetic theories of Trofim Lysenko had gained Stalin's favour.

The offical Pavlovian revival effectively dates from a joint meeting of the Soviet Academies of Science and Medical Science which took place in Moscow from 28 June to 14 July 1950; this laid down that Pavlov's theory of 'higher nervous activity' was henceforward to be made the foundation of all Soviet medicine, physiology and psychology.[116] The intended implications of the new line for psychology were perhaps most fully spelled out at a further conference held in Moscow two years later at which one of the main speakers was Professor A. A. Smirnov. Smirnov repeated the call for 'a *radical* reconstruction of psychological science' (emphasis in original). Repudiating earlier official views, he said categorically that 'the teaching of I. P. Pavlov on temporary connections [that is, conditioned reflexes] is a firm foundation for the understanding of *all* man's conscious activity' (emphasis in original). Smirnov was at pains to explain that the new line did not mean a denial of the reality of mind – because human consciousness both reflected and influenced the external world. Therefore psychology as an independent discipline was to be maintained. (Smirnov's remarks caused some confusion amongst his audience at the time.) Nevertheless it seemed to follow from his argument that the human mind was itself devoid of any inner autonomy and could be made totally subject to external regulation. Smirnov called for an end to 'attempts to seek the ultimate causes of psychological facts in mental phenomena themselves' and insisted that psychology had to be 'purged of all traces of idealism, subjectivism, introspectionism'.[117] (In other words, the empirical study of motivation evidently had no role in Soviet neo-Pavlovianism.) External influences, including those of the social system, were what shaped the mind. But these in turn were mediated through the brain; and Pavlov's doctrines were indispensable because they explained what the relevant brain mechanisms were.[118]

Did this new line therefore, signify an officially-inspired attempt to use Pavlov's methods for the purposes of indoctrination? There were passages in Smirnov's speech which were capable of being interpreted in that way. He said that 'Soviet psychologists are confronted in all definiteness with the problem of the formation of the personality of man' and also deplored the fact that efforts to date had been 'totally inadequate'.[119] But the crux of the matter is how this declared objective of forming the personality was supposed to be achieved. Did the neo-Pavlovian line represent some kind of genuine scientific breakthrough in methods of indoctrination? Or was it – like Lysenko's theory of genetics – an essentially pseudo-scientific, bogus theory? This question, as already noted, is far from irrelevant – bearing in mind the intellectual atmosphere in Stalin's last years. Freedom of scientific inquiry was at its lowest ebb in those years. It may be significant that neo-Pavlovian doctrines were being openly bracketed in the Soviet press with those of the new genetics.[120]

The goal of changing human nature was, of course, not new. The strikingly novel feature of neo-Pavlovianism was its preoccupation with questions of linguistics. This itself may provide a clue to the doctrine's scientific genuineness or otherwise. Pavlov, towards the end of his life, had written about the connection between thought and language. He had observed that the crucial difference between animals and humans was the latter's ability to respond to words; and he had described language as 'the second signalling system of reality' – as opposed to the 'first signals', which consisted of external stimuli perceived by animals and humans alike.[121] This aspect of Pavlov's writing had, until 1950, attracted relatively little official attention. After that date, however, the official attitude changed sharply.

But at this point, politics – as opposed to science – intruded. In June and July 1950, at exactly the time when the first conference on Pavlov was being held in Moscow, Stalin made a number of widely publicized pronouncements on the subject of 'Marxism and Linguistics'. He said, amongst other things, that thought without language was impossible[122] – which might have had the implication that thought itself could be made subject to control, through the control of language. It is unclear whether Stalin had this in mind; but what is clear is that soon afterwards Soviet psychologists expressly linked Stalin on linguistics with Pavlov on reflexes. Thus, Stalin's 'brilliant work' on Marxism and linguistics was extolled by Smirnov as providing 'the only correct prospect' for psychology's further development. Pavlov's 'theory of the second signal system, which in interrelationship with the first signal system plays an exceptionally important role in people's lives', was, so Smirnov said, 'wholly in accordance with what Stalin has pointed out with regard to the significance of language'. Furthermore, Pavlov was said to have demonstrated the way in which 'external influences' (including, of course, language) 'acquire a signalling function . . . and by virtue of this regulate the behaviour of man'.[123]

The 'regulatory' function of language thus seems to have been a key element in the neo-Pavlovian argument. But it is precisely at this point that the argument becomes obscure. There is, of course, a familiar sense in which language does have a 'regulatory' function: human beings are constantly adjusting both their ideas and their behaviour in response to messages conveyed to them through language. But regulation in this sense is perfectly compatible with individual autonomy: people are quite free to select which messages they respond to. It is all very far removed from the Orwellian notion of language as an instrument of 'thought control', by means of which rulers can supposedly shape public opinion according to their will. It is conceivable that 'neo-Pavlovians' of the early 1950s did have some such Orwellian notion in mind; one cannot be sure. But such a notion does not appear to derive from the ideas of Pavlov; nor indeed does it have any evident foundation in either science or common sense.

The most convincing explanation (to my mind at least) of what led to the neo-Pavlovian movement in this period is to be found in a well-documented study by Professor Robert Tucker, on which the above material is to some extent based. Neo-Pavlovianism, in Tucker's view, was essentially 'a theory of semantics constructed on a physiological basis'.[124] It did not, he concludes, 'grow spontaneously out of the scientific investigations of Soviet physiologists, pathologists and psychologists ... It was, on the contrary, imposed on them from above by political authorities whose interest in the matter was non scientific.'[125] Tucker sees the whole phenomenon – taken together with that of Lysenkoism – as a symptom of the regime's gradual drift in Stalin's last years into 'the realm of political fantasy and wish-fulfilment'.[126]

The political, rather than scientific, motivation behind the neo-Pavlovian line also tends to be confirmed by Soviet evidence. Some psychologists in the USSR were bewildered or hostile even at the time. One of their number wrote an article openly protesting at the new approach on the grounds that 'we are thereby equating the salivation of a dog at the sound of a metronome with the most intricate phenomena of the spiritual life of man.'[127] This same article also quoted the story of how a speaker at a conference sometime after 1950 got a note signed by 'a group of psychologists seeking the subject of their science'. It is true that in the years following Stalin's death Soviet psychology continued to have a Pavlovian orientation. This was approved at a major conference held in Moscow in May 1962, which did, however, severely criticize the 'Pavlov' conference held 12 years earlier. In the words of the speaker who opened the 1962 meeting: 'The Stalin personality cult made its imprint ... It fettered the creative initiative of scientists [and] gave rise to dogmatism, an attitude of uncritical acceptance of certain particular, dubious and inaccurate formulations.'[128] What was apparently discarded in the post-Stalin years was, in Tucker's opinion, the 'idea of finding in Pavlov the scientific key to mind control'.[129] There is, in any case, no evidence that neo-Pavlovianism ever came up with any recommendations of any practical use for propagandists; nor that it had any visible impact on the Soviet propaganda output. Later on, in 1971, a Soviet book on psychology expressly denied that the authorities had *ever* sought to make use of Pavlovian reflexes for indoctrination purposes. This is difficult to reconcile with Smirnov's remarks quoted above. But it provides still further evidence that neo-Pavlovianism was discarded by Stalin's successors. According to this book:

> Apart from a few impulsive pupils of . . . Pavlov . . . nobody supposed that man's vital activity [*zhiznedeyatel' nost'*] could be reduced to systems of conditioned reflexes. Still less did such an approach serve as a guideline for the Communist Party, which was engaged in . . . the goal-directed education of social consciousness in the working people. It is necessary to emphasize this because the story is still popular among psychologists in capitalist countries that the support given by the party and government to I. P. Pavlov is to be explained as an attempt to use his ideas so as to devise a state plan for the management of people on the basis of conditioned reflexes.[130]

It remains to add one short footnote. In the mid-1960s a Soviet psychologist, V. M. Yakushev, apparently did attempt to elaborate a theory of propaganda with the help of Pavlovian doctrine. His detailed argument appeared in an unpublished dissertation and is not entirely clear. However, his arguments were criticized as unrealistic,[131] and found no official support. Yet, rather surprisingly, Yakushev (to judge by the published abstract of his dissertation) was, in effect, scathingly critical of Soviet propaganda as it then was. He addressed himself to Pavlov not Stalin. He stressed the importance of relating the message to existing motivation. He maintained that prohibitions could be counter-productive. He strongly advised against the use of excessive repetition as an effective way of winning over an audience, because, he said, this could produce 'passivity or even hidden resistance' on the audience's part; and 'the atmosphere of slumber in such cases operates as a defensive reaction by the organism against zero information which adds nothing to what is already known.'[132] Yakushev, indeed, was one of the authors quoted at the end of chapter 2 who said that practically no attention had been given in the USSR to the psychology of propaganda.

From all that has been said in this section, two broad conclusions seem to follow: first, that the Soviet interest in Pavlov has had very little to do with propaganda methods (except, possibly, in the period 1950–3); secondly, that the doctrines of Pavlov, insofar as they do provide insights into propaganda method, have far more to do with the reinforcing or rewarding of positive motivation than with the kind of punitive methods associated with 'brainwashing'. This seems to be implied in Yakushev's argument. Pavlovianism and Stalinism, in other words, may have less in common than is sometimes supposed.

Conclusion

The purpose of this chapter was not to attempt yet another survey of the Stalinist system as such, but to concentrate on one particular question which has often been raised in connection with Stalinism, and which might be termed 'the myth and reality of thought control'. There are, needless to say, many imponderables about Soviet propaganda in the Stalin era. Neither the intentions behind it nor the impact which it made can be known with anything approaching certainty. Nevertheless – if one goes by the weight of the evidence presented above – two paradoxical conclusions seem to emerge.

The first concerns the question: did Stalin attempt to use psychology for propagandist or political purposes? The answer seems to be 'No'. There is little to suggest that Stalin's regime was, after the 1920s, in the least interested in the psychological aspects of propaganda. (The only possible exception was the apparently fruitless discussion of Pavlov in the early 1950s.) The then leadership, for all its proclaimed goal of changing human beings, became actively hostile to the empirical study of motivation. Psychology – far from being harnessed for the purposes of indoctrination – was severely and increasingly handicapped by political interference from above. The rise of 'thought control' was accompanied at every stage by a down-grading of the status of psychology.

The second paradox is underlined by the ban imposed in the 1930s on opinion surveys; and this, in turn, highlights the crucial problem of feedback in the Stalinist system. Stalinism has frequently been portrayed as 'totalitarian', which implies a system of near-total control imposed from above over everything – including opinion. But it is not as simple as that. Effective control presupposes effective feedback. How, for instance, can a regime control public opinion if it has no reliable way of finding out what the public really thinks? It is therefore especially noteworthy that when, in the early 1930s, the regime began to impose tighter controls, it immediately clamped down on feedback (such as opinion research), against the advice of some of its own social scientists. As a result, the system increasingly developed a weakness even in its own terms; that is, it became more and more deprived of any mechanism for self-correction in the light of mistakes.

This would seem to have happened with the propaganda machine; and it fits into what we know about the regime more generally. The system of controls was ruthless but also lop-sided. The regime proved itself to be strong on mobilization but, as we have said, weak on feedback. Therefore its achievements were sometimes on a large scale; but so, equally, were its blunders (and crimes). Even the successes were often achieved by inefficient means, at an unnecessarily high cost. Stalin's leadership in the Second World War is a well-known example. Mobilization was a key factor in the final Soviet victory. But when war broke out, lack of feedback led to near-total disaster – because Stalin had been able to disregard the warnings of an impending German attack. The Soviet writer Ilya Erenburg recalled this latter episode in his memoirs and succinctly expressed the feedback problem in these words: 'I had thought that truthful information would help to determine policy: it turned out, on the contrary, that information was required which would confirm the correctness of the chosen policy.'[133]

It does not, of course, follow that Stalin's propaganda 'failed'. He made an enormous psychological impact and enjoyed substantial public admiration, although the attitudes of ordinary Russians at the time must surely have been shaped as much by events or personal experience as by pure propaganda. In any case, Soviet achievements in the Stalin era were not all propaganda myths. The reasons for the success of the Stalin cult in the USSR remain to be fully explored. They probably had far more to do with a popular acceptance of the need for a strong leader to prevent anarchy[134] than with any special propaganda skill on the part of Stalin (who relied heavily on crude censorship and downright falsehood). In any case it is apparent that the then methods of indoctrination were extremely primitive; and it would be wrong to credit the Stalinist indoctrination system with psychological skills which it quite clearly did not possess. And that leads back to the central theme of this book.

It has become commonplace to say that Stalin had no interest in persuasion. And on at least one occasion in the Khrushchev era, the Soviet communist newspaper *Pravda* endorsed this opinion. In 1962 the paper printed a favourable review of Solzhenitsyn's first published account of the *Gulag*; then it added this unusual comment: 'The tyranny and the brutality – which were corollaries of the [Stalin] cult – were directed against working people, against the people. This, above all, is the message of *One Day in the Life of Ivan Denisovich*. Stalin did not believe in the masses, he regarded them with scorn.'[135]

The price paid for Stalin's attitude has been high – not only, of course, for the victims, but for the system itself.

Notes

1 The annual production of paper had fallen by 1920 to 37,000 tons compared to 219,000 tons in 1913. In the 1920s Soviet newspaper circulation increased sharply, but only in 1923 did the country regain the 1913 level of 21 copies of newspapers for every 1,000 inhabitants in Russia. See *Pechat's SSSR za 50 let. Statisticheskie ocherki* (Moscow, 1967), pp. 156, 158. A more detailed account of the problems then facing the Soviet press is given in Peter Kenez, *The Birth of the Propaganda State: Soviet Methods of Mass Mobilization, 1917–1929* (Cambridge University Press, 1985), esp. ch. 10.

2 See Pavel Gurevich and Vsevolod Ruzhnikov, *Sovetskoye radioveshchanie. Stranitsy istorii* (Moscow, 1976), p. 40. Occasional or experimental broadcasts had, however, begun earlier.

3 See Valentin Talovov, *O chitatel'skoi psikhologii i teoreticheskikh osnovakh eë izucheniya* (Leningrad, 1973), p. 27.

4 Ya. Shafir, *Ocherki psikhologii chitatelya* (Moscow/Leningrad, 1927), p. 85. Further information about empirical research into readers' interests in the 1920s is provided in R. F. Ivanova, 'The first experience of concrete sociological investigation of the Soviet press', in *Vestnik Moskovskogo Universiteta* (Seriya zhurnalistiki), 2 (1967), pp. 43–55.

5 See Ivan Kuznetzov, *Vyacheslav Alekseyevich Karpinskii* (Moscow, 1974), p. 5. The text of Lenin's letter appears in *PSS*, vol. 54, pp. 143–4.

6 Talovov, *O chitatel'skoi psikhologii*, pp. 29–30. This was said to compare with a total of only 90 books, pamphlets and articles on this theme published in Russia between the middle of the nineteenth century and November 1917.

7 Ibid., citing *Sbornik postanovlenii i rasporyzhenii Glavpolitprosveta* (Moscow, 1921), p. 26.

8 Ibid., p. 27.

9 Ibid., p. 51, citing *Knigonosha*, 19 (1925), p. 3.

10 See V. N. Kolbanovskii and Yu. A. Sherkovin (eds), *Problemy sotsial'noi psikhologii i propaganda* (Moscow, 1971), pp. 117–18.

11 A. B. Zalkind, *Pedologiya v SSSR* (Moscow, 1929), p. 60.

12 See Talovov, *O chitatel'skoi psikhologii*, pp. 16, 50, 56.

13 Details of Rubakin's biography are taken, except where otherwise shown, from S. Simsova (ed.), *Nikolai Rubakin and Bibliopsychology* (Clive Bingley, London, 1968) and from Alfred Senn, *Nikolai Rubakin: A Life for Books* (ORP, Newtonville, Mass., 1977).

14 *PSS*, vol. 25, p. 112.

15 See *BSE*, 1st edn, vol. 49 (Moscow, 1941), p. 511; ibid., 2nd edn, vol. 37 (Moscow, 1955), p. 276; ibid., 3rd edn, vol. 22 (Moscow, 1975), p. 339.

16 Reprinted in Lenin Library Archive, *Zapiski otdela rukopisei*, vol. 26, (Moscow, 1963), p. 79.

17 Quoted in V. A. Kuz'michev, *Pechatnaya agitatsiya i propaganda* (Moscow/Leningrad, 1930), pp. 60–1.

18   Simsova, *Nikolai Rubakin* p. 10

19   See, for biographical details, Kuznetsov, *Vyacheslav Alekseyevich Karpinskii*.

20   Lenin Library Archive, pp. 401–3.

21   Nikolai Rubakin, *Psikhologiya chitatelya i kniga* (Moscow, 1929), quoted in Kuz'michev, *Pechatnaya agitatsiya i propaganda*, pp. 59–61.

22   See Lenin Library Archive, p. 80.

23   A. V. Petrovskii, *Istoriya Sovetskoi psikhologii* (Moscow, 1967), p. 176.

24   Talovov, *O chitatel'skoi psikhologii*, pp. 50–1.

25   Ya. Shafir, *Rabochaya gazeta i eë chitatel'* (Moscow, 1926), esp. pp. 25–30, for details of the survey and of the questions.

26   Ibid., p. 107.

27   Ibid., p. 222.

28   Ibid., p. 112.

29   Ibid., pp. 109–10.

30   Ibid., pp. 187–8.

31   Ibid., pp. 178–81.

32   Ibid., pp. 14–16.

33   Ibid., p. 162.

34   Ibid., p. 16.

35   Ibid., p. 241.

36   Shafir, *Ocherki psikhologii chitatelya*, p. 85.

37   Shafir, *Rabochaya gazeta*, p. 21.

38   Ibid., p. 91.

39   Shafir, *Ocherki psikhologii chitatelya*, p. 85.

40   Ibid., pp. 72ff.

41   V.A. Kuz'michev, *Pechatnaya agitatsiya i propaganda* (Moscow/Leningrad, 1930).

42   Ibid., pp. 200–4.

43   Ibid., pp. 207–8.

44   Ibid., p. 211.

45   Ibid., pp. 215, 246.

46   V. A. Kuz'michev, *Organizatsiya obshchestvennogo mneniya* (Moscow/Leningrad, 1929). The reference to Lippman is on p. 5.

47   Ibid., p. 61.

48   This account is taken from ibid., pp. 6–16.

49   See *Stroitel'stvo kommunizma i preodolenie religioznykh perezhitkov* (Moscow, 1966), p. 16; also *Voprosy nauchnogo ateizma* 4, (Moscow, 1967), pp. 43–4.

50   K. N. Kornilov, in Carl Murchison (ed.), *Psychologies of 1930* (Clark University Press, Worcester, Mass. and Oxford University Press, 1930), p. 271.

51   See Petrovskii, *Istoriya Sovetskoi psikhologii*, pp. 88–9, quoting Klara Tsetkin, *Vospominaniya o Lenine* (Moscow, 1955), p. 44. For an English translation, see Klara Zetkin, *Reminiscences of Lenin* (Modern Books, London, 1929) p. 52.

52   It appeared in *Pravda*, 14 June 1925; see Petrovskii, *Istoriya Sovetskoi psikhologii*, p. 88.

53   See Petrovskii, *Istoriya Sovetskoi psikhologii*, pp. 79–84, for a Soviet account of these 'Freudo-Marxists'.

54   Petrovskii, *Istoriya Sovetskoi psikhologii*, p. 142.
55   See article on 'Behaviourism' in *BSE*, 1st edn, vol. 6, (Moscow, 1927), pp. 434–43.
56   See Raymond A. Bauer, *The New Man in Soviet Psychology* (Harvard University Press, Cambridge, Mass., 1952), ch. 5, esp. pp. 80–1). This book provides a detailed survey of Soviet official thinking on psychology between 1917 and the beginning of the 1950s.
57   Petrovskii, *Istoriya Sovetskoi psikhologii*, pp. 67–8.
58   Ibid., pp. 140–1.
59   Shafir, *Rabochaya gazeta*, p. 12.
60   R. F. Ivanova, 'The first experience of concrete sociological investigation of the Soviet press', in *Vestnik Moskovskogo Universiteta* (Seriya zhurnalistiki), 2 (1967), p. 55.
61   See Alec Nove, *An Economic History of the USSR* (Allen Lane, The Penguin Press, London, 1969), pp. 144, 154.
62   See the then official party history: *Istoriya Vsesoyuznoi Kommunisticheskoi partii (bol'shevikov)* (Moscow, 1942), p. 291. This book had first been published in 1938.
63   The change in the Soviet intellectual climate in the early 1930s is thoroughly documented in Gustav A. Wetter, *Dialectical Materialism; A Historical and Systematic Survey of Philosophy in the Soviet Union*, tr. Peter Heath (Routledge & Kegan Paul, London, 1958), esp. part II, ch 6 and 9. Further documentation is provided in Bauer, *The New Man in Soviet Psychology*, esp. from ch. 6 onwards.
64   Wetter, *Dialectical Materialism*, p. 175.
65   *Pravda*, 4 February 1962, p. 3.
66   Petrovskii, *Istoriya Sovetskoi psikhologii*, p. 138.
67   See Wetter, *Dialectical Materialism*, esp. ch. 9; Bauer, *The New Man in Soviet Psychology*, esp. pp. 97ff.
68   A. Zalkind in *Pedologiya*, 3 (1930), pp. 318–20.
69   A. S. Zaluzhnyi in *Pedologiya*, 3 (1932), p. 17, quoted in Bauer, *The New Man in Soviet Psychology*, p. 106.
70   B. M. Teplov, *Sovetskaya psikhologicheskaya nauka za 30 let* (Moscow, 1947), p. 31.
71   Ibid., p. 20.
72   Ibid., pp. 17–18.
73   Petrovskii, *Istoriya Sovetskoi psikhologii*, p. 120.
74   See A. B. Zalkind in *Pedologiya*, 3 (1930), p. 318.
75   A. B. Zalkind, *Pedologiya*, 2 (1930), p. 163.
76   *Pedologiya*, 2 (1930), p. 293.
77   This account of the 'method of collisions' and the attacks on it is taken from G. Gak, 'Concerning a harmful method', *Kommunisticheskaya Revolyutsiya*, 8 (1931), pp. 19–26.
78   See Aleksandr Afinogenov, 'Fear', translated into English in Eugene Lyons (ed.), *Six Soviet Plays* (Gollancz, London, 1935), pp. 585–6.

79 See *BSE*, 2nd edn, vol. 3 (Moscow, 1950), p. 508; ibid., 3rd edn, vol. 2 (Moscow, 1970), p. 430.

80 Lyons, *Six Soviet Plays*, pp. 588–9.

81 See V. N. Kolbanovskii, 'The current tasks of Soviet psychology', *Pedagogicheskoye obrazovanie* 5 (1936), pp. 7–21, esp. pp. 10 and 12.

82 See *Voprosy psikhologii*, 6 (1970), pp. 184–5.

83 The party Central Committee resolution 'On perversions in the system of the People's Commissariat of Education' appeared in *Pravda*, 5 July 1936 and was reprinted in, inter alia, *Khrestomatiya po istorii sovetskoi shkoly i pedagogiki* (Moscow, 1972), pp. 143–6. The meaning and consequences of this resolution are discussed in John McLeish, *Soviet Psychology: History, Theory, Content* (Methuen, London, 1975), esp. pp. 148–9; and also in Bauer, *The New Man in Soviet Psychology*, esp. ch. 8.

84 B. A. Chagin, *Ocherk istorii sotsiologicheskoi mysli v SSSR* (Leningrad, 1971), p. 178. A historical survey of the origins of sociological studies in Russia, their curtailment in the 1930s and revival after Stalin's death can be found in Elizabeth Ann Weinberg, *The Development of Sociology in the Soviet Union* (Routledge & Kegan Paul, London, 1974), ch. 1.

85 *Novyi Mir*, 6 (1965), p. 272 (S. Epshtein).

86 See McLeish, *Soviet Psychology*, pp. 159, 226. The gap began with the closing of the last remaining psychological journal, *Sovetskaya psikhotekhnika*, in 1934; it ended in 1955 with the appearance of the new journal *Voprosy psikhologii*.

87 S. A. Ratner, *Voprosy sotsial'noi psikhologii v 20–30e gody v SSSR. Avtoreferat* (published abstract of unpublished dissertation). (Leningrad, 1968), pp. 3–4.

88 Petrovskii, *Istoriya Sovetskoi psikhologii*, p. 175.

89 B. D. Parygin, *Sotsial'naya psikhologiya kak nauka* (Leningrad, 1965), p. 49.

90 B. D. Parygin, 'Sovremennoye sostoyanie sotsial'noi pskihologii', in *Materialy k nauchnoi sessii, posvyashchennoi 50-letiyu Velikoi Oktryabr'skoi sotsialisticheskoi revolyutsii* (Leningrad, 1967), p. 122.

91 See Talovov, *O chitatel'skoi psikhologii*, p. 11 where it is said that in the field of journalistic studies between the mid-1930s and mid-1960s not a single Soviet book was known to have appeared which dealt specifically with the psychology of the reader.

92 K. N. Kornilov, *Psikhologiya* (Moscow, 1935), p. 38.

93 K. N. Kornilov, B. M. Teplov and L. M. Shvarts (eds), *Psikhologiya* (Moscow, 1938), pp. 3–4.

94 As to the ending of what was called 'anti-scientific' work on psychotechnics, see Teplov, *Sovetskaya psikhologicheskaya nauka za 30 let*, p. 24. As to the ending of the study of children's sexual development, see Petrovskii, *Istoriya Sovetskoi psikhologii*, pp. 93–4. A more recent Soviet book on sex education says that the study of child sexuality was never banned but that 'psychologists and teachers themselves avoided this', apparently because they felt unable to put forward counter-arguments to the views of Freud, whose theories had by the 1930s become unacceptable. See D. V. Kolesov, *Besedy o polovom vospitanii* (Moscow, 1986), p. 158.

95   *Voprosy psikhologii* 3 (1969), p. 133 (L. M. Zyubin).

96   See Alec Nove, 'Was Stalin Really Necessary?', *Encounter*, 103 (April 1962), pp. 86–92, esp. p. 90.

97   Soviet psychological research in the late 1930s and in the 1940s is summarized in McLeish, *Soviet Psychology*, esp. pp. 168ff.

98   See Petrovskii, *Istoriya Sovetskoi psikhologii*, p. 294, citing a resolution passed by a plenum of the Moscow Psychological Society on 10 October 1936.

99   Ibid., p. 294.

100   This point was made, e.g. in *PS*, 12 (1971), p. 63.

101   For a biography of Makarenko and account of his ideas, see James Bowen, *Soviet Education: Anton Makarenko and the Years of Experiment* (University of Wisconsin Press, Madison, 1965).

102   See Merle Fainsod, *Smolensk Under Soviet Rule* (Macmillan, London, 1959) esp. pp. 246ff.

103   See *Sotsial'naya psikhologiya lichnosti* (Moscow, 1979), pp. 262–3.

104   Sidney and Beatrice Webb, *Soviet Communism: A New Civilisation*, 3rd edn, (Longmans, Green, London, 1944) p. 653.

105   This book first appeared in London on 8 June 1949 and in New York five days later. See Bernard Crick, *George Orwell: A Life* (Penguin Books, 1982), p. 563.

106   First details appeared in the *International Herald-Tribune*, 3 and 4 August 1977. The story of these experiments is recounted in John Marks, *The Search for the Manchurian Candidate: The CIA and Mind Control* (McGraw-Hill, New York, 1980).

107   See Robert Conquest, *The Great Terror: Stalin's Purges of the Thirties* (Macmillan, London, 1968), ch. 5, 'The problem of confession'.

108   See, in particular, Robert J. Lifton, 'Thought reform of Chinese intellectuals', *Journal of Social Issues* (USA), 13 (1957), pp. 5–20, partly reprinted in Marie Jahoda and Neil Warren (eds), *Attitudes* (Penguin Books, Harmondsworth, 1966), pp. 196–209.

109   See, in particular, Robert C. Tucker, *The Soviet Political Mind: Studies in Stalinism and Post-Stalin Change* (Praeger, New York, 1963), esp. ch. 5 'Stalin and the Uses of Psychology'. See also B. P. Babkin, *Pavlov: A Biography* (Gollancz, London, 1951). The author was a former pupil of Pavlov.

110   See, on this point, Babkin, *Pavlov*, esp. pp. 161–2. Babkin says that although Pavlov had believed the Bolshevik revolution to be 'the greatest misfortune sustained by Russia', nevertheless in 1935 he praised Soviet rule as a 'historic social experiment'. Possibly, Babkin suggests, this change of attitude was influenced by the appearance of the Nazi threat. As late as 1930, the Soviet psychologist Konstantin Kornilov had denounced what he called Pavlov's 'obviously counter-revolutionary' political pronouncements – but was immediately criticized by colleagues for taking up an attitude 'to the left' of the Communist Party Central Committee. See *Pedologiya* 3 (1930, pp. 422–3).

111   The text of this decree, dated 24 January 1921, is reproduced in English in

E. A. Asratyan, *I. P. Pavlov: His Life and Work* (Moscow, 1953), p. 33; also in Babkin, *Pavlov*, p. 165.

112 See McLeish, *Soviet Psychology*, pp. 223–4.

113 See *Pedologiya* 3 (1930), p. 320.

114 Teplov, *Sovetskaya psikhologicheskaya nauka za 30 let*, p. 14.

115 See A. A. Smirnov, 'The state of psychology and its restructuring on the basis of the teaching of I. P. Pavlov', *Sovetskaya Pedagogika*, 8 (1952), p. 89.

116 The circumstances of this meeting are recounted in Wetter *Dialectical Materialism*, pp. 477–8; and in McLeish, *Soviet Psychology*, p. 204.

117 Smirnov, *Sovetskaya Pedagogika*, 8 (1952), pp. 76–8.

118 Ibid., p. 67.

119 Ibid., pp. 65, 78.

120 *Pravda*, 27 September 1949, quoted in Tucker, *The Soviet Political Mind*, p. 102. The article linked Pavlov's ideas with those of the biologist I. V. Michurin, which Lysenko had developed.

121 See McLeish, *Soviet Psychology*, p. 119.

122 In an interview given on 29 June, and published in *Pravda* on 4 July 1950, Stalin had expressly denied the notion that 'thoughts exist in the mind of man prior to their being expressed in speech' and had gone on to insist: 'Whatever the thoughts that may arise in the mind of man, they can arise and exist only on the basis of the language material, on the basis of language terminology and phrases.' The text of this interview can also be found in Robert H. McNeal (ed.), I. V. Stalin, *Sochineniya*, vol. 3 (Hoover Institute on War, Revolution and Peace, Stanford University, California, 1967), p. 153.

123 Smirnov, *Sovetskaya Pedagogika*, 8 (1952), p. 68.

124 See Tucker, *The Soviet Political Mind*, p. 111.

125 Ibid., p. 101.

126 Ibid., p. 97.

127 Ibid., pp. 106, 108, quoting *Voprosy Filosofii*, 1 (1953), pp. 195, 197.

128 See *Filosofskie voprosy fiziologii vysshei nervnoi deyatel'nosti i psikhologii* (Moscow, 1963), p. 10. Also quoted in Tucker, *The Soviet Political Mind*, p. 118.

129 Tucker, *The Soviet Political Mind*, p. 118.

130 M. G. Yaroshevskii, *Psikhologiya v XX stoletii* (Moscow, 1971), p. 266.

131 See V. M. Yakushev, *Gnoseologicheskie i psikhologicheskie osnovy propagandy i agitatsii*, Avtoreferat (published abstract of unpublished dissertation, Lvov (1967), referred to and criticized in V. D. Pel't (ed.) *Problemy teorii pechati* (Moscow, 1973), pp. 77–8, partly on the ground that 'the present state of the physiology of the higher nervous system provides no possibility of building a model for the formation of convictions, setting out from Pavlovian reflexes.'

132 Yakushev, 'Gnoseologicheskie i psikhologicheskie osnovy', pp. 10–11.

133 See Ilya Erenburg's autobiography, 'People, years, life', final instalment, *Novyi Mir*, 6 (1962), pp. 145–6.

134 The fear of anarchy and sense of need for a strong leader is mentioned in

Nadezhda Mandelstam *Hope against Hope* (Penguin Books, Harmondsworth, 1975), p. 113. A rather similar view was expressed in a discussion in *LG*, 18 May 1988, p. 6.

135 *Pravda*, 23 November 1962, p. 7 (V. Yermilov).

5
From Stalin's Death to Gorbachev's Accession

The old methods no longer work. But new ones have not yet been fully developed.

Viktor Mikheyev, *Sotsial' no-psikhologicheskie aspekty upravleniya* (1975, p. 286), on the psychology of management

Introduction

Between March 1953 when Stalin died and March 1985 when Gorbachev came to power, Soviet society underwent enormous changes. The improvements during those 32 years were in many ways vast – in living standards, in education and also in the media, which became more open and honest than they had been under Stalin. Yet it was an epoch when solutions increasingly failed to keep pace with problems. Intellectual life went through more than one period of 'thaw' followed by 'freeze'. The later years of the Brezhnev era which ended in November 1982 were widely associated with the loss of a sense of direction (both by the leadership and in society), the abandonment of reforms previously attempted, authoritarianism, cynicism, and both economic and intellectual stagnation. It is true that the country's unsolved problems were discussed, to some extent, in Soviet publications (thus providing outside observers with a good deal of information). But the admitted problems were not tackled; and this was true not only of the economy but of many other areas of society, including the media. It was the accumulation of all these unsolved problems which finally precipitated the much more radical Gorbachev reforms – including the policy of greater openness or *glasnost'* in Soviet society.

Despite all the changes which occurred between Stalin and Gorbachev,

Soviet society during that time could fairly be described by two expressions which are not mutually incompatible: 'non-liberalization' and 'de-terrorization'. By 'non-liberalization' is meant the failure to allow debate on basic issues and the non-reform of the political system, which continued to be based on one-party rule and one-candidate elections. At no time, even at the height of Khrushchev's anti-Stalin campaign after 1956, did Soviet society regain even the limited intellectual diversity of the 1920s. The campaign against Stalin, for all its enormous consequences, never developed into a critique of the system: it mainly purported to deal with the exposure of past abuses by one man (Stalin) now allegedly put right. Party control became more benevolent, but not more accountable. In 1957 Khrushchev had warned Soviet writers that 'we cannot put the organs of the press in unreliable hands. They must be in the hands of the most faithful, the most trustworthy, those most steadfastly devoted to our cause.'[1] And this expressed a resolve which Brezhnev no less than Stalin would have fully endorsed.

But the other, no less important, side of the coin was what we have called 'de-terrorization', that is, the abandonment of reliance on indiscriminate mass coercion. Khrushchev – by freeing millions of prisoners from labour camps – effectively ended the terror. His successors showed no inclination to re-impose it; and in this sense the Brezhnev era cannot correctly be described as neo-Stalinist. The repression of dissidents was sometimes vicious, but it was targeted selectively against minorities. This was probably due in part to the influence of Yurii Andropov, who headed the KGB from 1967 to 1982. By and large, Brezhnev is remembered not for having carried out mass purges, but rather for having allowed indiscipline, alcoholism and corruption to grow unchecked and for having culpably failed to dismiss corrupt or incompetent subordinates.

The ending of mass terror went hand in hand with an overall decline in the atmosphere of fear, which itself had significant consequences. From the late 1960s, dissidents began, for the very first time, to talk openly to foreign journalists. Soviet Jews from that time began openly to campaign for the right to emigrate. Even in Soviet books and journals, limited reforms of the system (including the extension of *glasnost'* and the idea of contested elections) were occasionally discussed.[2] Indeed, as noted in chapter 1, the principle of *glasnost'* as well as 'constant responsiveness to public opinion' were expressly mentioned in the Soviet constitution enacted in 1977. They may have produced few immediate results, but clearly the ideas behind the Gorbachev reforms did not appear from nowhere.

At all times between Stalin and Gorbachev, the party was insistent that its control must be maintained. But if mass coercion was no longer an acceptable instrument of control, then what was to replace it? This became one of the basic underlying problems of Soviet politics. And it has a direct bearing on the theme of this book, namely propaganda methods and persuasion.

The Khrushchev years: propaganda and de-Stalinization

Stalin's attitude, it may fairly be said, had been marked by an increasing reliance on propaganda, an indifference to persuasion and an implacable hostility to debate. Khrushchev's approach was notably different. He modified the ideology (as distinct from the political system) by proclaiming at the 20th congress of the Communist Party in February 1956 that war was not inevitable and that communist parties might conceivably win power in other countries without violent revolution. The implications of this for propaganda and persuasion were obvious. Khrushchev's entire style – his travels in the non-communist world and his sometimes boorish lectures to audiences both at home and abroad – did indeed suggest a genuine if perhaps naive belief in proselytization.

Khrushchev, logically enough from his own point of view, was recurrently preoccupied with revitalizing the official propaganda message. Indeed, this became particularly important in 1961 when the Soviet Communist Party adopted a new programme, in which the creation of a 'New Man' figured prominently. Yet, paradoxically, it was precisely in the field of propaganda *method* (the central concern of this book) that Khrushchev made the least impact. In its content, of course, the official message changed very greatly – with the ending of the Stalin cult and the sometimes sensational revelations about Stalin's abuses of power. But insofar as Khrushchev made any impact on propaganda method he did so mainly in an indirect way – by creating a freer atmosphere in which others were stimulated to think. In matters of method, Khrushchev was, by and large, a traditionalist.

It was under Khrushchev, in the 1950s, that the campaign of anti-religious propaganda intensified (following the relative relaxation which Stalin had introduced during the Second World War).[3] With regard to propaganda in general, Khrushchev's innovations had broadly speaking two aspects. First, he carried out a huge expansion of the political education system: as noted in chapter 2, the number of pupils in the system is said to have risen from 4 million just after Stalin's death in 1953 to some 35 or 36 million at the time of Khrushchev's dismissal in 1964. The propaganda apparatus itself underwent a number of re-organizations.

Secondly, Khrushchev as an integral part of his de-Stalinization campaign launched an all-out drive against the influence on propaganda work of those whom he described as 'dogmatists'.[4] He took pleasure in ridiculing 'people who pose as theoreticians but whose theoretical "wisdom" essentially boils down to the juggling of quotations . . . These sorry scholars cannot understand the important Marxist truth that people must first of all eat, drink, have homes and clothe themselves.'[5] The practical result of this approach was, on the one hand, a greatly increased emphasis on the harnessing of propaganda for economic tasks (although ideology continued to be stressed in principle); and, on the other hand, a general attempt in the propaganda field to 'brighten things up'. It was by methods such as these – rather than by the study of audience psychology – that Khrushchev evidently hoped to strengthen the impact of the party's message.

However, Soviet evidence even in that period suggests that the party's message frequently failed to get across. According to a Communist Party resolution of 9 January 1960, one of the main shortcomings of propaganda was 'the narrowness of its sphere of influence, its weak mass character and its not always intelligible form of presentation'. Political study, so this resolution indicated, was often a lifeless business where 'the main stress is laid on the mechanical memorization of bookish formulas'.[6] A very similar picture emerged from the discussion at an All-Union Conference of Ideological Workers held nearly two years later, in December 1961, when one speaker observed that political lectures at universities and other institutes of higher education were often 'grey, dull, dogmatic and remote from life' and that this had to be fought against as 'the greatest evil'.[7]

Nevertheless, neither the 1960 resolution nor the 1961 conference said anything that was really new about methods of propaganda in the psychological sense. The resolution insisted that propaganda must reach everyone and re-affirmed the traditional policy of a 'differentiated approach' to various social groups. It had much to say about the content of the party's message – stressing, for example, the importance of economic tasks whilst at the same time saying that it was wrong to reduce the number of lectures on Marxist–Leninist theory. A passing mention was made here (as well as at the 1961 conference) of the social sciences, but again in regard to propaganda content, not method. The question of method did get a passing mention at the 1961 conference, in the opening speech by Leonid Ilyichev, who at that time had overall responsibility for ideology. But the context of his remarks made it plain that he did not mainly have psychology in mind. The crux of the matter, he said, was 'the profoundly thought out *organization* of all ideological work' (emphasis added).[8]

Khrushchev's de-Stalinization campaign did, however, eventually influence propaganda in a more indirect way – by paving the way for the gradual revival of the social sciences, which Stalin had so ruthlessly suppressed. But this revival took some years and was not outwardly very visible until the early 1960s. Entrenched opposition to empirical inquiry was still strong within the Soviet establishment – as shown by the fact that as late as 1957 the *Large Soviet Encyclopedia* – in a volume covering the letter 'S' – criticized Stalin, but also printed articles describing 'social psychology' as 'a branch of bourgeois psychology' and insisting that 'the only scientific sociology is historical materialism.'[9] Continuing opposition to opinion research was underlined by the appearance in 1959 of an article which maintained that the questionnaire survey method 'cannot be accepted as a scientific method of studying public opinion, particularly in the form in which it is now used by public opinion institutes in bourgeois countries'.[10] One indication of a change of climate came in June 1958, with the setting up of a Soviet Sociological Association. But this was only a modest beginning – since the Association had no journal of its own until 1974,[11] and one of its main initial functions was simply to maintain contact with foreign sociologists.

It appears that the first move to revive attitude research in the USSR was made in the non-Russian Baltic republic of Estonia, where the newspaper *Edasi* began systematically to study its readers' preferences as early as 1956,[12] although this fact was reported only much later. The reason for this particular project almost certainly had to do with countering the challenge of foreign broadcasts. Estonian audiences were able to pick up programmes from Finland, both on radio and, in some areas, on television; and they could easily understand them because of the close similarity between the two languages. (The pioneering of audience research is an interesting example of a small non-Russian minority having a major influence on Soviet thinking.) Another landmark came in May 1960 when the Moscow newspaper *Komsomol'skaya pravda* printed apparently the first-ever Soviet opinion poll. (A thousand people all over the country were asked whether 'mankind can successfully prevent war' and 96.8 per cent replied in the affirmative.)[13] Between then and 1967 the paper carried out a number of other surveys, although none of them dealt with controversial political issues.[14] During the early sixties there were similar developments elsewhere. It is said that Moscow television began audience research in 1962 and Leningrad television did so two years later.[15] It was only by degrees, however, that the Soviet authorities came to recognize any direct connection between the social sciences and persuasion. Both the 1960 resolution, already mentioned, and the party programme adopted in October 1961 had spoken in very general terms about the role of the social sciences in promoting 'communist education',[16] but neither document made any specific reference to propaganda or empirical research. But in 1963 Leonid Ilyichev effectively acknowledged the lack of any adequate propaganda theory:

> The main thing is that we still lack any serious scientific elaboration
> of the problems of communist education [*vospitanie*]. Up until now,
> theoretical works on problems of education have been written in

isolation from the concrete analysis of facts and real processes. The authors of such works often proceed not from life, but from an abstract schema. They begin by creating some ideal edifice and afterwards select a few examples in order to confirm ready-made conclusions.[17]

A little earlier, in October 1962, Ilyichev, in an address to the Soviet Academy of Sciences, made a direct call for empirical research and expressed regret at the fact that social psychology had not been studied in the USSR. Contrary to what the *Large Soviet Encyclopedia* had written in 1957, he observed that 'it would be incorrect to cast doubt on the actual need for truly scientific, Marxist, research in the sphere of social psychology.' The 'main reason,' Ilyichev continued, why the social sciences had gained in importance was because of the considerably greater demands imposed 'both on the scientific guidance of our country's development and on the party's ideological work as a whole'. The Academy of Sciences then passed a resolution expressly calling for 'concrete social research' extending, *inter alia*, to both sociology and psychology.[18] This appears to have been the point when the authorities expressly endorsed the revival of the empirical social sciences. In 1963, when a congress of Soviet psychologists was held, the study of social psychology was one of the subjects on the agenda.[19]

The Brezhnev era: new thinking about propaganda method

Khrushchev was removed from power by his colleagues in October 1964. One of his successors' first steps – in the propaganda field – was drastically to cut down the number of pupils in the political education system, which, as we have said, then stood at somewhere between 30 and 36 million people. Two years later, the numbers had been more than halved and comprised no more than 13.5 million, the majority party members. The new leadership's evident purpose was not to de-emphasize oral propaganda – which was later stepped up – but to improve its apparently poor quality. According to one Soviet author: 'The mass scale of party study which had been attained ... rendered almost impossible the universal adoption of strictly regulated and systematic forms of instruction.'[20]

Of more direct concern here is the interest which the new leadership under Brezhnev began to show specifically in propaganda method. What was apparently the first book to deal specifically with this subject appeared only in the spring of 1966 under the title *The Scientific Principles of Party Propaganda*. It placed considerable stress on social psychology and called

for empirical research into the impact of propaganda so as to 'help reveal
shortcomings and discard in good time all that cuts it off from life, deadens
it and lowers its effectiveness'.[21] A year later, in February 1967, a book
written by the then Head of the Propaganda Department, Vladimir Stepakov,
gave an authoritative endorsement to this view – and made it clear by
implication that method had not so far been a conspicuous feature of the
Soviet approach to propaganda:

> the assertion can still be heard that it is, supposedly, enough to have
> a profound knowledge of content . . . and that method will come of
> its own accord. It goes without saying that such a view is untenable.
> The propagandist who possesses no skill in method can count only
> on individual successes, attained by chance or intuition. But one
> cannot rely only on intuition and personal experience. A sound
> knowledge of method is required of all propagandists.[22]

Stepakov observed that 'Knowledge of psychology is very important for the
propagandist';[23] and that 'We often allow an excessive "rationalism" in our
propaganda; we exert insufficient influence on people's emotions and
feelings.'[24] He suggested it would probably be useful to study 'bourgeois'
(that is, Western) propaganda methods and the conditions in which it
achieved results: 'It is necessary to know all this in order to intensify our
counter-propaganda, make it more versatile and reduce to a minimum the
influence of bourgeois ideology on individual citizens in our country.'[25]

Much else in Stepakov's book dwelt on the traditional Soviet approaches
to propaganda (such as content, organization etc). But the book's greatest
significance lay in the more or less explicit approval, from an authoritative
source, and for the first time since the early 1930s, of attitude research in
propaganda work:

> There is one further extremely important condition without which
> the true effectiveness of propaganda is unthinkable. What we have
> in mind is constant and reliable information about the results of
> propaganda work, the existence of a so-called feedback. In this
> respect, concrete research plays a great role.

Already by that time (1967), so Stepakov's book said, a research centre
existed at the Communist Party's Academy of Social Sciences to investigate
the effectiveness of propaganda.[26] A further step to organize research on
a permanent footing came in 1970 or 1971, with the creation under the
Academy's aegis of two bodies specifically concerned with propaganda
method. They were: first, a 'Faculty on the theory and methods of
ideological work'; and, secondly, a 'Department for research into the
effectiveness of party propaganda and political information'.[27] (This followed

a party resolution on the subject in November 1970.)[28] The mandate of the 'Faculty on theory and methods' was said to cover, among other things, the 'study of the theoretical heritage of Marx, Engels and Lenin', the 'analysis of the structure, effectiveness, functions and methods' of 'ideological work', the 'study of the social-psychological problems of ideological work' and a 'critical analysis of the conceptions of imperialist [i.e. Western] propaganda' and the 'preparation of recommendations on foreign policy propaganda and counter-propaganda'.[29]

This concern with propaganda method was part of a more general change. The empirical investigation of public attitudes towards the media did indeed reach a new peak in the Soviet Union, soon after Khrushchev's successors came to power. A number of research findings were published, even if in an abbreviated form. They included a survey of the audience of Leningrad television (1967),[30] as well as surveys of the readership of, among others, the Estonian newspaper *Edasi* (1967),[31] *Izvestia* (1968),[32] the trade union daily *Trud* (1968),[33] *Literaturnaya gazeta* (1969)[34] and, not least, of the party daily *Pravda* (1969).[35] Many of their findings have been published in English,[36] and we shall not set them out in detail. In general, they confirmed what Shafir had noted 40 years earlier: a high degree of public interest in international affairs as well as a fairly low level of interest in economics.[37] And although they did not indicate any high degree of opposition to the political system, they did highlight certain marked discrepancies between the preferences of the public and those of the editors. It transpired, for example, that only 18 per cent of *Izvestia* readers regularly read 'propaganda articles', whilst 72.6 per cent of the Estonian readers of *Edasi* said they would have welcomed more news of 'accidents and other occurrences'.[38] Amongst Leningrad television viewers, 17.4 per cent listed 'frankness' as one of the things most of all lacking in programmes.[39]

All this revival of research clearly reflected Communist Party policy – since the post-Khrushchev leadership did not curtail the social sciences. In March 1966, in a speech at the 23rd party congress, Brezhnev stressed their importance;[40] and in August of the following year, their further development was expressly enjoined in a party resolution.[41] An important step in this direction was taken in June 1968 with the creation, inside the USSR Academy of Sciences, of an Institute of Concrete Social Research. In February 1969, another party resolution instructed this new body 'systematically to carry out the study of public opinion' – including the attitudes of different groups of the Soviet public towards the party's domestic and foreign policy – and to convey the findings together with conclusions and suggestions to the party's Central Committee.[42] It has to be added that not very long afterwards this institute became the target of official attacks because of its alleged ideological unorthodoxy. In 1972 it was extensively re-organized and given a new name: The Institute of Sociological Research.[43]

But despite all the upheavals, the offical support in principle for empirical social science research was not in doubt. The year 1974 at last saw the establishment of a separate journal of sociology (*Sotsiologicheskiye issledovaniya*), which comes out four times annually. Opinion research (in theory at least) became an accepted feature of the Soviet system.

Propaganda, opinion research and the question of liberalization

The question naturally arises at this point: why did the authorities give support to this empirical research? And how did the new-found concern with methods of persuasion tie up with the more general question of political liberalization? The short answer is that the two issues *were* related, but not in any simple way. For one thing, the attitude of the top establishment under Brezhnev changed over time and became more conservative. Apart from that there were, as we shall see, evident disagreements among Soviet specialists over the purposes of empirical research, even though these disagreements seldom came out fully into the open.

In the Khrushchev period, the social sciences found favour as an antidote to the 'dogmatism' of the Stalin cult. After Khrushchev was removed, his successors gradually de-emphasized and then halted the attacks on Stalin. They did, however, continue to favour the social sciences for another reason – as an antidote to what they called 'voluntarism and subjectivism', which were the standard official code names for describing the ill-thought-out economic crash programmes and re-organizations for which Khrushchev had been blamed. As an article in the party theoretical journal *Kommunist* expressed it in early 1965 soon after Khrushchev's removal:

> Unfortunately, we have had the sad experience of hastily adopting and immediately introducing on a nationwide scale thoughtless and untested ideas and proposals. Such 'experiments' are expensive; they lead to waste of efforts and means ... The organization of social experimentation and working out methods for it are one of the responsible tasks of sociological science.[44]

The stress on experiment did, of course, mean the encouragement of consultation and debate; and from that point of view the revival of sociological research did signalize a measure of liberalization. And in the early post-Khrushchev period, that is, in the mid-1960s, Soviet sociological literature became more lively and informative than in any subsequent period of the Brezhnev era. But the whole Soviet intellectual climate became more illiberal after 1968 – following the Soviet intervention in Czechoslovakia to halt the liberal experiment led by Alexander Dubček, and following the appearance inside the USSR of dissident protest. From then on Soviet sociological research – although still officially supported – lost its earlier momentum. At all events, it was much more difficult for challenging or original ideas to get into print.

However, quite apart from these changes in the general political climate, there were at all times disagreements between Soviet social science specialists themselves. And although the disagreements were never absolutely clear-cut (since everyone was ostensibly arguing about how to strengthen rather than change the Soviet system), one can nevertheless tentatively discern three Soviet schools of thought. First were the 'old-guard conservatives', who were generally hesitant if not hostile towards empirical research as a whole. Second were the liberals, many of them outspokenly anti-Stalinist, who believed that empirical inquiry would sweep away dogma and make the system more responsive to public opinion. In retrospect, their ideas have acquired a special significance – because, in spirit at least, they anticipated many of the ideas of the Gorbachev era. Third, and eventually most influential in the Brezhnev era, were what one might term the 'new hardliners', who wanted to use the social sciences as a weapon in the 'ideological struggle' with the West, and who believed that sociological (including opinion) research, was needed as an instrument not of liberalization, but of more effective social control by the party. (This was in many ways at odds with the policy of encouraging initiative from below, which was later to be advocated by Gorbachev.)

The 'old-guard' attitude was exemplified by the views of the well-known Soviet political commentator, Yurii Zhukov, whose journalistic career had begun in the 1930s. At the time of the *Pravda* readership survey in the mid-1960s, Zhukov, as a member of the paper's editorial board, privately expressed his strong opposition to the whole project. However, when the survey was completed, it showed Zhukov to be one of the most popular journalists of all. (I was told of this by Dr Vladimir Shlapentokh, one of the main organizers of the *Pravda* survey, who emigrated in 1979 to the United States.) This is a reminder that the Soviet public is at times more conservative than its leaders. Zhukov emerged from the survey with his authority on the paper's editorial board strengthened; he apparently stuck to his original view and argued in *Pravda* some years later that questionnaire surveys deserved 'by no means the decisive place' in the study of public opinion.[45]

As to the 'liberal' school among social scientists, one – relatively moderate – example is the work of Professor Boris Parygin of Leningrad University, whose book entitled *Social Psychology as a Science* appeared in 1965 in a small edition of 3,400 copies and was sold out within a week. Parygin, in the course of a wide-ranging survey of his subject, insisted that social psychology had the right to an autonomous existence; and he criticized what he called 'the vulgarization of the theory of historical materialism in a spirit of purely economic determinism'.[46] He illustrated what he meant in a later book, with reference to one of the USSR's most serious problems, the breakdown of marriage. This, he said, had much more to do with 'lack of mutual understanding between spouses' than with any economic factors.[47] More generally, Parygin argued:

> Applied social psychology will produce an undoubted impact and valuable results. Even bourgeois social psychology, which has evolved on a false theoretical foundation, is capable of providing effective practical recommendations, for example with regard to the study of consumer demand or the organization of public opinion polls. It is another matter that these recommendations and technical devices can be used to the detriment of the people's interests.[48]

It was precisely over the question of public opinion research that the Soviet liberals in the 1960s made the greatest inroads on Soviet thinking. We have already noted in chapter 3 the traditional Soviet notion of public opinion as a sanction against deviance rather than as a force which can influence government; and this notion continued to hold sway. But this does not in any case exhaust the subject of public opinion studies. From the 1960s, other important aspects of public opinion began to be discussed in print in the USSR. In particular the issue was openly raised: how far could the doctrine of a 'unanimous' public opinion be accepted at face value?

In 1967, in one of the very first monographs on public opinion ever to appear in the USSR, the sociologist Boris Grushin (who had organized the *Komsomol'skaya pravda* surveys which started in 1960) directly challenged the assumption of unanimity; and his approach in many ways foreshadowed the 'socialist pluralism' of the Gorbachev era. Grushin's book included an entire section entitled 'Monism or Pluralism of Opinions?'[49] – a significant thing in itself, since the word 'pluralism' was never much liked by the authorities in the Brezhnev era. The essence of Grushin's thesis was that Soviet public opinion was, in different contexts, both monistic *and* pluralistic.[50] There was no scope in Soviet society for politically organized opposition, so Grushin insisted, because there were no groups whose opinions were permanently opposed to the opinions of other groups.[51]

Nevertheless, having said that, Grushin proceeded with considerable force, and not a little sarcasm, to demolish the Soviet notion of unanimity in its traditional form. He attacked in particular the claim put forward in an earlier book by the Soviet writer Aleksandr Uledov that: 'In our country, ever since the victory of socialism, a common opinion has been formed on all questions affecting the interests of all classes and social groups.'[52] To this Grushin retorted that opinion surveys in Russia to date had produced 'not a single survey where opinions were in fact unanimous'. This, he said, was a perfectly obvious fact which could be ignored only 'through a great disregard for the empirical evidence'. And he went on to argue with thinly veiled sarcasm that:

> In reality, if public opinion is united at all times and on all questions, then there is no point in studying it; it is enough to ascertain the view of some leader, speaking in the people's name, or of some representative of the people itself, and then reach the conclusion: that is what the entire nation thinks![53]

Divisions within public opinion, according to Grushin, arose not just through membership of a class but from all kinds of other factors – such as profession, income, age, sex, residence in different parts of the country and much else besides, although people with particular views did not constitute fixed groups but varied according to the issue under discussion.[54]

Grushin's argument is of particular interest because of the glimpses which it provides into the way that Soviet conservatives regarded public opinion. Even they, it appeared, were obliged to recognize that conflicts of view sometimes arose; but they then tried to define the problem out of existence, by denying that such conflicts were a true manifestation of public opinion. Thus Uledov had been willing to concede that: 'When public opinion is being formed, a struggle between opposing judgements is inevitable. Such a struggle also occurs in socialist society . . . The actual process of the formation of opinion cannot be described as one of unanimity. But it is a different matter when we are dealing with an opinion already formed.'[55]

According to this interpretation, so it would seem, debate in Soviet society was to be treated as an *intermediate* stage on the road to reaching an ultimately unanimous verdict. But Grushin immediately insisted that this was an untenable interpretation – because it was impossible to draw any clear demarcation-line between the 'process' and the 'result' of opinion-formation. 'The process of opinion-formation', he said, 'occurs without interruption at any time. It can . . . move from pluralism to unanimity as well as the other way round.' The implication of Uledov's argument, Grushin observed, was that 'an opinion with a plural structure does not constitute a fully fledged public opinion.'[56]

Another argument of Uledov's which Grushin attacked was Uledov's attempt to explain differences of opinion as due to 'the difference between the level of awareness of the broad masses and that of the vanguard – the Communist Party', or, as Grushin paraphrased it, the difference between knowledge and ignorance, or consciousness and lack of consciousness. Grushin conceded that some opinions were indeed more competent than others and that the party was indeed 'the conscious section of the people'. But, he then asked, 'how can it be claimed that literally every member of the party is superior in knowledge and awareness to all the non-party members of society?!' And he went on to object to Uledov's view for reasons which go to the heart of the subject which concerns us here because:

> the impression is created ... that people's views are supposedly changed not primarily by changing their conditions of life [bytie] through economic and social development and so forth, but by changing their awareness through increased education, through intensified upbringing work and so on [that is, propaganda – DWB.] However, it can easily be understood that the situation is exactly the other way round.[57]

This dictum, made only in passing, was a rare example of a direct challenge to conventional Soviet assumptions about the key role of propaganda in the formation of public opinion.

Grushin then went on to attack the (unattributed) view that only the 'progressive' classes constituted public opinion, whereas the reactionary or exploiting classes did not. But this argument, Grushin observed, 'involves truly insoluble contradictions', because 'public opinion' if defined in this way would be unanimous even in a capitalist society.[58] He then dealt with a closely similar argument which sought to restrict the term 'public opinion' to the opinion of the majority which 'expresses views corresponding ... to the true interests of the working masses'. (This leads back to the problem of interests which we mentioned in chapter 3.) Grushin rejected this concept as well. Unusually, for a Soviet writer, he went on to probe its implications:

> Suppose that the majority of the people express a point of view (for example, by voting for a reactionary bourgeois politician or a reactionary bourgeois party) which constitutes a distorted or ... perverted or mistaken reflection of the true interests of the popular masses (and such a mistake may arise for the most varied reasons: the low level of development of the masses' self-awareness, the

influence of hostile ideology and so on), then it follows that such an opinion is not 'public'. So what is it in such a case? Is it a 'fictitious' or a 'non-genuine' public opinion or a fake . . .?

On the contrary, Grushin retorted, the fact that a view was mistaken in no way prevented it from being an expression of authentic public opinion. Indeed, he said, 'for the purposes of understanding . . . mass awareness, such an opinion is of no less value than a valid opinion which corresponds to the true interests of the person expressing it.'[59] (All this, it may be seen, marked a revival of the arguments for opinion research of the kind put forward in the early 1930s, which the authorities had at that time so angrily rejected.)

Grushin's basic thesis seems to have won official acceptance. It was he who wrote the very first article on public opinion to appear in the *Large Soviet Encyclopedia* (in 1974). Grushin in this article repeated that public opinion could be either 'monistic' or 'pluralistic'; and the context implied that this referred both to Soviet and Western society. But he added that Soviet public opinion was 'united on basic problems of social development'.[60] From the late 1960s onwards, Soviet doctrine ceased to insist on the supposed unanimity of public opinion in literally all respects; and this represented a permanent gain for the Soviet liberals.

Soviet liberals made their influence felt in other ways too in the 1960s, following the revival of the social sciences. Conferences on this theme proliferated. Particular mention should be made of three meetings of sociologists specializing in mass communication which took place at the Estonian university of Tartu in 1966, 1967 and 1968. The atmosphere at these gatherings was evidently unusually relaxed – quite unlike the more familiar gatherings of ideological functionaries. (The report of the first meeting actually mentions in print how out of 53 anecdotes told in between the sessions, only six were decent!)[61] However, the discussions touched on basic issues and seemed, at times, to be questioning orthodox views at their foundation. Several speakers at the Tartu meetings in effect challenged the whole doctrine of the role of propaganda and of the malleability of human nature. For example, one social psychologist, V. A. Mansurov, expressed agreement, in this respect, with the findings of research on mass communication in the United States:

The communicator can influence the behaviour of the recipient [that is, the listener – DWB] only if he imparts information which the recipient can use to satisfy his own wishes and needs . . . the audience is not a passive recipient, a lump of clay in the hands of experienced propagandists. On the contrary, it consists of individuals who make their own demands on communications and select what they need.[62]

The speaker stopped short of asking how far the Soviet media actually met these requirements. What was, however, particularly noteworthy was his insistence that Western findings about the impact of communication were valid for Soviet society. Another speaker, the sociologist L. N. Kogan, when discussing the impact of television, said that 'the only broadcast which will not be switched off is the one which gives pleasure.'[63] The notion of human malleability was also challenged at a more basic level by Professor Yurii Levada, then of the Soviet Academy of Sciences, who voiced doubts as to how far a person's convictions could be regulated by mere exposure to factual information. 'Knowledge and values,' he pointed out, 'are different things.' And, he asked, 'What about the man who has, for example, learned about atheism in our environment but who is himself religious?' Nor was this at all surprising, Levada went on. Lenin, for instance, had been a convinced atheist, although he had won the highest marks for religious knowledge when at school. 'A certain formal conformism,' Levada rather pointedly added, 'is essential for anyone who disagrees with society but is nevertheless obliged to live and work in it.'[64] But convictions, he went on, are resistant to change because they lie close to the 'nucleus' of the personality: 'Convictions take a long time to develop, they develop firmly and in general they change comparatively rarely . . . They can change, let us say, once in a lifetime. [But] if anyone changes his convictions for the second time, I do not think he has any convictions left.'[65]

Also in the course of the Tartu meetings, Levada had gone even further in voicing his liberal sympathies – by mentioning the threat of the 'monopolization' of the media. (What he had in mind, so he said, was the disappearance of newspapers owing to economic competition in Britain, France and the USA.) However, he also maintained that an audience would continue to be selective towards what they were told even 'under a complete monopoly of information'. Levada based this assertion on Western findings, arguing first that all information is mediated through informal groups (a subject to which we shall return) and secondly that audiences tend to absorb what they find congenial and to discard or forget what they find uncongenial.[66]

On a more practical level, the Tartu discussions offered some highly relevant insights into the difficulties, under Soviet conditions, of actually conducting attitude research and opinion surveys. In particular, a Leningrad sociologist, A. N. Alekseyev, devoted an entire paper to the motives of those who were unwilling to answer survey questionnaires; and he forcefully argued that if their views were left out of account, this could seriously distort survey findings. He then went on to describe a survey specifically focused on people who had *failed* to answer a postal questionnaire – about the effectiveness of criticism in the press. The non-respondents, it turned out, were 'much more pessimists than optimists'. Thus:

> Half expressed an obviously sceptical attitude to questionnaires in
> general (including this one); the remainder said that they had been
> too busy or had attached no importance to the questionnaire form (a
> milder form of scepticism or lack of interest). Only one person, who
> had failed to reply owing to illness, wholeheartedly welcomed the
> editors' initiative. One person said that he had not received the
> questionnaire form.[67]

Failure to respond to a questionnaire is, of course, common in the West
as well as in the Soviet Union. Alekseyev did, however, make the point
that a respondent's beliefs about the aim and content of the survey were
crucial in securing his co-operation. He quoted the case of a survey in a
village settlement in the far north of the Soviet Union which had caused
'great irritation', because people were asked what they thought of a proposal
to provide winter gardens and enclosed passages between certain buildings
– in a place where even the most elementary amenities were lacking!
Alekseyev used this apparently trivial example in order to make a much
more basic criticism: 'We constantly discourage people from replying
because we ask about things which do not worry them very much, whilst
we do not ask them about what does worry them. Or else, we ask in such
a way as to undermine confidence in the investigation as such.'[68] In order
to ensure co-operation, Alekseyev went on, the questions should be
formulated in a neutral way and the findings should be published.[69]

The Tartu meetings, although to a considerable degree preoccupied
with concepts and theories, did also make two specific and very serious
criticisms of the Soviet media. Sociological findings were quoted confirming
the 'low popularity' of the political educational system, both before and
after its re-organization in 1965.[70] Another and no less serious criticism
was made of Soviet television, and it came from the Leningrad sociologist
Boris Firsov, who had pioneered Soviet television audience research. Firsov
(like a number of other Soviet communications specialists on other
occasions) voiced concern about the day when foreign television would be
accessible to audiences in the USSR:

> in the very near future, our airwaves will become open to television
> programmes from other states. And I am not convinced that our
> Soviet television programmes, in the form in which they exist today,
> will withstand direct competition from other programmes. There will
> probably be two phases: at first, a general curiosity; but even after
> this curiosity has passed, many of our programmes will scarcely be
> able to compete with those of certain other states, unless changes

are made in some of the methods and principles on which the programmes are produced.[71]

Firsov then mentioned the difficulties which Czech television had had to face when adapting to competition from West German and Austrian television. He made all these points in order to stress the growing role of sociology in making programmes more attractive. But he added one last rider: unless the findings of audience research were acted upon, 'then there is no point in carrying out research'.[72]

It remains to mention that one participant at these meetings, A. I. Goryacheva, a member of Tartu University, anticipated the views of Mikhail Gorbachev by nearly 20 years when she urged a policy of greater openness (*glasnost'*) in the media so as to counteract the spreading of false rumours. She went on to argue 'It was Lenin who associated *glasnost'* with the participation of the working masses in the building of a new life.'[73]

Even after 1968, when, as we have already said, Soviet debates became less free, the liberal views (of those who wanted to reform the system gradually and from within) never totally disappeared from print. One quite well-known Soviet advocate of opinion research was Rafael Safarov (a member of the staff of the Institute of State and Law of the USSR Academy of Sciences), whose writings on this topic went back to the 1960s. In a book published in 1975 he urged the use of polls to assess the performance of the authorities – even suggesting that the role of public opinion should not be 'restricted only to a range of secondary questions'.[74] And in September 1981 (still in the Brezhnev era) he wrote an article in *Pravda* arguing that the social sciences could not function unless they could answer the question: 'what does the people think and what does it want?' In the same article Safarov called for a study to be made of the time-lag between the making of suggestions 'from below' and the taking of decisions by the authorities on the strength of these suggestions.[75] In a further article on public opinion (which appeared in a book approved for publication in July 1982, only four months before Brezhnev's death) Safarov developed his ideas with even more outspokenness. Whilst claiming that Communist Party supremacy was 'the guarantor of democracy' he expressed sentiments which (in the Brezhnev era) verged on heresy. Although, Safarov said, Soviet public opinion was influenced by the political system, 'nevertheless public opinion is not devoid of autonomy, since it is primarily guided by the social needs, interests and expectations of particular social groups.' Furthermore, 'Popular supremacy is impossible unless public opinion is revealed, expressed and taken into account in the process of the functioning of the political system.' Responsiveness to public opinion under socialism 'means nothing other than the subordination of the state to the interests of society.' (The very hint that the two could ever be in conflict was most unusual in Soviet literature.) An increased influence of public opinion 'is conducive to an even greater decentralization of decision-making'; and 'The principle of consensus [*konsensus*] in domestic political relationships in no way requires the absolute unanimity of all citizens.' Safarov also maintained in this later article that 'stability is not a synonym for the immutability of the political system.'[76]

The literature just quoted should help to dispel the mistaken impression of the Brezhnev era as consisting only of grey, neo-Stalinist uniformity. That is in no way to suggest that intellectual freedom prospered under Brezhnev. The expression of liberal views in print was, in the later Brezhnev period, very much the exception. At least one of the people quoted above – Professor Yurii Levada – was publicly attacked for lack of 'party-mindedness'.[77] The Tartu meetings were not continued and the discussions there were criticized for supposedly relying too much on 'the conception of bourgeois sociologists'.[78] All of which brings us to the third – and most powerful – tendency among Soviet social scientists in the 1970s, represented by what we have termed the 'new hardliners'. Far from opposing the development of the social sciences, as Stalin had done, they saw social science as an increasingly important instrument, not of liberalization, but of social control over society by the Communist Party.

One of the key concepts of the 'new hardliners' was, it seems, the concept of what was termed 'scientific management'. The 1967 party resolution on the social sciences (see p. 140 n. 41 above), called among other things for 'the drawing up of methods for the scientific management of social processes',[79] and this idea was soon extended to include propaganda and the media. A Soviet book of 1971 argued, apparently for the first time, that 'the problem of social management in connection with the practical functioning of the mass media is at present becoming especially urgent and important.'[80] A textbook for higher party schools later claimed: 'Socialism, for the first time in the history of mankind is carrying out the planned, scientific management of all spheres of social life: economic, social-political and spiritual.'[81] Another writer claimed, not long afterwards, that management if properly validated 'regulates the spiritual life of society in a goal-directed way'.[82] This, clearly enough, was in marked contrast to the liberal views expressed at the Tartu meetings which had questioned the notion of the malleability of human nature. The new hardliners also differed from the liberals in adopting a much more condescending attitude towards public opinion. For example, a member of the party's Propaganda Department, Valentina Baikova, stressed what she called the 'goal-formulating' role of the party and she continued:

Plate 12.   *Great Patriotic War 1944–1945: between battles.*

Plate 13.   *Victory Parade, Moscow, 1945.*

Plate 14.　*1950s Social Realism. The Chernyakhovsky bridge in Vilnius, Lithuania.*

Plate 15. *Red Square, Moscow, 1 May 1973.*

Plate 17. 'Western Europe': Soviet foreign policy poster of the mid-1980s. Western Europe seen carrying US rockets while the 'Soviet t-t-threat' is beaten out on a drum.

Plate 16. 'For the Motherland, Party, Communism! The bloc of Communists and nonparty people is unbreakable!' Election poster of the 1970s.

Plate 18. *Reading the news on Soviet television.*

Plate 19. *Week of action for disarmament, October 1982. The Kazakh SSR, Alma-Ata. Workers of the toy factory of the Kzyl-Tu firm signing the appeal of the participants in the Soviet movement of peace champions addressed to the 37th session of the United Nations General Assembly.*

Plate 20. An 'agitpunkt' for local Soviet elections on the outskirts of Moscow, 1987. For the very first time, voters in some districts had a choice of candidates. The poster on the left reads 'Citizens of the USSR! Participate actively in the further democratization of our society! Be the masters of the country!'

Plate 21.   *'We will fulfil the decisions of the 27th CPSU Congress'. Slogans in Vilnius, Lithuania, 1988.*

Plate 22.   *Reading the government newspaper 'Izvestiya' on a display board.*

The absence of a 'clear consciousness' demobilizes the masses and gives rise to negative features in their psychology – vacillations, passivity, indecisiveness, gullibility, a propensity towards illusions of petty-bourgeois compromise and so forth.

As the historical practice of the CPSU [Soviet Communist Party] has shown, the formulation of goals, based on scientific foresight, is of enormous significance in guiding the process of social transformation.[83]

One of the leading proponents of the theory of 'scientific management' was Viktor Afanasyev, appointed Editor-in-Chief of *Pravda* in 1976, who said it involved 'bringing people's subjective activity into accordance with the requirements of the objective laws of the functioning and development of society'.[84] (All this merely illustrates the general Soviet claim that only the official ideology can provide a scientific basis for running society in the interests of all and in freedom from blind forces.) On another occasion Afanasyev developed his argument as follows:

The functioning and development of socialist society are based, in effect, on the conscious, creative actions of millions of people – working people. Hence the unusual complexity and responsibility of managing people in conditions of socialism. It includes the rational organization of their work, and of their economic, social, political and spiritual life, their upbringing in the spirit of communist ideals, the observance of the norms of socialist law and communist morality.[85]

What was essentially new in this concept of 'management' was not the emphasis on party control as such, but the belief that such control could not be effective without reliable feedback. As one Soviet psychologist succinctly put it: 'Management without information is impossible; and information without management is pointless.'[86] It was even suggested that cybernetics and information theory were relevant to propaganda 'management',[87] though this line of research does not seem to have produced any practical recommendations. But it was in any case apparent that 'management' and feedback of the kind just described necessarily involved reliance on the social sciences. As one Soviet author observed: 'The management of the ideological process cannot be effectively implemented without adequate and reliable information.'[88] Afanasyev, in the article just quoted, emphasized his view that 'widely organized, systematic, well-thought-out concrete social investigations [were] essential for the organization of effective ideological work.'[89] Another Soviet author wrote that 'social psychology, as we understand it, belongs to the sciences concerned with management.'[90] A not untypical statement of the orthodox

Soviet attitude towards opinion research in the 1970s came from an Estonian party secretary, V. I. Vyalyas, who said: 'The study of the opinion of the masses is essential both in order to solve the problems which worry them and for the correct orientation of public opinion itself, for the perfection of the mechanism of social and political management.'[91] This attitude differed markedly from that of the Soviet liberals, who wanted public opinion to be more diverse and to have a greater influence on government, and it was also, of course, quite different from the Stalinist view of the 1930s and after, which effectively denied that the empirical social sciences had any function at all.

'Scientific management' was apparently seen by the authorities in the Brezhnev era as providing a sense of future direction for Soviet society. For instance, political information, according to Afanasyev, fitted into this scheme because 'it emerges in the first place as an implement for man's management of himself, by influencing his awareness and behaviour and through man, through his thoughts, deeds and actions [influencing] the management of social processes.'[92] The importance of this passage is the light it sheds on the kind of society which the authorities in the Brezhnev era hoped eventually to bring about. The aim, as we noted in chapter 3, was to create not a pluralistic society, but rather a society which would be collectivist and increasingly self-regulating; one where external coercion would more and more be replaced by internalized political 'awareness' and self-discipline, although of course under continuing party guidance. The norms of communist morality would, so it was said, be turned into 'the inner regulators of behaviour'.[93] And the notion of such a self-regulating society was even bracketed with the old Marxist–Leninist notion of the 'withering away' of the state:

> Lenin, when assessing the role of habit in the life of society, said that the state would wither away and be replaced by popular self-management when people gradually became accustomed to observe the elementary rules of communal living. Ideological-educational work must be conducted in such a way that knowledge is turned into convictions and that they in turn become habits.[94]

For the then Soviet establishment, such a theory must have had obvious ideological attractions. The concepts of 'system' and 'self-regulation' – which were implicit both in the 'managerial' and still more in the 'cybernetic' approaches – conformed well with Marxist-Leninist ideas. Nevertheless, so far as propaganda *method* was concerned – that is, in regard to the question of exactly *how* people were to be persuaded to think and act in the way desired – none of these theories seemed to take matters very much further forward. In this context, one other point should be noted. Even the most conservative of the 'new hardliners' recognized that empirical research would be of little value for the purpose of social control if it skirted round society's unsolved problems. Indeed in 1967 the then Head of the Communist Party's Propaganda Department, Vladimir Stepakov, made the point very forcefully:

> The task consists in profoundly and systematically studying the causes and manifestations of survivals [of capitalism]. No matter how unpleasant the facts and conclusions that we arrive at, only such an approach will help us effectively to build up our entire policy and our entire propaganda.[95]

Stepakov was no liberal: he had worked in the Ministry of State Security during the last months of Stalin's life.[96] His argument was prompted purely by realism. However, one of the main failings of the Brezhnev leadership as time went on was precisely its readiness to turn a blind eye to society's unsolved problems. To this we shall shortly return.

Media research from the late 1960s: pluses and minuses

The 'new hardliners', so we have argued, were determined to maintain the party's control over society, but believed that this required the use of much more sophisticated methods than in the past. Hence, from their point of view, 'non-liberalization' and the pursuit of opinion research were perfectly compatible, indeed mutually complementary, policies. Certainly, the later Brezhnev period (from the end of the 1960s until 1982) did see the continuation of media and opinion research – involving a small number of major projects and a host of minor ones. The following selective examples will give some idea of their scope.

    One of the most fully reported of these projects was a lengthy study of 'public opinion' undertaken between 1967 and 1974 and largely focused on the adult population of the southern Russian city of Taganrog (which was apparently chosen by the sociologists because it was a representative medium-sized industrial centre in the Russian Federation). The study – one of whose aims was 'the enhancement of the effectiveness of ideological work' – was organized under the aegis of the Institute for Sociological Research and is said to have entailed 76 individual sub-projects. The overall findings did not appear in book form until 1980.[97] The project was directed by the liberal sociologist Boris Grushin, and there is no reason to doubt its professional competence. Grushin gave at least a hint of being subject to political constraints by saying that the impact of foreign broadcasts was outside the scope of the inquiry.[98] But whatever the constraints may have been, the published results of the survey did contain significant information. Although they said little about the basic political attitudes of Soviet citizens, and emphasized that the Soviet media, particularly the press, enjoyed a high prestige with the Soviet public, the findings did, all the same, highlight some of the authorities' unsolved problems. It transpired that although more than 99 per cent of the adult population were exposed to one or more channels of the mass media (newpapers, radio or television), nevertheless almost one-third (32.6 per cent) of adults were entirely outside the audience for lectures and other kinds of oral propaganda.[99] The public's knowledge of international affairs was found to be significant, although uneven. Many people supposed (wrongly, as the survey pointed out) that living standards in Czechoslovakia were 'many times higher' than in America, Sweden and West Germany.[100] On the other hand, 95 per cent of the sample had heard of President Lyndon Johnson and 96 per cent had heard of President de Gaulle. (The British personalities most often mentioned were Winston Churchill, Harold Wilson, John Gollan, the then British Communist leader, Sir Laurence Olivier and the Beatles; the survey revealed, in passing, that the British communist *Morning Star*, which was of course the only available British newspaper, sold 40 copies a day, retail.)[101]

One noteworthy feature of the survey was its use of specially devised comprehension tests aimed at discovering how far Soviet audiences understood the most common political jargon words. The results showed, among other things, that 46 per cent of respondents either did not know the meaning of the term 'imperialism' or else gave an incorrect definition; 58 per cent were similarly at a loss over the meaning of 'monopoly' and 68 per cent over the meaning of 'reactionary'.[102] Clearly enough, the official message was frequently failing to get across. But this ignorance of political terminology may not necessarily have been due to lack of interest in politics. The sociologists involved pointed to another possible explanation, namely that clichés came up against audience resistance because they were 'meaningless ... and therefore dysfunctional'. Among the expressions which, so it was said, 'readers were sick of', were, for instance, the terms 'creative initiative' and 'fulfilment (or overfulfilment) of the plan'.[103]

Another major opinion survey, also under the aegis of the Institute for Sociological Research, was carried out in 1977. Rather unusually, it was conducted on a nationwide scale (in 375 areas of the country) and it was based on a sample of 9,672 people over the age of 16, of which 2,099 were readers of *Pravda*. (One purpose, apparently, was to compare those who read the paper with those who did not.)[104] This survey did attempt to probe attitudes towards the Soviet system – by inviting respondents to compare the Soviet and capitalist ways of life with particular reference to such issues as educational opportunities, medical care, facilities for free holidays and so on. (The choice of questions may well have been prompted by the signing of the Helsinki agreements on 1 August 1975 and by President Carter's human rights campaign, launched just over a year later.) The survey reported that people of all social groups were 'virtually unanimous' in regarding the Soviet way of life as superior; but the unanimity was not entirely unqualified. Attitudes to the West were not totally uniform. The survey is said to have discovered that some aspects of life in the capitalist world were given 'a considerably higher than average evaluation' by young people (especially students and older schoolchildren) and by those who got their information from foreign sources, such as broadcasts or films.[105] Even *Pravda* did not emerge with an entirely clean bill of health: as many as six out of ten of the paper's readers said that it ought to contain more critical items. A Soviet book of 1980 which reported this finding commented: 'The dissatisfaction of many readers with critical articles is primarily due to the fact that by no means all negative phenomena are adequately reflected on the pages of *Pravda*'.[106] The findings of this survey almost certainly helped to precipitate the very sharply-worded party resolution on the failings of propaganda which was adopted in April 1979 and which we quoted in chapter 2 (see p. 35 *ante*).

These projects did not stand alone. Between 1979 and 1985 the Institute for Sociological Research conducted further surveys of the readers of *Izvestia*, *Sovetskaya Rossiya* and *Literaturnaya gazeta*. In the late 1970s and early 1980s, the Institute is said to have conducted more than 20 pieces of empirical investigation related to 'the role of the mass information media in the formation of public opinion',[107] although the findings do not appear to have been published. Quite apart from this centrally organized activity, research into the impact of propaganda had been widely carried out on a local or *ad hoc* basis for many years. As early as 1968 it was said to be going on in more than 40 areas of the country.[108] As time went on this local activity proliferated; by 1980 it was said that as many as 250 groups in the USSR were engaged in sociological research into the effectiveness of propaganda work.[109] One of the most frequently mentioned examples of this locally sponsored research was the work of the 'Council for the Study of Public Opinion' set up in 1975 in Georgia under the aegis of the republican party central committee. This body (which was upgraded in 1981 to the status of a 'centre'),[110] is said to co-operate closely with the faculty of applied sociology of the university of Tbilisi, the Georgian capital, and also to draw on the advice of visiting sociologists from abroad. The original establishment of the council centre dated from the time when the party first secretary in Georgia was Eduard Shevardnadze – who later became Soviet Foreign Minister and a close colleague of Gorbachev.

Shevardnadze's appointment as the Georgian party leader had itself followed a period of notorious local corruption; this was one of the problems which Georgian opinion surveys sought to investigate. For example, a survey conducted in Georgia in 1978–9 tried to probe public attitudes towards the persistence of what were described as 'private property tendencies' (an apparent reference to corruption). The findings were reported as showing that although the public clearly understood the danger of these tendencies, nevertheless more than half of those polled (55 per cent) voiced scepticism as to whether the measures being taken against them would succeed in the near future. They blamed the trouble on a whole number of causes, ranging from the influence of family and school to unsolved economic problems and the behaviour of the law-enforcement agencies themselves.[111]

To judge from all these examples, opinion research in the USSR was, even during the late Brezhnev period, conducted on a significant scale and yielded a sizeable amount of information, much of it critical of the status quo. It should, however, be pointed out that opinion surveys were by no means the only, or indeed the main, method used by the authorities for monitoring public attitudes. More traditional (and less sophisticated) methods were still heavily relied on. These included, in particular, the study of letters and complaints addressed by members of the public to newspapers or to the authorities. In 1979, apparently in response to a growing volume of citizens' complaints, a new 'Letters Department' was set up within the secretariat of the Communist Party Central Committee in Moscow,[112] though this was reported to have been abolished under Gorbachev. Another traditional method of keeping in touch with public opinion was (as we noted in chapter 2) the study of questions put to lecturers and propagandists by their audiences. This method continued to be used: for example the Communist Party in Estonia recorded and analysed nearly 60,000 such questions during the second half of the 1970s.[113] It was also reported that questions put to Soviet lecturers by foreign tourists were sometimes studied – so as to build up counter-propaganda.[114] And in addition to such sources as these, local party authorities – as one Soviet propaganda official pointed out – also have access to other kinds of information, concerning, for example, the functioning of the propaganda system, the turnover of political literature in public libraries and also so-called 'negative information', such as the level of church attendance, the size of church revenues and the level of crime, especially among minors. (The Soviet author made this juxtaposition without any trace of irony.)[115]

But even granted that Soviet opinion research proper expanded at this time more than at any previous period of Soviet history, what about the weaknesses of such research? These have been widely recognized since

Gorbachev came to power, but they were apparent from Soviet sources even in the pre-Gorbachev period. One weakness – often highlighted by Western critics – has been the potential conflict between empirical investigation of any kind and the need to arrive at ideologically orthodox conclusions. This problem certainly existed – as was shown by the attacks on certain sociologists in the 1970s for allegedly relying on 'bourgeois' concepts;[116] and by the re-organization in 1972 of the Institute for Concrete Social Research. The consequences – for propaganda research as well as for many other areas of inquiry – were that criticism was largely directed at local or secondary problems rather than at basic questions affecting the Soviet system. Nevertheless, as we have seen, diverse views continued to be expressed – presumably because the leadership needed the expertise of social scientists. Indeed, on one occasion a senior party official criticized 'the inclination of certain sociologists to adopt a didactic, lecturing attitude towards . . . ideological workers',[117] which presumably meant that sociologists had tendered advice which the authorities found unacceptable.

A second, widely recognized weakness of Soviet opinion research was its lack of co-ordination and uneven professional quality. It was only under Yurii Andropov, in late 1983, that steps were taken to set up a nationwide public opinion research centre.[118] The following complaint from a Soviet author in the late Brezhnev era is not atypical:

> Unfortunately, the professional level of sociological research has not, so far, by any means always satisfied the requirements of practice. Research is still carried out in a fragmentary way with the use of different methods within the framework of one subject. The data obtained are seldom comparable . . . Profound theoretical generalizations from the results of research are still a rarity.[119]

A third weakness of Soviet opinion research – which has been openly mentioned in Soviet literature – stemmed from the difficulty of ensuring frank answers from members of the public to politically or otherwise sensitive questions. The published findings of the Taganrog survey contain an oblique reference to this problem: they actually listed the topics on which, in the opinion of the local authorities, greater or lesser frankness was to be expected. For example, the authorities thought that Soviet citizens were more willing to speak openly about the failings of public transport than about the problems of industrial enterprises (presumably because employees would be reluctant to criticize employers).[120] Some years later, in 1985, a Soviet author revealed that during the Taganrog survey of public attitudes towards the media 'some respondents said . . . that they would not reply to questions in the interview if they knew that they would have to provide detailed information about themselves'; and this author strongly advised against asking for personal details from respondents in polls 'especially if they touch upon negative phenomena, [or] contain sharp questions, since this raises doubts about guarantees of anonymity in the survey'. The problem which particularly concerned this author was the reluctance of many Soviet citizens to admit listening to foreign broadcasts – something which is viewed with official disfavour – unless their anonymity was ensured. To demonstrate his point he quoted from an experimental survey which showed that people were much more likely to reply frankly on this subject if interviewed at their place of work (where they presumed that the survey was sanctioned by the management) than if they were interviewed at home (where they might think their identity could be more easily discovered). Surveys at places of work, he went on, did reveal a higher number of listeners to foreign broadcasts than surveys done in the home. By contrast, when people were asked about what they listened to on domestic radio (which was not a sensitive subject), replies were statistically much the same, regardless of where the interview was carried out.[121]

All this was only one example of a wider problem: the fear of victimization. (It may be noted that 'persecution for criticism' was an evil widely recognized even under Brezhnev.)[122] Although some people were increasingly willing to speak openly, many others were reluctant to do so. And this reluctance would have been sufficiently widespread to cast doubt on the statistical validity of any poll on a sensitive issue.

One of the most direct obstacles to polling or any other kind of sociological research under Brezhnev is not really in dispute. His successors have made it abundantly clear that he allowed a vast accumulation of malpractices – including, not least, corruption – to be swept under the carpet. In this atmosphere of officially-sanctioned 'cover-up', it is hardly surprising that opinion research should have run into difficulties. Very often, the obstruction was caused by local authorities, as a Soviet writer pointed out in 1983:

> There are a good many places where public opinion surveys are known only by hearsay ... So what is the trouble? It consists in the fact that the necessary organization of public opinion studies ... is hindered by a kind of conservatism and inertia on the part of some leaders, by the fear that the findings of public opinion surveys will uncover various shortcomings in their work. In other words ... some members of the managerial *apparat* still avoid sociological investigations.[123]

One of the most telling signs of 'cover-up' can be found in a Soviet handbook for party workers published in 1980, that is, in Brezhnev's lifetime. It records that in 1978 elections took place in 402, 128 primary party organizations throughout the USSR. However, in only 72 cases was the work of the party bureau or its secretary found to be unsatisfactory.[124] Gorbachev in his report to the 27th party congress in February 1986 put matters in a different light; he said that 'at some stage, some republics, territories, regions and cities were placed out of bounds to criticism.'[125] It later became clear that malpractices were widespread and were not confined only to particular regions.

Meanwhile, as *glasnost'* gathered momentum, the Soviet press became much more brutally frank about the past weaknesses of the country's sociology. Writing in *Pravda* in early 1987, one of the best-known advocates of reform, Academician Tatyana Zaslavskaya, said that Soviet sociology was 'much more weakly developed than, say, in Poland or Hungary, not to mention the developed capitalist countries'. She noted that in 1989 it was planned to complete the training of no more than 100 sociologists with a higher education in the USSR, whereas 6,000 comparable specialists were trained annually in the United States; and she referred to 'the bitter formula "sociology without sociologists"' to describe the state of affairs in the Soviet Union. She complained about the lack of published Soviet statistics on such problems as the crime rate, the suicide rate, alcohol consumption, drug use and illness; and she also complained about the topics 'out of bounds to sociological research'. 'Let me say frankly,' she continued, 'so long as such restrictions are maintained it is impossible seriously to expect any effective recommendations from science.'[126] It only remains to add that a year later Academician Zaslavskaya was designated as the head of a newly formed Centre for the Study of Public Opinion on Social and Economic Questions, which was attached to the State Committee on Labour and the Soviet trade unions, with Boris Grushin as deputy.[127]

However, the Soviet press made it clear that opinion research in the Brezhnev era had indeed been a risky business. The Moscow *Literaturnaya gazeta* in 1987 published an account of the harassment of the sociologist Aleksandr Alekseyev (presumably the same as the participant at the Tartu conference mentioned earlier). In the late 1970s he had drawn up a pilot questionnaire asking people whether they expected changes in Soviet society. The questionnaire was at that time officially deemed to be 'politically harmful', and it was made one of the grounds for Alekseyev's expulsion from the Communist Party, the Soviet Sociological Association and the Soviet Union of Journalists. By 1987, however, he had been reinstated in the Soviet Sociological Association[128] and I am told that he has also regained his party membership.

The evidence therefore indicates that the Soviet media and opinion research in the late Brezhnev period was of an extremely uneven quality.

It was sometimes highly professional and sometimes informative; but it was seriously vitiated for all the reasons just given. It could not possibly have been anything like as efficient as the kind of research in this field which has become commonplace in the West. Therefore, the problem of getting reliable feedback in Soviet conditions still remained a problem.

Soviet propaganda research: conclusions and results

So much then for the general scope of Soviet media research. How far was it translated into practical results? How far did it produce any change in the Soviet theoretical approach to propaganda? There is of course no doubt that the Soviet media, between the 1950s and the 1980s, did undergo significant changes (as also did the media in the West). Much of the change was due to changes in Soviet society as a whole – such as the growth of education, the rise of television, the greater exposure of Soviet audiences to foreign broadcasts and the undoubted increase in contacts between the USSR and the outside world. How far the evolution of the Soviet media was directly due to sociological research is much less clear. Certain trends both in the development of the Soviet media and the development of Soviet thinking should, however, be noted.

First, as to organization. As already stated in chapter 2, the 1960s and 1970s saw a steady and deliberate expansion of the political education system and oral propaganda network. (Only in 1981 did the Brezhnev leadership seem to have second thoughts and even then the doubts mainly concerned organization, and not the necessity for oral propaganda as such.) In other words, new thinking about propaganda was accompanied by a new emphasis on traditional Bolshevik propaganda methods.

Secondly, as to style and content. The Soviet press did indeed become more journalistic. It is a remarkable fact that until the late 1950s even the term 'news' (*novost'*) was not commonly used in Soviet journalism because it was equated with the 'bourgeois' concept of 'sensationalism'.[129] Topicality had not been the prime journalistic consideration: indeed, it was only in January 1960 that the official news agency TASS was specifically enjoined to give information to the radio prior to publication in newspapers.[130]

We shall make no attempt at any detailed content analysis of the Soviet media during these years. Nevertheless, detailed comparisons which have already been made between the Soviet press of the early 1950s and of the early 1970s do indicate that at the later time criticisms and proposals were much more factual and more directed against general problems than against the misdemeanours of individuals chosen as scapegoats.[131] Moreover, in the 1960s and 1970s, some Soviet newspapers, at least, published a substantial amount of sociologically interesting material – for example, on the causes of divorce, on demography, on labour relations and, latterly, on corruption. (The regular coverage of corruption in the press can be traced at least as far back as New Year's Day 1979, when *Literaturnaya gazeta* began a new feature on 'Economics and Morality'.)[132] There were even occasions when politically controversial proposals were printed. For example, during the press discussion in 1977 of the draft of the new Soviet constitution, one letter in *Pravda* proposed a more specific constitutional guarantee that decrees of the government should be published if they were of general importance. (The writer made the pointed remark that 'in order to observe the laws, one must first of all know what they are'.[133] This idea was not adopted by the authorities.) Another proposal was that public opinion should be more fully consulted when managers were appointed.[134] This proposal was not incorporated into the constitution but it foreshadowed a change which was realized after Gorbachev came to power.

It should also be mentioned that the Soviet government – especially after signing the Helsinki agreements on 1 August 1975 – became much more anxious to defend its own record on human rights. It did so by emphasizing its own interpretation of human rights (with particular reference, for example, to full employment, free education and free medical care).[135] This was reflected in the Soviet media, which also became more informative about the Soviet record over cultural and tourist exchanges. The expansion of contacts with the outside world, although limited, was nevertheless real. Whereas over half a million Soviet citizens were said to have gone abroad in 1956, the numbers who did so in 1976 had risen to between 2.6 and 3 million (in the years 1975–6, some 40 per cent of Soviet citizens who travelled abroad were said to have visited non-communist countries).[136] Another expansion in contacts resulted from the suspension of the Soviet jamming of Russian-language broadcasts of the BBC and the Voice of America: jamming was suspended in September 1973 but was resumed in August 1980 following the rise of Solidarity in Poland.[137] However, Soviet audiences were able, if they wished, to listen to Western radio stations during most of the 1970s, at a time when those stations were giving great prominence to the views of Soviet dissidents.

The limited East–West detente of the 1970s did make the Soviet public more exposed to critical information from abroad; but the Soviet media reacted not by admitting that it might be partly true, but by hitting back more vigorously at the West. In particular, the Western human rights campaign was met by Soviet counter-accusations of human rights violations in the West. The Soviet press did, almost for the first time, give prominence to the dissidents – no doubt as a response to foreign broadcasts beamed to the USSR. But the dissidents were attacked in the Soviet press in harsh language; and the charge that they were sometimes imprisoned in psychiatric hospitals was met by the Soviet reply that some of the dissidents were indeed mentally ill, (this was a claim which the then head of the KGB, Yurii Andropov, once made).[138] On the issue of human rights, the Soviet media no doubt became more sophisticated, but certainly not more liberal or self-critical.

How far the journalistic changes just described were due to media research is difficult to say. Dr Vladimir Shlapentokh, who in the 1960s helped to conduct research into the readership of Soviet newspapers, told me he believed his findings had had the greatest influence on *Literaturnaya gazeta* – which was widely regarded as the liveliest Soviet newspaper of the Brezhnev era.[139] Following the *Pravda* survey in the 1960s, Dr Shlapentokh had submitteed a report to the paper's editorial board, at the latter's request. In this report he had indicated, among other things, that criticism in the paper would lack credibility with readers if it was directed only at minor figures (such as chairmen of collective farms) and was not permitted in regard to people of really senior rank. Dr Shlapentokh's recommendations were, it appears, never acted upon. The innovations in the media were real, but so also were the traditional taboos. And this leads us to one of the basic (although unwritten) guidelines of Soviet journalism throughout this entire period. Hedrick Smith, the Moscow correspondent of the *New York Times* in the early 1970s, said it was expressed in the motto quoted to him by a Soviet journalist: 'Criticize but Don't Generalize': in other words, it is all right to find fault in a particular situation but don't write general conclusions because that is politically dangerous.[140] This taboo did not invariably apply to Soviet specialized literature.[141] And towards the very end of Brezhnev's era, as complaints of shortages and corruption multiplied, even Soviet newspapers conveyed an impression that all was not well. Nevertheless, during the Brezhnev era, it remained true, so far as the Soviet mass media were concerned, that most criticism related either to secondary issues or to local misdemeanours or else was orchestrated from above, as with the anti-corruption campaign.

It is hardly necessary, however, to recall the unsolved problems of the Soviet media in the early 1980s, since these are a matter of common knowledge. In 1983, it took the Soviet authorities six days to admit in public their responsibility for the shooting down of the South Korean airliner which had been overflying Soviet territorial airspace on 1 September. At about the same time, there had been prolonged official silence over the last illnesses of Brezhnev in 1982, of Andropov in 1983–4 and of Chernenko a year later.[142] This lack of openness had unleashed an entirely predictable torrent of rumours and allegations which the Soviet authorities were unable to control. These episodes represented the crowning disasters of the traditional policy of media secrecy. They were highly damaging to Soviet prestige; and they can only have strengthened the hand of those, like Gorbachev, who believed that reform of the media was imperative.

Judged, therefore, in purely practical terms, media research in the Brezhnev era did not produce any really basic improvement in the media's performance. But it remains, having briefly discussed the changes in the media's organization, style and content, to say something about the state of Soviet *thinking* on propaganda method. Here again, there was little sign of any radical innovation. Nevertheless Soviet literature revealed an increasing awareness of unsolved problems in the propaganda field. Propaganda was no longer governed solely by the traditional, or ideological, guidelines described in chapter 3. As from 1968 a new annual publication on propaganda was published.[143] New topics and problems were raised in print. It is to these that we now turn.

One criticism which was made again and again both in Soviet literature and in official statements was focused (rather paradoxically, in view of what we noted earlier) on the Soviet media's lack of promptness in reporting news. According to one Western researcher, this criticism was first levelled as far back as 1957.[144] In 1965, the Soviet communist theoretical journal *Kommunist* was complaining that 'bourgeois information agencies have achieved a high operational efficiency, immediately responding to everything happening in the world, while we are sometimes late,' and added that 'complacency is inadmissible.'[145] In February 1969, a party resolution included a specific directive to the media 'to take concrete steps to improve the promptness' of its domestic and foreign reporting.[146] Brezhnev himself criticized the media's lack of prompt reporting in a speech in 1973,[147] and he did so again in a major speech five years later.[148] Promptness was once more enjoined in the party resolution of April 1979,[149] and also, during the Andropov era, in a party resolution of June 1983 which called for greater promptness in reporting on television.[150] Yet the practical results, as we have seen, were less than impressive.

Official strictures were continually echoed during these years in more specialized Soviet literature. For example, in 1970 a propaganda specialist argued in some detail that one of the most effective forms of persuasion consisted in pre-empting opponents by getting one's own version in first:

> Under conditions when the population does not get reports from domestic sources, the first report given by bourgeois propaganda often achieves an openly subversive aim – the planting of rumours ... That is why it is so important to strive for maximum speed and completeness in our propaganda.

Radio, so this author argued, was the ideal vehicle for fast news. Therefore:

When drawing up the schedule of radio broadcasts, the fact must also be remembered that our ideological adversaries pay great attention to using the time for propaganda most suited to our audience, particularly stepping up their activity during the morning and evening hours. Therefore, when considering how to intensify our counter-propaganda, we must do everything possible to deprive our adversary of the advantage of giving the first report – in order that later on, when an individual is at work or meeting friends and so forth, he discusses the facts which he has heard in our interpretation. In that case, hostile propaganda will be 'superimposed' on an already formed opinion, and will meet with a reaction which is not hard to guess.[151]

Quite clearly then, the question of more *glasnost'* in the media was being raised in the Soviet Union long before the Gorbachev era; and the disadvantages of secrecy were being pointed out even by hardliners such as this particular author apparently was. The dilemmas of secrecy were obvious even then. Suppress a piece of information – and the listener could tune in to foreign broadcasts. Publish the information – and this would be a big step towards the abolition of censorship. Either way, under conditions where jamming was less than fully effective, the listener could compare the official version of the news with the versions given abroad.

Nevertheless, opposition to prompt reporting was sometimes openly expressed in print. For instance, a Soviet book of 1973 admitted that 'unfortunately our information is by no means always prompt' and that 'this does definite harm,' but it added the warning: 'Promptness in political information has nothing in common with hastiness. Unnecessary haste sometimes leads to the distortion of real events, so that information in this case is founded not on facts but on forecasts and guesses.'[152] One of the basic obstacles to promptness was, of course, the authorities' reluctance to release politically sensitive news stories before an official interpretation of those stories had been worked out. In August 1981, a *Pravda* article indirectly touched on this difficulty and came close to implying that journalistic promptness was not invariably the wisest thing. In words which succinctly expressed the kind of opposition to *glasnost'* which Gorbachev later overruled, the article, whilst acknowledging the value of promptness, argued: 'Whereas delay with the correct interpretation of an event carries the risk of the ideological adversary gaining the initiative, a superficial or, still worse, a wrong interpretation of an event may result in the loss of important positions in the battle of ideas.'[153] However, the obstacles to prompt reporting were often not political but simply bureaucratic – the result of an editorial reluctance to act without instructions. One example – quoted some years later – concerned the death in an air crash in August 1985 of Samantha Smith, the American schoolgirl whom Yurii Andropov had once invited to the Soviet Union. This was obviously not a politically sensitive story. But when news of the death reached Moscow television, the duty editor, despite protests from journalists on the spot, refused to let the report be broadcast without prior approval from above.[154]

Another topic of discussion in Soviet specialized literature from the 1960s onwards was the psychology of propaganda. Some of this literature focused on 'educational' psychology (or 'pedagogy', in Soviet parlance) rather than on the psychology of persuasion proper; that is, it concentrated on the problem of how to ensure that the subject-matter of Marxism-Leninism was clearly and coherently grasped by the audience.[155] (This was not always an easy matter, as we shall see later.) A number of books focused on the art of lecturing or public speaking or on the art of presenting an argument in a logical, convincing manner.[156] Other books dealt with the relevance of social psychology to propaganda and sometimes discussed the findings of Western communication research in this area. A book which appeared in Moscow in 1971 described Western findings on the psychology of propaganda in some detail and remarked: 'A critical analysis of these data will help us to make communist propaganda more efficient, more conducive to results.'[157] Later books on propaganda intended for lecturers and party workers also included, for the first time, sections on social psychology, sometimes borrowing from Western concepts.[158] All this marked a change of emphasis from Soviet writings of an earlier period, which had often merely condemned Western social science. Whether Western communication research made any great impact on Soviet thinking about propaganda may be doubted. (We shall return to this point later.) But certain Western concepts – in particular those of 'attitude' and 'selective attention' became recognized as valid by Soviet propaganda specialists. So also did the notion of 'image' or 'stereotype'.[159]

Soviet writings on the social psychology of propaganda have tended to be long on generalization and rather shorter on practical recommendations. But sometimes, even though not very often, Soviet writers did give specific advice about psychological methods of persuasion. For example, a book entitled *Propaganda and Young People*, published in 1981, included a contribution by the social psychologist V. M. Yakushev (whom we quoted in the last chapter), in which he advised lecturers that they should avoid seeming to 'impose' their views and should relate their message to the audience's 'motivational sphere of consciousness', that is, to their interests.[160] More noteworthy was Yakushev's challenge to the traditional view of what makes Soviet propaganda effective:

Some propagandist-beginners naively suppose that, if they repeat a certain idea day in and day out, then the listener will eventually accept it as his own. Such a view is in no way confirmed by the findings of science . . .

It is possible and in some cases necessary to repeat certain basic propositions ... especially if they were previously unknown to listeners; but to repeat in the very same words what everyone has already heard several times before serves no purpose. The propagandist who behaves in this way creates a passive attitude on the part of the audience towards what he says.[161]

In the same general context, even hardline Soviet propaganda specialists have urged that the Soviet audiences should be familiarized with anti-communist arguments so as to lessen their impact.[162] One Georgian psychologist, when explaining this concept in a book published in 1978, explicitly drew the analogy with medicine:

In order to acquire the capacity to fight infectious diseases, the organism requires certain injections or vaccinations ... It has been found that a certain parallel can be drawn between this kind of immunization and the process of making people resistant to hostile propaganda. In order to exclude the possible influence of hostile propaganda, it is not enough ... to reinforce the system of views which is acceptable to us. It has, furthermore, been proved necessary to develop immunity against the influence of the attitudes of opposing propaganda through a process of preliminary familiarization with the opposing point of view. It is moreover essential, just as in the case of innoculations, for society to grow accustomed to 'weakened doses' of opposing, hostile views. In that case, it will not be totally unprepared for, or lacking in immunity against, the influence of hostile propaganda.[163]

In a similar vein, another Soviet author, writing in 1981 about propaganda addressed to young people, strongly urged that greater use should be made of a 'two-sided' presentation of facts, particularly in lectures to students:

The point is that a message based on a two-sided presentation of the arguments has a greater influence on an educated person than an argument with a one-sided exposition of the facts. This means that the higher the educational and political level of the audience and the more it is able to discern all the artful designs [khitrospleteniya] which underlie complex social phenomena, the more the teacher can trust them. It therefore seems expedient (within appropriate limits, of course) to rely on a two-sided presentation of arguments to a student audience.

This method, the author went on, would help students to rebut opposing views 'in a well-argued fashion, from Marxist-Leninist positions', which they were not always able to do. Furthermore:

The two-sided presentation of information, or two-sided arguments, are particularly effective in work with audiences exposed to counter-communication, that is, hostile propaganda. The increasing contacts between the student youth of our country and the representatives of the bourgeois world ... make the task of developing ideological 'immunity' an especially pressing one.[164]

These remarks clearly show how pressure for the modernization of propaganda sometimes came not from Soviet liberals, but from Soviet conservatives, concerned to build more effective defences against alien ideas. The idea of 'two-sided' presentation was borrowed from the American psychologist Carl Hovland, although the Soviet author did not mention him by name. Western ideas on the psychology of propaganda were also quoted in Soviet books with a view to discrediting Western broadcasts to the USSR in the eyes of the Soviet public. For instance, it was argued that these broadcasts should be combated by a twofold strategy of 'pre-emption' and 'exposure'; the latter included 'demonstrating the psychological and social-psychological mechanisms on which the propaganda of the ideological adversary relies' besides showing the hostile aims behind the broadcasts.[165] (Indeed an American book on 'Psychological Warfare' was apparently published in Moscow in a Russian translation as far back as 1962.)[166]

Some Soviet writers have also urged – although in rather general terms – the use of psychological methods for the purpose of appealing to the emotions as well as the rationality of the audience. Here too, Western findings were sometimes mentioned. Thus, one writer in 1971 (whilst repeating that communist propaganda 'is addressed above all to man's awareness, to his reason') nevertheless criticized what he called 'the one-sided intellectualism' of some party propaganda.[167] A *Propagandists' Handbook* for 1974 indicated that besides invoking logic, it might be sometimes justifiable to resort to what the handbook called 'suggestion' (*vnushenie*), that is, some kind of non-rational appeal involving reliance on 'assertions made without any particular validation or proof'. This was apparently a reference to factors such as the audience's respect for an authoritative source or simply the power of an emotional appeal. Nevertheless this book did go on to say that such methods would not have a long-lasting effect unless backed up by facts and arguments.[168]

Another related topic which Soviet propaganda specialists touched on after the 1960s was the question of audience resistance to propaganda. Scepticism about the power of communication to alter opinions was voiced, as we noted earlier, at the sociologists' meetings at Tartu. The importance of 'attitudes' and 'selective attention' in modifying the impact of a propaganda message was pointed out in an article in 1969 in the journal *Questions of Psychology* (which appears to have been the very first published article concerned specifically with the psychology of persuasion). The author, Yurii Sherkovin, himself a psychologist, made, *inter alia*, the far from trivial point that 'propaganda activity produces effects only when it gives satisfaction to listeners.'[169] Writing in 1971, he went out of his way to deny the 'omnipotence' of propaganda and said it was likely to fail if, for instance, it ran counter to what he termed 'the stable tendencies of the development of society', or the audience's attitudes.[170] Psychological resistances to persuasion also got mentioned in specialized literature for party workers. For example, a book which appeared in 1974 under the title *Communist Propaganda: Questions of Theory and Methods* contained a warning that every individual reacts to information 'selectively, depending above all on his or her life experience' and that if the information runs counter to the audience's previous notions then 'there may be a negative reaction'. However, the book did not offer any very clear guidance as to how such audience resistances were to be overcome. It merely said that bearing them in mind 'propaganda seeks to operate in a differentiated manner, to be active, to take the offensive, and to impart to people a scientific view of the objective world.'[171]

The Soviet response to the evidence of psychological resistance to propaganda took different forms. On the one hand, some Soviet writers argued that these resistances had been overrated or misunderstood. Thus, one writer observed: 'Whilst justly emphasizing the role of attitudes as regulators of behaviour, American social psychology and sociology excessively exaggerate their importance,' since attitudes can change under the impact of new information about changes in the environment.[172] The same problem was also discussed in a Polish book called *The Psychology of Political Propaganda*, which appeared in a Russian translation in Moscow in 1981. The Polish author, Leslaw Wojtasik, quoted the widely accepted Western view formulated by Joseph Klapper the American sociologist to the effect that propaganda is much more likely to strengthen attitudes than to change them. But Wojtasik then qualified this by adding that Klapper was not totally denying the possibility of such change. And, this Polish author went on:

It may therefore be said that *good*, scientifically based propaganda can successfully change people's attitudes. Klapper's assertions should not be interpreted in the sense of the fatal impossibility of changing attitudes through the influence of propaganda or other educational work; they merely point to the difficulties which exist in this area. But such change requires prolonged influence which is organized in a special way [emphasis in original].[173]

A second and notably different Soviet reaction (corresponding to what we described earlier as the 'liberal' tendency) has been one of scepticism towards the power of propaganda. As one Soviet book briefly noted in 1986, 'Some researchers suppose that propaganda cannot by itself radically alter an individual's convictions.' But, thirdly, even the 'hardline' school of thought came increasingly to recognize that propaganda by itself was not the decisive, nor even the prime moving force, as Brezhnev had once implied (see p. 69 ante). A book of 1980 observed in passing: 'Propaganda is only one of many factors which influence ... people's minds and behaviour.'[174] A similar message was conveyed even more forcefully in another book of 1980 by Vadim Medvedev, who later became a secretary to the Communist Party Central Committee and a member of the Politburo under Gorbachev. As Medvedev then put it:

> The idea that the problems of education can be resolved *wholly or mainly by ideological methods* may in practice give rise to discrepancies between word and deed and thereby inflict harm on the work of education. Equally, it is unjustified to regard shortcomings in educational work as the only reason for the continuance of negative phenomena in socialist society. Of course, these phenomena are not engendered by the socialist system; however, it cannot be said that they have no basis in real life [emphasis added].[175]

Comments like this foreshadowed a significant change of emphasis in the party's attitude to propaganda – a change which under Gorbachev became of great importance. By degrees, the problems of political socialization were increasingly blamed on the unsolved problems of society itself rather than on mere failures of propaganda or 'educational' work.

Political socialization, the 'micro-environment' and the 'work collective'

So far in this chapter we have focused on Soviet thinking on propaganda in the mainly verbal sense. However, as mentioned in chapter 3, the Soviet doctrine of socialization has also laid great stress on the role of group influence over the individual. From this point of view Soviet thinking did undergo a certain refinement. In the late 1960s, a distinction came to be drawn between the influence of the overall 'social environment' and that of the so-called 'micro-environment' (that is, the individual's immediate surroundings, his family, friends, those he comes into contact with at work and so on). This distinction, apparently first formulated in Soviet literature in 1968 by the sociologist L. P. Buyeva was soon afterwards endorsed as being of 'very great importance'.[176] In 1974, Viktor Afanasyev, the future Editor-in-Chief of *Pravda*, explained the importance of the concept as follows:

> It is essential resolutely to have done with the notion that the social environment – socialist production or other social relationships, or the prevailing ideology in society – will themselves automatically lead to the formation of a new personality. It is important to study thoroughly the empirical conditions of the life of the particular individual, his 'micro-environment'. It is important to seek to change this environment, to try to ensure that it 'works' in the same direction as the general social environment.[177]

For Soviet conservatives in particular, this theory had obvious attractions. It offered a politically acceptable explanation of what went wrong in Soviet society by blaming the environment, but not the system as such. It was stated by one author, for example, that a lecturer, when explaining the causes of immoral behaviour in Soviet society, 'should analyse the micro-environment in which it arose, [and] show that it is atypical of the new social relationships'; whereas, when discussing the negative aspects of the capitalist world, 'it is essential skilfully to expose all attempts . . . to separate individual amorality from the amorality of capitalist society as a whole.'[178] Over and above that the theory of the 'micro-environment' did seem to offer an explanation of some practical use to the authorities; for the citizen's behaviour and opinions are undoubtedly influenced, to some extent at least, by the immediate group to which he belongs. It all tied up with the traditional Soviet notion of public opinion as a sanction against deviance. One Soviet author writing in 1974 spelt this out quite explicitly:

> In a small collective, a tremendous importance attaches to the power of public opinion, which is displayed not only in such forms as workers' meetings, comrades' courts, wall newspapers, and so on, but also in less official ways. Thanks to the evaluations and judgements of the collective, a certain continuity of social control is established over individual behaviour. All this turns the opinion . . . of the immediate entourage into an effective moral force, capable of regulating mutual relations between people and of preventing . . . anti-social manifestations.[179]

The immediate environment, so this writer went on to argue, was an especially powerful influence on young people with 'a low level of social maturity'. Therefore, he maintained, 'It is important to keep control over those "channels" which can become a source of bad influence on the younger generation (neighbours, circles of friends, family relationships, the immediate environment at work and during times of rest, etc.).'

The doctrine of the 'micro-environment' is a notable example of the way in which Soviet theoreticians have partly drawn on Western findings, (in this case about the importance of small groups).[180] From the Soviet point of view, these findings seemed useful – because they suggested methods of social control to which the Soviet authorities were inclined anyway. The theory also provided a powerful new reason for the stepping up of oral propaganda to which we referred in chapter 2. We shall return in the next chapter to the defects of this theory; nevertheless it should not be dismissed as a mere ideological 'ploy'. The theory of the micro-environment, as will later be seen, can provide a significant insight into the strengths and weaknesses of Soviet persuasion.

All that we have just described was related to an even more prominent development in Soviet thinking of the Brezhnev era. This was the emphasis on the role of the so-called 'work collective' (*trudovoy kollektiv*), that is, the managers and staff at the individual's place of employment, one of whose functions was to be that of political socialization. Brezhnev himself had mentioned it at the party congress in 1971.[181] Article 8 of the 1977 Soviet Constitution was specifically concerned with 'work collectives', one of whose tasks was said to be 'to educate their members in the spirit of communist morality'.[182] According to Mikhail Suslov, speaking as a member of the ruling Politburo in 1979, the Communist Party required that 'the main effort in the development of ideological-educational work should be concentrated in the work collective.'[183] None of this meant, of course, that the role assigned to the work collective was connected only with propaganda. On the contrary, the development of the work collective became associated with a much wider range of issues and was the subject of new laws in 1983 and in 1987.[184] (It gave rise to a sizeable amount of literature on labour relations and management and was associated, even before Gorbachev came to power, with modest trends towards industrial democracy, but this lies outside the scope of our discussion.) There was, however, no doubt, certainly during the Brezhnev era, that work collectives were intended to play a key role in political socialization. *Pravda* on one occasion spoke of their 'tremendous mobilizing and educative power'.[185] Geidar Aliev, later to become a member of the ruling Politburo, once went so far as to describe the work collective as 'the main educator of Soviet man'.[186] It was here in particular that the official propaganda effort was concentrated and intensified.

Propaganda, psychology and method

It remains, when examining the Soviet approach to propaganda during the Khrushchev and Brezhnev eras, to bring the subject back once again to the central theme of this book, namely the question of psychological method, or the 'how' of Soviet persuasion. We have argued that for a number of reasons, including, not least, the abandonment of Stalinist mass coercion, the Soviet authorities were much more interested than previously in propaganda method. As we have just seen, a number of new approaches were embarked upon. But the question then has to be asked: how far did all these various approaches represent an attempt at a viable or coherent propaganda strategy? How far if at all did the new thinking involve any radical re-appraisal of traditional methods, with their heavy emphasis on correctness of propaganda content and efficient organization?

The answer appears to be 'Very little'; and this, in spite of the considerable, even if chequered, development of opinion polls and social science research. Although lip service was quite often paid to the role of psychology in relation to persuasive methods, remarkably little emerged in the form either of improved propaganda performance or of useful practical recommendations. Exhortations to the media to improve their style produced little effect, judging from the frequency with which the same criticisms recurred from year to year. Calls for greater promptness, for less bald repetition and for a greater reliance on a 'two-sided' presentation of facts represented a change from the Stalin era, but they did little more than point to obvious weaknesses in the existing propaganda system. They hardly amounted to a comprehensive strategy.

The nub of the problem was how far the mere fact of an individual's being constantly exposed to a propaganda message or to essentially partisan information could itself guarantee the individual's successful political socialization. Certainly as far back as 1967 Stepakov, the head of the party's Propaganda Department, had raised this problem and implied that it had not been solved. As he put it: 'We still have little knowledge . . . of the ways of turning people's knowledge into their convictions and motives for behaviour.'[187] In the early 1980s, another Soviet author noted that despite the fairly wide range of literature in the USSR relating to ideology, nevertheless 'the questions of the "mechanism" of the formation of convictions . . . have been the questions least explored.'[188] That suggested that the problem was not much nearer to solution.

Earlier in this book, at the end of chapter 2, we drew attention to the disparity between the vast scale of Soviet propaganda activity and the remarkably little attention apparently devoted to psychology. At the end of the Brezhnev era, the psychological aspects of propaganda still remained greatly under-explored. The best evidence of this can be found in the complaints on this very point in Soviet statements and writings. Thus an author in 1977 expressed regret that although social psychology was widely studied, nevertheless 'you will not find on the bookshelves a single book on the social psychology ... of propaganda and ideological work as a whole.'[189] Another author in the same year wrote of the need to develop what he termed the 'pedagogical approach' to propaganda, but went on to complain that books specifically concerned with this subject 'can be counted on one's fingers'.[190] In 1980, a Soviet textbook on social psychology said that 'up until now the mass information and propaganda media have had no relationship on an organized basis with social psychology.' The author suggested that the media and propaganda systems should regularly seek the advice of psychologists, which they were not doing. Most of the literature on social psychology and propaganda – so this book claimed – dealt more with theoretical or experimental questions than with applied research, much or most of which remained unpublished and therefore inaccessible to specialists. The book reached the conclusion that: 'Taken as a whole, the situation which has arisen in regard to applied research in the sphere of mass communication and propaganda can in no way be considered satisfactory ... A mass audience, its reactions, and the influences exerted upon it can only be studied "in the field". And the carrying out of research at this level needs resources, cadres and time.'[191]

A very similar point – that psychological method had played little part in propaganda – was made at a conference of ideological workers held in Moscow in April 1981, when one of the main speakers observed: 'Our sociology, our pedagogical science and psychology are turning only slowly towards the investigation of questions of the communist education of the working people and of propaganda work.'[192] The subject was again raised in June 1983, when Konstantin Chernenko, in a speech to a plenum of the Communist Party Central Committee devoted to ideology, called among other things for 'a further strengthening of the scientific method base of ... all propaganda' and made the criticism that 'so far there has been an obvious lack of depth and planning in the elaboration of sociological, psychological and pedagogical problems' in this area.[193] A conference of public opinion specialists held in Moscow in March 1984 noted that up until then attempts to study public opinion from the angle of social psychology had been rare. The conference also expressed the view that 'the development of research is being held back by the inadequate analysis of theoretical problems.'[194]

Thus the evidence indicates yet again that Soviet propaganda specialists, certainly up until the 1980s, were little concerned with the empirical study of motivation. This lack of concern applied in particular to the study of *political* motivation. Indeed, the subject of 'political psychology' (which increasingly won attention among social scientists in the West) was hardly discussed at all in Soviet literature until 1980. In that year, however, a Soviet author did raise the subject – possibly because it had been the theme of a number of papers delivered at the Eleventh World Congress of the International Association of Political Science, which in 1979 had been held in Moscow.[195] This Soviet author wrote a résumé of Western studies in this area, and added: 'The lack of attention to political psychology in our country, both among political scientists and, still more, among psychologists, cannot be considered justified.' He nevertheless urged 'an extremely cautious and sharply critical approach' on the Soviet side to Western findings and said that Soviet specialists should evolve their own approach to the subject.[196]

In short, then, the evidence presented in this chapter all tends to confirm that the study of psychology and of public opinion played a far less important part in Soviet persuasion than they did in the persuasive techniques used in the West in the same period. And this itself is worth bearing in mind when finally trying to evaluate the realism of the traditional Soviet approach to propaganda – the subject to which we shall now turn.

Notes

1   *Kommunist*, 12 (1957), p. 23, quoted in Alex Inkeles, *Public Opinion in Soviet Russia: A Study in Mass Persuasion*, 4th imp. (Harvard University Press, Cambridge, Mass., 1962), p. 327.

2   See Ronald J. Hill, *Soviet Politics, Political Science and Reform* (Martin Robertson/M. E. Sharpe, Oxford/New York, 1980) for reviews of Soviet writings in the Brezhnev era on *glasnost'* (pp. 71–2, 136) and on contested elections (pp. 24–30).

3   See David E. Powell, *Antireligious Propaganda in the Soviet Union: A Study of Mass Persuasion* (MIT Press, Cambridge, Mass., 1975), pp. 38ff.

4   See Khrushchev's public report to the 20th party congress reported in *Pravda*, 15 February 1956, p. 10.

5   *Kommunist*, 12 (1957), pp. 3ff. quoted in Inkeles, *Public Opinion in Soviet Russia*, p. 330.

6   See the Communist Party resolution 'On the Tasks of Party Propaganda in Contemporary Conditions', *Pravda*, 10 January 1960, p. 1.

7   See speech by V. P. Yelyutin, the then Minister of Higher and Secondary Special Education, reported in *Pravda*, 29 December 1961, p. 2. The proceedings of this conference were published in *XXII s"yezd KPSS i voprosy ideologicheskoi raboty* (Moscow, 1962).

8   *XXII s"yezd KPSS*, p. 78.

9   See *BSE*, 2nd edn, vol. 40 (Moscow, 1957), pp. 196 and 207.

FROM STALIN'S DEATH TO GORBACHEV'S ACCESSION   175

10   *Voprosy filosofii*, 3 (1959), p. 44 (A. Uledov).
11   Ibid., 8 (1958), pp. 185–6. The journal *Sotsiologicheskie issledovaniya* first appeared in 1974.
12   See *Zhurnalist*, 2 (1967), p. 51 (Boris Firsov).
13   Results were reported in *Komsomol'skaya pravda*, 19 May 1960.
14   Details of these surveys (which dealt, *inter alia*, with free time, students' aspirations, attitudes towards the family and attitudes towards *Komsomol'skaya pravda*) are set out in Elizabeth Ann Weinberg, *The Development of Sociology in the Soviet Union* (Routledge & Kegan Paul, London, 1974), ch. 6 and appendix II, pp. 123–37.
15   See E. P. Prokhorov (ed.), *Sotsiologiya zhurnalistiki* (Moscow, 1981), p. 55, n7.
16   See *Pravda*, 10 January 1960; and the *Programme of the Communist Party of the Soviet Union* (Moscow, 1961), part II, Section V 3(a), p. 115.
17   See Leonid Ilyichev, *Obshchestvennye nauki i kommunizm* (Moscow, 1963), p. 36.
18   See *Stroitel'stvo kommunizma i obshchestvennye nauki* (Moscow, 1962), esp. pp. 10, 35–6, 303.
19   See E. S. Kuz'min and V. E. Semyonov (eds), *Sotsial'naya psikhologiya* (Leningrad, 1979), p. 39.
20   F. G. Krotov, *Shkola ideinoi zakalki* (Moscow, 1978), p. 143.
21   A. G. Efimov and P. V. Pozdnyakov, *Nauchnye osnovy partiinoi propagandy* (Moscow, 1966), p. 8.
22   V. I. Stepakov, *Partiinoi propagande – nauchnye osnovy* (Moscow, 1967), pp. 283–4.
23   Ibid., p. 189.
24   Ibid., pp. 86–7.
25   Ibid., p. 266–7.
26   Ibid., pp. 263ff.
27   Reported in *Voprosy teorii i metodov ideologicheskoi raboty*, 1 (Moscow, 1972), p. 3.
28   The resolution 'On measures for the improvement of the training of theoretical cadres in the Academy of Social Sciences attached to the CC of the CPSU' was adopted on 12 November 1970 and is summarized in *Ob ideologicheskoi raboty KPSS. Sbornik dokumentov* (Moscow, 1977), pp. 474–9.
29   *PS*, 12 (1971), pp. 65–6.
30   *Zhurnalist*, 10 (1967), pp. 42–5 (Boris Firsov).
31   Ibid., 2 (1967), pp. 50–2 (Boris Firsov).
32   Ibid., 2 (1968), pp. 23–5 (Vasilii Davydchenkov and Vladimir Shlyapentokh).
33   Ibid., 7 (1968), pp. 46–8 (Yurii Skvortsov).
34   See F. Burlatskii et al. (eds), *Problemy sotsiologii pechati*, vol. 2 (Novosibirsk, 1970), pp. 92–136. This volume, as well as its predecessor which appeared under the same editors in 1969, deals at length with the problems of empirical communication research.
35   See *Zhurnalist*, 10 (1969), pp. 34–7 (Boris Evladov, Anatolii Pokrovskii and Vladimir Shlyapentokh).

36 See, in particular, Gayle Durham Hollander, *Soviet Political Indoctrination: Developments in Mass Media and Propaganda since Stalin* (Praeger, New York, 1972) esp. pp. 62–9; Ellen Mickiewicz, 'Policy applications of public opinion research in the USSR', *Public Opinion Quarterly*, Winter 1972–3, pp. 566–78; Stephen White, *Political Culture and Soviet Politics* (Macmillan, London, 1979), esp. pp. 136ff.

37 See, in particular, White, *Political Culture* p. 139, quoting *Sotsiologicheskie issledovaniya*, 3 (1975), p. 59.

38 See Hollander, *Soviet Political Indoctrination*, pp. 65, 69, quoting *Zhurnalist*, 2 (1968), p. 24, and 2 (1967), p. 51.

39 *Zhurnalist*, 10 (1967), p. 44.

40 *Pravda*, 30 March 1966, p. 9.

41 See the resolution 'On measures for the further development of the social sciences and the enhancement of their role in the building of communism', summarized in *Pravda*, 22 August 1967.

42 This resolution 'On the state of party-political information and on measures to improve it' was adopted on 7 February 1969 and is summarized in *Ob ideologicheskoi raboty KPSS*, pp. 297–304. The passage cited above is on p. 303.

43 For a brief official account of this, see *Sotsiologicheskie issledovaniya*, 1 (1974), esp. pp. 7–9. A more detailed account based partly on unofficial sources can be found in Mervyn Matthews and T. Anthony Jones (eds), *Soviet Sociology, 1964–75: A Bibliography* (Praeger, New York, 1978), pp. 11–15.

44 *Kommunist*, January 1965, quoted in Paul Hollander (ed.), *American and Soviet Society: A Reader in Comparative Sociology and Perception* (Prentice-Hall, Englewood Cliffs, NJ 1969), pp. 524–5.

45 See, for an account of this episode, my interview with Dr Shlapentokh published in *The Listener*, 20 May 1982, pp. 18–19. (Note: since emigrating from the Soviet Union in 1979, Dr Shlapentokh adopted this transliteration of his name, although the reader of his works published prior to his emigration will find a different transliteration, Shlyapentokh, which is used here in reference to these earlier writings.) Yurii Zhukov's article appeared in *Pravda*, 29 August 1974, p. 4.

46 B. D. Parygin, *Sotsial'naya psikhologiya kak nauka* (Leningrad, 1965), p. 164. The preface to the book's second edition, which appeared in 1967, states that the first edition was sold out within a week.

47 B. D. Parygin, *Osnovy sotsial'no-psikhologicheskoi teorii* (Moscow, 1971), p. 341.

48 Parygin, *Sotsial'naya psikhologiya kak nauka*, p. 166.

49 B. A. Grushin, *Mneniya o mire i mir mnenii* (Moscow, 1967), pp. 172ff.

50 Ibid., p. 191.

51 Ibid., p. 186.

52 Ibid., p. 174, quoting A. K. Uledov, *Obshchestvennoye mnenie sovetskogo obshchestva* (Moscow, 1963), p. 75.

53 Grushin, pp. 175–7.

54 Ibid., pp. 184–6.

55 Uledov, *Obshchestvennoye mnenie sovetskogo obshchestva*, pp. 88–9, quoted in Grushin, *Mneniya o mire*, p. 177.
56 Grushin, *Mneniya o mire*, p. 178.
57 Uledov, *Obshchestvennoye mnenie sovetskogo obshchestva*, pp. 32–3, quoted in Grushin, *Mneniya o mire*, pp. 179–80.
58 Grushin, *Mneniya o mire*, p. 192.
59 Ibid., p. 194–5.
60 *BSE*, 3rd. edn, vol. 18 (1974), p. 242–3.
61 See Yu. V. Vooglaid et al. (eds), *Materialy vstrechi sotsiologov* (3 vols, Tartu, 1967–9): vol. 1 *Metodologicheskie problemy issledovaniya massovoi kommunikatsii*, 1967; vol. 2, *Tsennostnye orientatsii lichnosti i massovaya kommunikatsiya*, 1968; vol. 3, *Lichnost' i massovaya kommunikatsiya*, 1969. For the reference to anecdotes, see vol. 1, p. 212.
62 Ibid., vol. 3, p. 107.
63 Ibid., vol. 3, p. 165.
64 Ibid., vol. 2, pp. 29, 30.
65 Ibid., vol. 2, p. 35.
66 Ibid., vol. 1, pp. 151–4.
67 Ibid., vol. 2, pp. 196ff.
68 Ibid., vol. 2, pp. 203–5.
69 Ibid., vol. 2, pp. 207–8.
70 Ibid., vol. 3, pp. 67–8.
71 Ibid., vol. 1, p. 78.
72 Ibid.
73 Ibid., vol. 1, pp. 94–5.
74 See R. A. Safarov, *Obshchestvennoye mnenie i gosudarstvennoye upravlenie* (Moscow, 1975), p. 67. His earlier writings are reviewed in Ronald Hill, *Soviet Politics*, *passim*. Safarov's post is given in the *Pravda* article cited in n. 75.
75 See R. A. Safarov, 'Public opinion: its study and effectiveness', *Pravda*, 25 September 1981, pp. 2–3.
76 See R. A. Safarov, 'Public opinion in the political system of developed socialism', in D. A. Kerimov et al. (eds), *Problemy partiinogo i gosudarstvennogo stroitel'stva*, vol. 2 (Moscow, 1982), pp. 160ff, esp. pp. 164–9.
77 See, for an account of this attack, Matthews and Jones, *Soviet Sociology 1964–75*, pp. 12–13.
78 See *Voprosy teorii i metodov ideologicheskoi raboty*, 7 (Moscow, 1977), p. 138.
79 This resolution was summarized in *Pravda*, 22 August 1967.
80 See S. Gurevich (ed.), *Problemy informatsii v pechati* (Moscow, 1971), p. 282.
81 See V. I. Danilenko (ed.), *Upravlenie sotsial'nymi protsessami v sotsialisticheskom obshchestve* (Moscow, 1978), p. 5.
82 *Voprosy teorii i metodov ideologicheskoi raboty*, 12 (Moscow, 1980), p. 25 (S. S. Vishnevskii).
83 *Nauchnoye upravlenie obshchestvom*, 11 (Moscow, 1977), p. 62.
84 *Problemy nauchnogo kommunizma*, 8 (Moscow, 1974), p. 83.
85 See, for the text of these remarks, G. L. Smirnov et al. (eds), *Problemy*

178   FROM STALIN'S DEATH TO GORBACHEV'S ACCESSION

kompleksnogo osushchestvleniya zadach kommunisticheskogo vospitaniya v svete reshenii XXV s'yezda KPSS (Moscow, 1978), p. 294.

86 V. M. Yakushev, 'Gnoseologicheskie i psikhologicheskie osnovy agitatsii i propagandy', Avtoreferat (published abstract of unpublished dissertation (Lvov, 1967)), p. 80.

87 See, in general, G. T. Zhuravlev, *Sotsial'naya informatsiya i upravlenie ideologicheskim protsessom* (Moscow, 1973), esp. pp. 7ff. See also Gurevich *Problemy informatsii v pechati*, p. 287.

88 Zhuravlev, *Sotsial'naya informatsiya*, p. 9.

89 See Smirnov et al., *Problemy kompleksnogo osushchestvleniya*, p. 301.

90 G. L. Smirnov et al. (eds), *Voprosy teorii i praktiki partiinoi propagandy* (Moscow, 1971), p. 78 (N. S. Mansurov).

91 See Smirnov et al., *Problemy kompleksnogo osushchestvleniya*, p. 319.

92 *Problemy nauchnogo kommunizma*, 8 (1974), pp. 84–5.

93 *PS*, 1 (1976), p. 21 (V. Zevin).

94 *Voprosy teorii i metodov ideologicheskoi raboty*, 4 (Moscow, 1975), pp. 48–9 (A. I. Yakovlev).

95 Stepakov, *Partiinoi propagande - nauchnye osnovy*, p. 125.

96 See, for Stepakov's biography, the 1965 *Ezhegodnik* (Yearbook) of the *BSE*, p. 603.

97 See B. A. Grushin and L. A. Onikov (eds), *Massovaya informatsiya v sovetskom promyshlennom gorode* (Moscow, 1980), pp. 3, 6. The reason why Taganrog was chosen is stated on p. 79.

98 Ibid., pp. 24, 44.

99 Ibid.., pp. 217, 219. The reference to the Soviet media's high prestige is on p. 250.

100 Ibid., p. 305.

101 Ibid., pp. 309–10. The reference to sales of the *Morning Star* is on p. 128.

102 Ibid., pp. 245–6.

103 Ibid., p. 247–8.

104 See V. S. Korobeinikov (ed.), *Pressa i obshchestvennoye mnenie* (Moscow, 1986), p. 6; G. P. Davidyuk and V. S. Korobeinikov (eds), *Effektivnost' sredstv massovoi informatsii* (Minsk, 1986), p. 24.

105 See A. K. Uledov et al. *Obshchestvennoye mnenie i propaganda* (Moscow, 1980), pp. 159–60.

106 Ibid., p. 156.

107 See Korobeinikov, *Pressa i obshchestvennoye mnenie*, p. 6.

108 *Zhurnalist*, 4 (1968), p. 78.

109 *Voprosy teorii i metodov ideologicheskoi raboty*, 12 (Moscow, 1980), p. 267, n. 2.

110 *Sotsiologicheskie issledovaniya*, 3 (1984), p. 31. The full title of the renamed institution was The Centre for the Study, Formation and Forecasting of Public Opinion.

111 See, for an account of this body, Uledov et al., *Obshchestvennoye mnenie i propaganda*, pp. 167ff; and for a description of its research, ibid., pp. 181–3.

112   For a mention of this department, headed by B. P. Yakovlev, see *Pravda*, 25 June 1979, p. 4. A well-documented analysis of the volume of citizens' letters to the authorities and to newspapers can be found in Stephen White, 'Political Communications in the USSR: letters to party, state and press', *Political Studies*, 31 (1983), pp. 43–60. Letters to the party Central Committee rose, with some fluctuations, from 482,100 in 1971 to 671,600 in 1980: see White, p. 47. White found little evidence that these communications from below made much impact on decision-making at the national or republican, as distinct from the local, level.

113   See V. I. Ivanov et al. (eds), *Sotsiologiya i propaganda* (Moscow, 1986), p. 36.

114   See V. A. Medvedev (ed.), *Sotsialisticheskii obraz zhizni i voprosy ideologicheskoi raboty* (Moscow, 1977), p. 371.

115   *Nauchnoye upravlenie obshchestvom*, 12 (Moscow, 1978), pp. 215–16 (V. G. Baikova).

116   See Matthews and Jones, *Soviet Sociology 1964–75*, pp. 11–15.

117   *Voprosy teorii i metodov ideologicheskoi raboty*, 4 (Moscow, 1975), p. 16 (M. T. Iovchuk).

118   A reference to a 'newly created All-Union Centre for the Study of Public Opinion' can be found in *Sotsiologicheskie issledovaniya*, 4 (1983), p. 7. The setting up of such a centre was envisaged in a party resolution 'On current questions of ideological and mass-political work' published in *Pravda*, 16 June 1983, pp. 2–3.

119   V. I. Volovich, *Sotsiologicheskie issledovaniya v ideologicheskoi raboty* (Kiev, 1981), pp. 18–19.

120   See Grushin and Onikov, *Massovaya informatsiya*, p. 426.

121   *Voprosy teorii i praktiki ideologicheskoi raboty*, 17 (Moscow, 1985), pp. 193–7 (V. S. Komarovskii).

122   This problem is well documented in Nicholas Lampert, *Whistle-blowing in the Soviet Union: Complaints and Abuses under State Socialism* (Macmillan, London, 1985).

123   *Nauchnoye upravlenie obshchestvom*, 16 (Moscow, 1983), pp. 83–4 (M. K. Gorshkov).

124   *Spravochnik sekretarya pervichnoi partiinoi organizatsii* (Moscow, 1980), p. 351.

125   *Pravda*, 26 February 1986. For an official English translation, see *Mikhail Gorbachev, Political Report of the CPSU Central Committee to the 27th Party Congress* (Moscow, 1986), p. 102.

126   *Pravda*, 6 February 1987, pp. 2–3.

127   *LG*, 9 March 1988, p. 1.

128   *LG*, 23 September 1987, p. 12 (Lidia Grafova).

129   See Gurevich, *Problemy informatsii v pechati*, p. 128.

130   See the Communist Party resolution of 29 January 1960 'On the improvement of Soviet radio broadcasting', summarized in *O partiinoi i sovetskoi pechati, radioveshchanii i televidenii. Sbornik dokumentov i materialov* (Moscow, 1972), pp. 530–6, esp. p. 536.

131   See Daniel Tarschys, *The Soviet Political Agenda. Problems and Priorities*

1950–70 (Macmillan Press, London, 1979), esp. p. 173; Jerry F. Hough, *The Soviet Union and Social Science Theory* (Harvard University Press, Cambridge, Mass., 1977), pp. 190–5.

132 *LG*, 1 January 1979, p. 10.

133 *Pravda*, 26 July 1977, p. 3 (V. Omel'chenko).

134 Ibid., 6 September 1977, p. 3 (A. Turikov); *LG*, 31 August 1977, p. 11, printed an article and a number of letters urging this reform.

135 See, e.g., the article 'Let us speak plainly' by the Editor-in-Chief of *Literaturnaya gazeta*, Aleksandr Chakovskii, in *Pravda*, 7 October 1978, p. 2.

136 See *Pravda*, 25 July 1957, quoted in Inkeles, *Public Opinion in Soviet Russia*, p. 338; *Pravda*, 29 January 1977, p. 4; ibid., 10 August 1977, p. 3, which gives the figure of over 2.6 million Soviet citizens going abroad in 1976.

137 See *Guardian*, 13 September 1973 and 21 August 1980. The Soviet jamming of Western broadcasts beamed to the USSR began in the late 1940s. Jamming of the BBC and Voice of America had been suspended in June 1963 and resumed in August 1968 following the Soviet-led invasion of Czechoslovakia. The jamming of Radio Liberty was continuous. The earlier history of Soviet jamming is described in Maury Lisann, *Broadcasting to the Soviet Union: International Politics and Radio* (Praeger, New York, 1975). See also p. 217 n. 2.

138 See *Pravda*, 10 September 1977.

139 See Hedrick Smith, *The Russians* (Sphere Books, London, 1976), p. 449.

140 Ibid., p. 451.

141 See Hill, *Soviet Politics* for a review of the specialized literature during the Brezhnev era.

142 The first official admission of the actual shooting down of the Korean airliner on 1 September was made in *Pravda* on 7 September. The deaths of Brezhnev, Andropov and Chernenko had not been preceded by any announcement that they were seriously ill. Andropov, who died on 9 February 1984, had not appeared in public during the previous autumn and no explanation had been offered for his failure to attend the anniversary celebration of the revolution on 7 November 1983.

143 *Voprosy teorii i praktiki massovykh form propagandy*, 1–3 (Moscow, 1968–70). For details of further volumes see the note on sources p. ix *ante*.

144 *Sovetskoye radio i televidenie*, 3 (1957), pp. 6–8, quoted in Lisann, *Broadcasting to the Soviet Union*, p. 12.

145 *Kommunist*, 10 (1965), pp. 76–7, quoted in Lisann, *Broadcasting to the Soviet Union*, pp. 36–7.

146 See the resolution of 7 February 1969 'On the state of party-political information and on measures to improve it', in *Ob ideologicheskoi raboty KPSS*, esp. p. 301.

147 *Pravda*, 16 August 1973, p. 2.

148 *Pravda*, 28 November 1978, p. 2.

149 See the resolution 'On the further improvement of the party's ideological, political-educational work' summarized in *Pravda*, 6 May 1979, p. 1.

150 See the resolution 'On current questions of the party's ideological mass-

political work', *Pravda*, 16 June 1983, pp. 2–3.

151 E. Nozhin, 'The law of pre-emption', in *Problemy radio i televideniya*, 2 (Moscow, 1970), esp. pp. 50–4.

152 See A. M. Rusakovich (ed.), *Politicheskaya informatsiya* (Moscow, 1973), pp. 35–6.

153 See A. Yakovlev, 'The Leninist principles for the perfection of ideological work', *Pravda*, 21 August 1981, p. 3. The author should not be confused with Aleksandr Yakovlev, who in June 1987 joined the Politburo but was then Soviet Ambassador to Canada.

154 *LG*, 13 August 1986, p. 14 (Vladimir Tsvetov).

155 See, e.g. A. S. Vishnyakov (ed.), *Metodika partiinoi propagandy* (Moscow, 1967), ch. 2, which deals with 'Elements of pedagogy and psychology in party propaganda'. See also B. Ts. Badmayev, *Elementy psikhologii i pedagogiki v partiinoi propagande* (Moscow, 1973) and 2nd rev. edn (Moscow, 1980). The same author also published a further monograph, *Psikhologiya i pedagogika v partiinoi propagande* (Moscow, 1985).

156 E.g., E. A. Nozhin, *Osnovy sovetskogo oratorskogo iskusstva*, 2nd edn, (Moscow, 1981); P. N. Fedoseyev et al., *Ob iskusstve polemiki* (Moscow, 1980; 2nd. edn, 1982).

157 V. N. Kolbanovskii and Yu. A. Sherkovin (eds), *Problemy sotsial'noi psikhologii i propaganda* (Moscow, 1971), p. 149.

158 See, e.g., M. A. Morozov (ed.), *Spravochnik propagandista* (Moscow, 1974), which includes (on pp. 140ff) a section on 'Propaganda and social psychology'; also P. K. Kurochkin et al. (eds), *Kommunisticheskaya propaganda. Voprosy teorii i metodiki* (Moscow, 1974), ch. 3.

159 See, as to changing Soviet attitudes towards the theory of stereotypes, Smirnov et al., *Voprosy teorii i praktiki partiinoi propagandy*, pp. 22–3.

160 See V. M. Yakushev, 'Psychology and propaganda' in E. M. Vorontsov et al. (eds), *Propaganda i molodyozh'* (Moscow, 1981), pp. 87–8, 91.

161 Ibid., pp. 89–90.

162 See, e.g., Morozov, *Spravochnik propagandista* (1974), p. 144.

163 Sh. A. Nadirashvili, *Psikhologiya propagandy* (Tbilisi, 1978), p. 119.

164 N. S. Nazarova, *Formirovanie kommunisticheskoi ubezhdyonnosti molodyozhi* (Kiev/Odessa, 1981), pp. 124–5.

165 Fedoseyev et al., *Ob isskusstve polemiki* (1980), pp. 298–9.

166 Kolbanovskii and Sherkovin, *Problemy sotsial'noi psikhologii i propaganda*, p. 55n., referring to P. Lainberger (Paul Linebarger) *Psikhologicheskaya voina* (Moscow, 1962).

167 Ibid., pp. 60, 62.

168 Morozov, *Spravochnik propagandista* (1974), pp, 144–5.

169 Yu. A. Sherkovin, 'Some social-psychological questions concerning the impact of propaganda', *Voprosy psikhologii*, 4 (1969), pp. 131–9. The quotation is taken from the English summary at the end of the article.

170 Kolbanovskii and Sherkovin, *Problemy sotsial'noi psikhologii i propaganda*, pp. 33–5.

171   See Kurochkin et al., *Kommunisticheskaya propaganda*, p. 181.
172   *Voprosy teorii i metodov ideologicheskoi raboty*, 7 (Moscow, 1977), pp. 251, 256.
173   Lesław Wojtasik, *Psikhologiya politicheskoi propagandy* (Moscow, 1981), pp. 113, 118. This book was originally published in Warsaw in 1975.
174   Uledov et al., *Obshchestvennoye mnenie propaganda*, p. 54; Ivanov et al., *Sotsiologiya i propaganda*, p. 191.
175   V. A. Medvedev, *Razvitoi sotsializm: voprosy formirovaniya obshchestvennogo soznaniya* (Moscow, 1980), p. 90. Medvedev did, however, go on to stress the importance of 'purposeful educational work'.
176   See L. P. Buyeva, *Sotsial'naya sreda i soznanie lichnosti* (Moscow, 1968), quoted with approval in G. L. Smirnov, *Sovetskii chelovek* (Moscow, 1971), p. 31.
177   *Problemy nauchnogo kommunizma*, 8 (1974), p. 120.
178   See, Smirnov et al., *Voprosy teorii i praktiki partiinoi propagandy* p. 104. The statement was made by V. Skatershchikov.
179   Yu. V. Sychev, *Mikrosreda i lichnost'*, (Moscow, 1974), p. 190.
180   One British political scientist has observed that 'it required elaborate investigation to discover that small groups are at least as important as mass communications in contemporary politics, democratic or dictatorial': see W. J. M. Mackenzie, *Politics and Social Science* (Penguin Books, Harmondsworth, 1967), p. 169.
181   *Pravda*, 31 March 1971. For an official English translation see *Report of the Central Committee of the Communist Party of the Soviet Union delivered by Leonid Brezhnev, 30 March 1971 (Moscow, 1971)*, p. 94.
182   *Konstitutsiya (Osnovnoi Zakon) Soyuza Sovetskikh Sotsialisticheskikh Respublik* (Moscow, 1977), art. 8.
183   *Delo vsei partii. Materialy vsesoyuznogo soveshchaniya ideologicheskikh rabotnikov, Moskva 16–17 oktyabrya 1979 g.* (Moscow, 1980), p. 37. Also reported in *Pravda*, 17 October 1979.
184   Article 8 of the 1977 Constitution gave work collectives the right to take part, *inter alia*, 'in training and placing personnel, and in discussing and deciding matters pertaining to the management of enterprises and institutions'. This was followed, during the Andropov period, by the enactment of a 'Law on Work Collectives and on the enhancement of their role in the management of enterprises, institutions and organizations', published in *Pravda*, 19 June 1983. This was in turn superseded by the Law on the State Enterprise, published in *Pravda*, 1 July 1987.
185   *Pravda*, 4 September 1980 (leading article).
186   *Aktivnaya zhiznennaya pozitsiya bortsov za kommunizm. Po materialam vsesoyuznoi nauchno-prakticheskoi konferentsii v Baku (25–7 aprelya 1979 g.)* (Moscow, 1979), p. 25.
187   Stepakov, *Partiinoi propagande – nauchnye osnovy*, p. 280.
188   Nazarova, *Formirovanie kommunisticheskoi ubezhdyonnosti molodyozhi*, p. 8.
189   *Problemy kommunisticheskogo vospitaniya i sotsialisticheskoi kul'tury* (Moscow, 1977), p. 93 (I. T. Levykin).
190   *Voprosy teorii i metodov ideologicheskoi raboty* 7 (1977), p. 166, (E. G. Andreyev).

191 G. M. Andreyeva, *Sotsial'naya psikhologiya* (Moscow, 1980), pp. 399–404.
192 See E. M. Tyazhel'nikov (ed.), *Za vysokoye kachestvo i deistvennost' ideologicheskoi raboty. Materialy vsesoyuznogo seminara-soveshchaniya ideologicheskikh rabotnikov. Moskva, 20–5 aprelya 1981 g.* (Moscow, 1981), p. 82. This statement was made by M. V. Zimyanin.
193 *Pravda*, 15 June 1983, p. 3.
194 *Sotsiologicheskie issledovaniya*, 3 (1983), pp. 28–9, (M. K. Gorshkov).
195 See S. K. Roshchin, *Zapadnaya psikhologiya kak instrument ideologii i politiki* (Moscow, 1980). This book included a chapter on 'Political psychology' (pp. 261–83) but was almost exclusively concerned with describing Western approaches. One previous discussion of political psychology can be found in Parygin, *Sotsial'naya psikhologiya kak nauka*, pp. 185–97. Parygin's general thesis was that western research in this field was often motivated by a wish to devise methods of social control over mass behaviour. He conceded that not all Western sociologists and social psychologists were 'cynical apologists for imperialism'. Some genuinely hoped to use psychology to further international understanding. However, Parygin said, it seemed 'Utopian at the very least' to suppose that international conflicts could be abolished by purely psychological methods, since this ignored 'the simple fact long since established by Marxism' that international political relations were determined not by psychology, but by differences between political systems and by 'the correlationship of class political forces', both domestic and international.
196 See S. K. Roshchin, 'Political psychology at the XI Congress of the International Political Science Association', in *Sovetskaya assotsiatsia politicheskikh nauk. Ezhegodnik 1979: Problemy politicheskikh nauk. K itogam Vsemirnogo kongressa Mezhdunarodnoi assotsiatsii politicheskoi nauki* (Moscow, 1980), esp. p. 133.

6

Propaganda and the Soviet System: A Critique

> The reverse side of bureaucratic zest is the tendency to regulate everything and anything. But, as experience shows, this does not by any means always lead to positive results. There are areas of human activity which are not in general amenable to regulation.
>
> Vasil' Bykov, Soviet writer in *Literaturnaya gazeta* (1 January 1986)

Introduction

Most books on Soviet propaganda by non-Soviet authors end with an attempt to evaluate the 'effectiveness' of this propaganda effort. These assessments are usually inconclusive. Clearly, the Soviet official message has sometimes made an impact at home; and, equally clearly, it has sometimes failed to do so, as will already have become apparent. To say that all this effort has been 'partially' or 'incompletely' successful would be a safe but nevertheless unsatisfying conclusion. Indeed, the problem of evaluating results sometimes baffles Soviet as well as foreign observers, since it raises difficulties not just of getting information but of clarifying concepts. One leading Soviet specialist on public opinion, Boris Grushin, has drawn a pertinent distinction between the 'effects' and the 'effectiveness' of the Soviet media, and has pointed out that the two do not coincide.[1] Neither of these variables is, in any case, at all easy to measure. To ask how far Soviet propaganda has been effective naturally raises the question: 'effective for what purpose?' It also raises the further question as to how far, in any society, unofficial attitudes are decisively shaped by official policies. This is one of the main issues to which this chapter is addressed; and it has as much to do with social psychology as with Soviet politics.

Only when this has been considered can one begin, even tentatively, to judge what role the Soviet media may have had.

Official goals and unofficial opinions

The Soviet media, as we saw it in the last chapter, were ostensibly concerned, at least in the Brezhnev era, with the 'scientific management' of public opinion. As can be seen from the quotation at the beginning of this chapter not all members of the Soviet establishment subscribe to this notion of 'management'. Admittedly, the idea that propaganda by itself is all-powerful was gradually repudiated, as we saw. Nevertheless some Soviet theorists do, or did, appear to believe that public opinion can *in principle* be 'managed' from above, provided only that the right means of doing so (in the form of policies, persuasive methods and so on) can be found. The theoretical basis for this claim seemed to be that public opinion, like everything else, must necessarily be causally determined, and could therefore be brought under control if only the causes which shape opinion could themselves be uncovered and brought under control.

Occasionally, Soviet writers made this line of argument explicit. For example, one author writing in the mid-1970s claimed that 'since the development of spiritual processes takes place on the basis of objective laws, [therefore] public opinion . . . possesses all the attributes of systems amenable to management', though he went on to admit that the scope for 'managing' opinion was, in existing circumstances, limited.[2] In a similar vein, a Soviet author writing in 1980 recognized that public opinion developed in accordance with 'certain laws which have not yet been uncovered or explained by science' but nevertheless maintained that: 'Socialism creates the objective conditions for the scientific management of all sides of the life of society. Here, the management of the process by which public opinion is formed becomes possible in principle.'[3] If Soviet public opinion specialists were even on the road to achieving this goal of 'management' then of course the 'thought-control' stereotype of Soviet propaganda might have some substance. Yet this leads back once again to our central question of exactly *how* such a goal is to be realized. As already noted in the last chapter, Soviet opinion research is, by any test, far behind that of other developed countries; and the lack of literature on propaganda method has been the subject of complaint in the USSR itself.

But, quite apart from this, the claim that opinion control is possible in theory can be met by at least one theoretical objection. For even if one were to concede that opinions, including public opinion, are governed by causal laws, one can equally argue that public opinion is to a considerable extent, and quite inevitably, shaped by causes *which are not amenable to direct control from above.* This proposition can be backed up by a good deal of empirical evidence and will be examined later. First, however, something needs to be said about two other related topics, namely, the state of Soviet unofficial opinion and the admitted problems of the traditional propaganda system.

One perennial difficulty about assessing the impact of the Soviet media on its own population has, of course, been the paucity of reliable evidence about what ordinary members of the Soviet public actually think. Even today, the state of unofficial Soviet opinion is to a great extent an unknown quantity: we shall not try to summarize the available evidence in any detail. Nevertheless, there is now a good deal more information on this subject than there used to be. Nationalism, both Russian and non-Russian, is emerging as a powerful force; but there are at least two other features of Soviet unofficial opinion which deserve to be pointed out. They are: first, a widespread lack of interest in the official ideology, Marxism-Leninism; and secondly, an equally apparent lack of mass support for democracy, in the Western sense of the word.

The absence of public enthusiasm for ideology (outside the ranks of the activists) was demonstrated already in the 1970s on the evidence of Soviet sociological surveys.[4] It was again confirmed by the findings of the 1977 *Pravda* survey, which carries particular weight since it was based, not on a local, but on a nationwide, poll – of 9,672 people including 2,099 *Pravda* readers (see chapter 6 above). In reply to questions put in this survey, no more than 30 per cent even of the *Pravda* readers (among whom party members are disproportionately represented) expressed an interest in 'Marxist-Leninist theory'; and among the sample as a whole no more than 9 per cent expressed such an interest. Considering the enormous effort expended by the authorities over many decades on the propagation of Marxism-Leninism, this was a remarkably low level of public response. (The topic of greatest interest was that of 'international life', mentioned by 75 per cent of *Pravda* readers and by 48 per cent of the sample as a whole. Next in popularity came the theme of 'morals and upbringing', where the respective figures were 69 per cent for *Pravda* readers and 47 per cent for the rest. No more than 33 per cent of *Pravda* readers and 13 per cent of the overall sample expressed interest in the topic of 'party life, the work of party organizations'.)[5]

Side by side with this lack of interest in ideology, there has been an almost equally visible lack of interest in political study – a fact which has been alluded to in Soviet literature over many years.[6] One of the clearest indications of this can be found in the results of a survey conducted in the Gorkii province in 1975 – a survey which was apparently thought

TABLE 2   *Pupils' attitudes to political study (replies %)*

Type of study	Study is interesting	Helps to solve production and other practical tasks	Attend because this is required by public organizations or by the administration	Difficult to reply
Party study	33.3	36.3	18.3	12.1
Komsomol study	18.3	35.3	30.5	15.9
Schools of communist labour	23.8	19.1	40.9	16.2
Average percentages for above	25.5	26.8	33.9	13.8

The different forms of political study are explained in chapter 2 above. Schools of communist labour were a form of propaganda intended for non-party audiences, mostly manual workers. These schools were abolished in 1987.

Source: M. F. Nenashev, *Ideino–vospitatel' naya rabota KPSS* Moscow, 1980, p. 78

typical, since it was said to 'coincide as a whole with the results of research in a number of other provinces'.[7] The results, reported in 1980, are shown in table 2.

It can be seen from the first column of replies that at the most no more than one-third of pupils expressed positive interest in study, whilst the replies in the third column revealed a very large minority who openly said that they attended under some form of compulsion. All this evidence makes it abundantly clear that Soviet propaganda is far from being all-powerful. It also helps to explain the increased official preoccupation with propaganda method, whilst equally demonstrating that the problem of method is far from having been solved.

Nevertheless, the evidence presented so far is only one part of the picture; it does not of itself provide grounds for inferring a widespread opposition to the Soviet system as such. The Taganrog survey, as already mentioned, spoke of 'the undoubtedly high prestige' of the media with its audience.[8] And according to a survey in Byelorussia reported in 1986, for example, 96.2 per cent of the sample said that they trusted the information in the media, whilst only 3.8 per cent said they did not do so.[9] Regardless of whether these findings are reliable, it would be wrong to suggest that Soviet sociological research invariably conveys a negative picture of the media's impact.

A second apparent feature of unofficial Soviet opinion is lack of mass support for Western-style democracy. Here some of the strongest evidence comes from non-Soviet sources. Particular mention should be made of the evidence provided by the American-controlled Radio Free Europe/Radio Liberty radio station, which is based in Munich and has broadcast to the USSR and Eastern Europe since the early 1950s. The gradual rise in the number of Soviet visitors to Western Europe has enabled this organization to conduct systematic interviews since the early 1970s, using standard polling techniques, with members of the Soviet public who are not, of course, émigrés.[10] These surveys have, as might be expected, shown substantial variations of unofficial opinion in the USSR, as well as a high degree of listening to Western broadcasts. Nevertheless, they have provided no evidence that the dissident or civil rights movement in the USSR commands anything approaching majority support. Thus a survey based on 3,821 interviews with Soviet citizens abroad in the early 1970s indicated that no more than 10.8 per cent of the Soviet adult population were sympathetic to *samizdat* activity, whilst no more than 3.8 per cent of this population was strongly sympathetic. (The finding also indicated that less than half the Soviet population – 43.8 per cent – were at that time aware of *samizdat*.)[11] This picture was substantially confirmed by a further survey of 3,310 Soviet travellers to the West in the late 1970s, intended, by indirect questioning, to discover unofficial attitudes to civil liberties. This survey made the tentative estimate that amongst Soviet urban adults (on whom the sample was eventually based) no more than one in seven could be seen as receptive to basic Western ideas of civil liberties, a figure which, as the survey's author observed, would be considered low by the standards of most modern industrial societies.[12]

This evidence of Soviet conservative attitudes at grass-roots level is corroborated from other sources. Vladimir Shlapentokh discovered it from his inside knowledge of the *Pravda* survey of the 1960s. (He told me that perhaps one-third of the respondents in that project were potentially liberal-minded.) David Shipler, who served as Moscow correspondent of the *New York Times* from 1975 to 1979, reached a similar conclusion. He warned against what he saw as the miscalculation of assuming that 'Russians form a captive nation yearning to be free', and added: 'I came away convinced of the Russians' discomfort with weak leadership and of their aversion to the West's pluralistic array of political ideas.'[13] All this makes it easier to understand the complaints by the Gorbachev leadership that its reform programme was being impeded by conservative attitudes from below.

The question of more immediate concern here is whether this conservatism should necessarily be attributed to the impact of official propaganda. No doubt propaganda has often served to reinforce conservative attitudes. Yet there are grounds for supposing that these attitudes are to some degree independent of the influence of the authorities. One of the best-known examples of spontaneous authoritarian attitudes is the apparently considerable popularity of Stalin. A former Soviet sociologist, Viktor Zaslavsky, has noted that 'a very large number of Soviet workers have a very positive opinion of Stalin and his record.'[14] This seemed to be confirmed by a British correspondent who visited Georgia in 1984 and reported that in that year over a million people visited the museum in Stalin's birthplace, Gori.[15] The reasons behind the admiration for Stalin are not entirely clear. What is clear, however, is that these attitudes could not possibly have been in response to official propaganda, since at that time the Soviet media had, by and large, studiously avoided the subject of Stalin for well over a generation.

The evidence concerning unofficial Soviet opinion does not therefore necessarily indicate demands for democratic reform although it does reveal substantial discrepancies between official and unofficial attitudes. How then does propaganda fit into the picture? And how far does it appear to be a net asset to the system? These questions cannot be answered directly, because it is always difficult to establish a causal link between propaganda and its effects. It is nevertheless possible to evaluate Soviet propaganda by more indirect means – that is, by examining its rationale and the apparent efficiency or inefficiency of its methods. And this is the subject to which we now turn.

The basic Soviet approach to this subject was examined in chapter 3. So far as ideology was concerned, we suggested that the official attitude was, in theory at least, possible to understand. The central importance which the Soviet leadership attaches to ideology did, so we argued, have a certain logic – so long as ideology was understood not simply as a set of dogmas, but as the foundation of a strategy intended to provide society with (among other things) cohesion and a sense of purpose and direction. After all if the majority of Soviet citizens really were wholeheartedly committed in thought and deed to the goals of the system, then many of Soviet society's problems would indeed be solved, and coercion would increasingly become superfluous. All this, we suggested, might explain the authorities' commitment to the mass conversion of public opinion, which, if fully won over to the party's cause, could act as a stabilizing factor and also as a moral sanction against deviance. To all this the objection might, perhaps, be made that ideology can never be a realistic basis for mass motivation; and that the only effective source of mass motivation in society lies in individual self-interest, material incentives and the market economy. It may be pointed out, however that not even the most avowedly capitalist societies base their philosophies on individual economic self-interest to the exclusion of everything else; they rely heavily on such non-economic values as religion, patriotism, freedom, respect for authority and so on. Intangible values play an essential part in the cohesion of all major social systems. Reliance on ideology (in a general sense) is therefore not peculiar to the Soviet system.

What has just been said is not, of course, intended as a moral judgement about Soviet ideology, but simply as an attempt to explain its rationale. However, even if the rationale behind the ideology can be understood, can the same be said of the rationale behind the traditional propaganda system? This brings us back yet again to the problem of method, that is, of exactly *how* the public is to be won over to the ideology. In the light of available evidence, how realistic have Soviet proselytizing methods proved to be?

The realism of Soviet propaganda method

At the end of chapter 3 we listed three distinctive Soviet methods of persuasion (apart from the party's monopolistic control of the media). They were: first, the didactic, repetitive explanation of the party's case, organized with the aim of reaching everybody; secondly, an attempt to secure the 'active involvement' of individuals by giving them practical assignments (such as delivering lectures) in the apparent belief that these assignments would increase the political commitment of those who performed them; and thirdly, the mobilization of group influence in support of the authorities against deviant behaviour.

It is not part of the present argument to suggest that these methods have never been effective, but the Gorbachev leadership itself has readily admitted that the traditional system was not working. Indeed, that is obvious even in the light of well-known facts. The talk in the Brezhnev era of the 'management' of public opinion, or of the 'scientific management' of spiritual processes, went hand in hand with the onset of massive corruption which seriously damaged the fabric of society and clearly showed that the authorities were not fully in control. Something evidently went wrong. And it is therefore not irrelevant to scrutinize the above-mentioned methods of persuasion in more detail. They were all subject to snags whether taken separately or taken together; and almost all these snags reflected the existence of low motivation on the part of those involved.

First of all, reliance on didactic repetition was clearly liable to become counter-productive, because it failed to provide new information and therefore bored the audience. The psychologist V. M. Yakushev, whom we have already quoted (chapter 5, note 160), drew particular attention to this problem, which has, however, been mentioned many times in Soviet literature. In the 1960s, as many as 55 per cent (1,200 out of 2,200) of a group of respondents, when asked what they saw as the main failing of the lecture system, replied 'Not enough new information'.[16] In 1970 a lecturer in the party's Propaganda Department argued that to try to convince someone of something he already believed merely spoiled matters, especially in the case of young people, because there was 'a sharper and more negative reaction among young people than among adults to the repetition of well-known truths. In such a situation, lectures, no matter how rich in content they may be, do not produce the desired results.'[17]

In the Brezhnev era, the situation showed no sign of improving. The 1979 party resolution on propaganda specifically deplored, among other things, 'the continual mechanical repetition of general truths, instead of their creative interpretation'.[18] In June 1983 in his speech to the party Central Committee, Konstantin Chernenko observed that 'long and dull, didactic monologues' were still continuing in propaganda work.[19] Nevertheless, the problem was to a considerable degree inherent in the party's policy of saturation coverage of an increasingly well-informed population. A textbook on propaganda published in 1974 did indeed acknowledge this difficulty by admitting that sometimes – for example at a political school – the propagandist might in certain respects be *less* well-informed than some of the audience. However, so this book continued, the propagandist 'teaches the art of thinking not through an abundance of information but through a wealth of ideas. And this is possible only on the basis of a perfect grasp of Marxist-Leninist theory, a constant renewal or self-renewal of the propagandist's knowledge.'[20] Lectures devoid of new information could hardly be expected to make any great impact.

The second persuasive method mentioned above – that of 'active involvement – was also subject to a number of snags. The requirement imposed in some political study courses that students should prepare *referaty* (papers or reports), as a practical way of gaining a better grasp of ideology, does not seem to have been highly effective. A Soviet author in 1981 described this method as 'a one-sided approach to the development of individual convictions', which is apparently not popular with students. This author agreed that the preparation of *referaty* could be of great value to the student concerned 'provided that the *referat* is not copied from a book or article and is not read out in an automatic, mindless way', but added that this method would not be a stimulus to thought unless there was a genuine exchange of opinions within the group. This, the author went on, did not always take place, 'Unfortunately, some teachers cannot or will not organize discussions. And if a discussion begins, such a teacher will suppress it, wrongly reacting to certain mistaken utterances of the students.'[21] Another fact which raised doubts about the value of practical assignments as a method of strengthening personal commitment relates to the work of political lecturers and 'propagandists'. It is well known that at least some of them have carried out their assignments only with reluctance. For example, according to a local survey conducted in 1977 in the province of Chelyabinsk, only 12.4 per cent of lecturers mentioned 'the creative role of lecture work' as one of their reasons for undertaking it; whilst a large minority – 36 per cent – said they did the work because it was a 'public assignment'; and 53 per cent merely said they gave lectures out of 'an awareness of the indispensability of lecturing activity.'[22] Being overloaded with other assignments was commonly mentioned by speakers as one of their main difficulties.[23] Factory managers and their aides are, as we mentioned in chapter 2, normally expected to deliver regular political reports to their work-force; but some have been criticized in the press for trying to evade this work on the grounds of having 'heavy work commitments' or of lacking 'propaganda experience'.[24] Perhaps even more unsatisfactory, from the authorities' point of view, were those speakers who readily delivered political reports but did so from texts prepared for them by others.[25] There has, indeed, been newspaper criticism of speakers who lose their thread when reading aloud from texts or journals. Yet even when the text was read fluently, *Pravda* understandably deplored it on the grounds that 'mechanical propaganda is merely counterfeit propaganda.'[26] It therefore appears that pressure from above to make people deliver political lectures can be directly counter-productive, besides going against the traditional Bolshevik insistence on the personal sincerity of the speaker as a precondition for winning converts. Indeed, as late as 1981 it was repeated that 'there must be no place for indifferent people' in propaganda work.[27] It is, however, not true that all such speakers are indifferent. One noteworthy example dating from the Brezhnev era was of a group of lecturers in Taganrog who argued that, besides giving audiences the view of current events presented in the Soviet media, they should also have the right to give audiences their own views, even if different from those officially endorsed. However, this claim was at the time expressly rejected – on the grounds that a propagandist must always regard himself, in Lenin's words, as 'a representative of state power, as a representative of the party which rules Russia'.[28]

The third distinctive Soviet method of persuasion – reliance on 'public opinion' or 'group pressure' against deviance – also raises a number of practical difficulties. One of them stems from the gradual process (not peculiar to the USSR) of urbanization, which inevitably makes the individual less amenable to surveillance. Whereas in 1926 no more than 18 per cent of the Soviet population lived in cities, by 1980 the figure had risen to about 70 per cent. This, as one Soviet author has pointed out, has substantially altered the influence of public opinion on individual behaviour, because public opinion 'loses the function of external coercion and control' and can do no more than prescribe general standards of behaviour. The author went on to observe: 'In the meantime, the whole complex mechanism of organizing a real public opinion in urban conditions is not entirely clear.'[29]

There is of course no doubt that in any society, and particularly within a small group, 'public opinion' can indeed be a powerful sanction; but this still leaves unanswered the question as to how far such opinion can be created from above. The Soviet sociologist L. P. Buyeva specifically mentioned 'unofficial' opinion as a force which could sometimes hamper 'the social activity of the individual', that is, work against the authorities;[30] and there is a good deal of empirical evidence from Soviet sources to confirm this. The influence of 'public opinion' in the work collective quite clearly failed to produce the improvement in labour discipline for which the Brezhnev leadership had hoped.[31] Such opinion can in fact work, to the disadvantage of the authorities – as was graphically illustrated by a letter to *Pravda* in 1978. The author had drawn attention to absenteeism at work, and then wrote to *Pravda* to complain that 'no one supported me at the meeting and moreover many people even ceased to greet me after my speech.'[32] The much-publicized 'comrades' courts' which are intended to be the voice of public censure do not always serve this purpose. Thus in 1979 *Pravda* reported a case at the Likhachev car factory in Moscow (one of the Soviet showpieces, frequently visited by foreign tourists), where an attempt to try a worker before a comrades' court for absenteeism and drunkenness was met by protests from the hall. ('Why weren't . . . we asked if we wanted to try him?') *Pravda* also reported that during the previous year at this factory, out of a total number of 1,033 cases brought before comrades' courts, no more than eight had been initiated from below; the remainder had all been initiated by the management. (The factory at about that time had a work-force totalling 70,000 people.)[33] On another occasion, *Pravda* described how sometimes an absentee from work would be severely censured by his colleagues – who would nevertheless later offer him their private sympathy, saying that they were only acting on instructions from above. 'The result,' so the paper said, 'is that the educative effect of the meeting is reduced to zero, and has the most negative consequences.'[34] It would, all the same, be wrong to depict unofficial opinion as a purely negative reaction to authority. When official and unofficial opinions coincide they are indeed highly effective. A Soviet author in 1984 brought this into relief by pointing out that although the theft of public property in factories was sometimes regarded with indifference, nevertheless a worker who stole from his colleagues was often subjected to boycott and might be forced to leave.[35]

A further snag about 'group pressure' should also be mentioned. Whilst it is true that an individual is often persuasible by group influence, he is usually influenced not so much by the group to which he happens in fact to belong as by the group to which he aspires, or to which he *chooses* to belong. It has been a notorious fact for many years that industrial slackers could quite often escape collective censure, simply by changing jobs. (It was reported in 1984 that some 25 million Soviet workers changed jobs every year, which was about one-fifth of the then labour-force.)[36]

The limitations of attempts to exert 'group pressure' from above have been particularly demonstrated by a body of little-known Soviet sociological research into the attitudes of schoolchildren. Already in the late 1960s, a survey of 1,600 older schoolchildren (*starsheklassniki*) had revealed that over 99 per cent preferred to spend their free time out of school, whilst over 92 per cent preferred to do so outside the home. One-third of this particular sample expressed dissatisfaction with the nature of 'social assignments' at school owing, among other things, to the 'lack of autonomy' and 'excessive regimentation of school life'.[37] Another sociological survey carried out amongst 600 adolescents aged between 14 and 16 and reported in 1977 found that over 90 per cent of the sample belonged to informal groups of friends, sometimes little connected with the school.[38] One of the leading Soviet authorities on the sociology of young people, Professor Igor'Kon (himself a liberal by Soviet standards) has pointed to the distinction between what he termed 'groups to which one belongs' (*gruppy chlenstva*) and 'referent groups' (*referentnye gruppy*) with which people identify.[39] Kon also noted that the 'official leader' in the classroom (the school prefect) was 'not always the most authoritative person', and that 'informal leaders' among the children could possess 'greater real influence'.[40] This may seem to contradict the findings of the American psychologist Urie Bronfenbrenner, who suggested that the influence of authority in Soviet schools was strong.[41] It appears, however, that the importance of informal groups sharply rises amongst pupils over the age of about 14.[42] These findings are yet another indication that attempts by the authorities to exert group pressure on individuals are by no means as effective as might appear.

For all the reasons just given, the traditional Soviet methods of persuasion are each subject to drawbacks, when taken separately. When taken together, they give rise to still further problems. For insofar as they rely on the use of pressure, rather than genuine persuasion, they fail to generate a positive response and can become counter-productive even from the authorities' point of view.

In the first place and most obviously, pressure from above tends to inhibit reliable feedback – as we noted at the end of chapter 4 in relation to Stalinism and as we noted in the last chapter in connection with the difficulty of getting frank replies in surveys on sensitive questions such as listening to foreign broadcasts. Lack of feedback, as we said, limits propaganda effectiveness – and is also a weakness in Soviet society as a whole. Already in the early 1970s, Jerome Gilison argued that the suppression of dissent and insistence on orthodoxy in the USSR had been 'detrimental to the development of the system *even within its own terms*' (emphasis in original) and added that 'the silencing of negative feedback ... can also be seen as a structural defect of the Soviet system which leads to inefficiency.'[43] The Chernobyl accident confirmed this. And it deserves to be noted that in a speech at the Soviet writers' congress in Moscow in 1986, the Soviet novelist Daniil Granin made precisely the same point as Gilison – although in more graphic language:

> Imagine, comrades, that you have been sent on a reconnaissance mission. After carrying out your assignment you come back and report that you counted a hundred enemy tanks. 'Ah,' you are told, 'that was too many. Report that there are no more than 20 tanks. It's more agreeable that way.' That was roughly the situation in our literature even quite recently. Over the past year and a half, this evil has been half-uncovered ... It has been revealed on a scale which we did not imagine.[44]

A second result of the traditional Soviet propaganda system, including the censorship, of course, is that it can – again to its own disadvantage – diminish its credibility and ultimately cease to perform its intended function. The much-used expression 'monopoly of information' would be misleading, even if Soviet society were entirely closed to information from outside. For the individual must always derive his information not just from the media but from the evidence of what he himself sees and hears. Propaganda which runs counter to the audience's personal experience (or predispositions) is liable to meet with distrust, as Soviet authors have recognized for many years. Nor is this a purely theoretical difficulty. Even in the Brezhnev era, the Soviet media were beginning publicly to admit that the gap between 'word and deed' was a source of weakness (see chapter 3). And, as already noted, soon after taking power Gorbachev made this a central issue when he criticized 'the inability to talk to people in the language of truth'.

Clearly, the credibility and therefore the effectiveness of the propaganda system were at issue. That was not necessarily to say that criticism of Soviet society was universally welcome with the public; the liberal writer, Vasil'Bykov, for example, noted that some people preferred 'to read about successes rather than difficulties' because it helped them to maintain 'a psychological balance'.[45] But the problem caused by the 'gap between word and deed' was perhaps most clearly brought into relief by the sociologist Professor V. Shubkin. Suppose, he said, that a student in higher education knows that the student at the next desk has gained his place through some kind of corrupt influence: in that case 'everything the teacher has to say about social equality and about the other great advantages of our society will merely irritate the audience.'[46]

There is a third side-effect of the Soviet propaganda system which makes it even more directly counter-productive in its own terms. It can produce exactly the kind of 'spontaneity' (*stikhiinost'*) which the controls are ostensibly designed to prevent. One familiar example of this process in the economic sphere is the appearance of a 'second economy' or black market as the result of excessively centralized economic planning. But an analogous phenomenon of 'spontaneity' can be seen in the public reaction to a controlled media system. This takes two notable forms: listening to foreign broadcasts, to which we shall return later, and the prevalence of rumours on a scale quite without parallel in Western society. The phenomenon of rumour and 'word-of-mouth' communication has long since been noted by Western Sovietologists.[47] We shall, however, focus here on the problem as it appears from Soviet official sources. These sources make it clear that rumours in the USSR have sometimes been remarkable indeed. There was, for instance, the rumour in Lithuania in 1967, at the time of the 50th anniversary of the Bolshevik revolution, that war would break out on the eve of the anniversary celebrations. The story is said to have been ridiculed on local television, but not before some people had begun queuing for emergency supplies of goods.[48] There have been other apparently spontaneous rumours over the years. Thus, in 1979 a deputy chairman of the USSR State Bank found it necessary to deny, as an invention, rumours of a Soviet monetary reform and currency devaluation.[49] Sightings of Unidentified Flying Objects from outer space are said to have been another topic of rumours.[50] It seems highly likely, however, that the most potent rumours are those which affect some particular town or district, and are not dealt with by the media on the spot. For it is self-evident that if, for instance, a local newspaper fails to report a local train crash or a local scandal, then the local population will soon realize that something is being hidden and will cease to trust official sources. Indeed, the lecturers and propagandists may be powerless to cope in such cases, simply because, as *Pravda* once observed, they 'sometimes know nothing whatever about such pieces of gossip' and 'talk to people only on the subjects they have prepared'.[51]

The prevalence of word-of-mouth communication is difficult to translate into reliable statistical terms. But according to a nationwide survey, reported in a Soviet book of 1986, more than half (51 per cent) of the Soviet adult population, 'quite often or even mainly get the fullest ... information' about domestic and international events, from talks with colleagues or acquaintances. This, the book continued, had two disadvantages. For one thing such conversations often relayed information 'whose origins are linked to sources which are unreliable and which may be directly hostile to us'. Secondly, interpersonal communication proved in some cases to be playing 'a considerably more important role' than the oral propaganda system, such as lectures.[52]

Another unusual Soviet account of the incidence of rumours appeared in a book published in 1983 based on a survey carried out in 1978–80 amongst inhabitants of Leningrad aged over 18.[53] This survey found that as many as 24 per cent of the sample encountered rumours 'fairly often', whilst 65 per cent encountered them 'sometimes' and only 11 per cent encountered rumours 'not at all'. Younger people were in general more familiar with rumours than pensioners. Rumours were by no means always disbelieved. A significant minority of the sample – 17 per cent – expressed the view that rumours were more often true than not. A larger minority – 36 per cent – expressed the opposite view, whilst nearly half the total – 47 per cent – found the question hard to answer.[54] The book correlated these findings with findings about the level of audience satisfaction with the *local* media. These showed among other things that 61 per cent of the sample thought local newspapers failed to provide sufficiently full information about the life of Leningrad; 47 per cent were similarly critical of the local radio; and 53 per cent of local television.[55] The survey also found that seven people out of ten thought there was not enough media information about 'law and order', the problems of drunkenness and hooliganism and court cases (that is, they apparently wanted more open reporting of crime).[56] When the respondents were asked an open-ended question about how they thought rumours ought to be dealt with, an unusually high proportion – 81 per cent – replied, though opinions were not unanimous. The majority thought the proper solution was for the local media to provide fuller and more up-to-date coverage of events. However, a conservative-minded minority thought rumours should be dealt with by punishing those who spread them.[57] (No precise percentages were given for either group.)

Listening to Western broadcasts has long been known to be widespread in the USSR, and is another example of the 'spontaneity' which the Soviet authorities traditionally disliked. Almost all the estimated figures for listening come from Western sources (usually based on the interviewing of Soviet visitors to the West, referred to earlier in this chapter). In 1984, the last year before Gorbachev came to power, it was estimated on the basis of such interviews that Voice of America programmes beamed to the USSR were heard at least once a week by 14–18 per cent of the Soviet adult population aged 16 or over. The corresponding figure for Radio Liberty was 8–12 per cent; and for the BBC Russian Service 7–10 per cent.[58] This, of course, was at a time when both the Voice of America and the BBC were still being jammed. This clearly enough represented a sizeable minority, which was all the more important since the audience was disproportionately concentrated amongst the more educated groups. In the 1970s, the Radio Free Europe/Radio Liberty organization estimated the Soviet audience for all Western broadcasts over the course of a year as amounting to 67.3 million adults over the age of 16.[59] This would have been equivalent to about 37 per cent of the total adult population at the time. Such figures can, of course, only be a general indicator, since it is impossible to be absolutely sure how far Soviet visitors to the West are politically representative of the Soviet population as a whole.

The Soviet authorities do their own research on this subject, but practically never publish audience figures. One exception, however, is to be found in a Soviet book of 1981 published in the Ukraine in a small edition of 2,000 copies. This book quoted surveys showing that 18 per cent of students derived political information from foreign broadcasts.[60] It said that the figure could be as high as 40 per cent amongst students dissatisfied with the way they were taught social science subjects.[61] Among the workers, so this book said, only 7.7 per cent turned to foreign radio as a source of political information. (It is difficult to extrapolate this figure on to the population as a whole, since it is unclear whether the figure refers only to workers or whether it should be extended to include members of their families, who presumably also listen to foreign broadcasts.) The book then went on – even more strikingly – to say that among schoolchildren as many as 21 per cent listened to foreign broadcasts. Apparently they did not do so out of a desire for purely entertainment programmes, because, as the book explained:

> One of the reasons for this is the growing interest on the part of older schoolchildren [starsheklassniki] in the variety of contemporary social life, in political information. If they fail to get satisfactory answers at school to the questions which concern them, they turn to other sources with a hostile ideological orientation.[62]

It would be difficult to imagine British or American schoolchildren, for instance, tuning in to Moscow radio in large numbers, out of dissatisfaction with the political information available to them at school. And this highlights one very important and little-noticed contrast between Soviet and Western audience behaviour. It has sometimes been claimed that censorship gives the Soviet authorities an entirely one-sided advantage – since Western audiences have access to the Soviet point of view, whilst Soviet audiences have no similar access to the views of the West. But this needs to be qualified. Success in conveying a message depends not just on physical access to an audience, but on audience receptivity. Soviet audiences often seem to be much more curious about the West than vice versa. Their curiosity automatically helps to overcome the barriers, such as censorship or jamming, which Soviet authorities have created. And because of this, paradoxically enough, the Soviet public may indeed sometimes be better informed about the West than the Western public is informed about the Soviet Union.

So much, then, for the purely practical difficulties of 'managing' public opinion from above. Most of the difficulties stem from lack of audience interest or trust in the official message or from an attempt to evade official controls. We have deliberately tried to show how all these traditional Soviet propaganda methods can be directly counter-productive from the authorities' point of view. The moral seems to be that coercive methods from above will not of themselves generate positive motivation from below; they can undermine rather than reinforce opinion control.

This is one side of the coin. Yet, as we have already seen, the system does show many signs of enjoying popular acceptance, no matter what areas of dissatisfaction exist. Does this therefore indicate that the propaganda system, for all its apparent weaknesses, really is highly effective after all? No doubt in many respects it has made an impact, especially where official and unofficial attitudes are in harmony. Yet this may not after all prove the success of the traditional propaganda system. The evidence may, on the contrary, simply indicate that propaganda is somewhat less important to the stability of the Soviet system than has often been supposed by communists and non-communists alike.

Official and unofficial factors in socialization: the family

A number of attempts have been made, both inside and outside the USSR, to gauge Soviet public opinion through studying the attitudes of Soviet citizens towards their own media. We shall now attempt a slightly different approach – by considering a body of little-known evidence as to the *relative* influence of official and unofficial factors in forming Soviet opinion. This has been made possible largely as a result of recent Soviet research on the influence of the 'micro-environment', referred to in chapter 5.

Some of these 'unofficial' factors – such as personal experience, word-of-mouth communication and informal groups – have already been mentioned. One thing which clearly emerges is that in the USSR as elsewhere, mass communication is not dealing with an audience of mutually isolated individuals.[63] Its message is almost always mediated through informal groups. In a book in 1980 Professor Igor' Kon emphasized that the media, even though themselves subject to 'social control', were 'not all-powerful' because:

> No matter how much time older schoolchildren spend in front of the television screen, they do not watch everything in succession and (most important of all!) they perceive and evaluate what they have seen and heard each in a different way. Their perceptions are powerfully influenced by the attitudes adopted in the family or in the circle of their closest comrades.[64]

And this must surely be true not only of schoolchildren but of adults as well. The factors involved in long-term political socialization are inevitably complex. It is, however, worth mentioning one unusual Soviet attempt to assess these factors, which was made in a survey of 1,059 people carried out under the auspices of the Komsomol, apparently at some time in the 1960s. Respondents were asked the question: 'Which of the things listed below has most of all influenced the formation of your character?'[65] The replies, in percentages, were as follows:

Preponderant influence	Percentage
The family	63.0
Artistic and political literature	38.1
Teachers	29.8
Comrades at school	29.6
The Komsomol organization	27.8
Domestic films	26.2
The work collective	21.2
Foreign films	12.0
The army	11.2
Work in a [study] circle	8.7
Comrades met out of doors	8.6
Neighbours	2.5

The book which quotes this survey gives no further information about how the respondents were selected. What it does, however, show is that official influences were far from being the major factor in socialization. Study circles (which presumably refer to political education classes) came very low on the list. Foreign films came surprisingly high. One would naturally not wish to lay undue stress on exact percentages. Even so, there is no doubt that by far the most important influence listed was not the school but the family. Indeed, Soviet authors make precisely this point. And it is specifically to the influence of the family that we now turn. This is not, of course, because the Soviet family is all-powerful (indeed its influence on children has been waning in recent years, largely because of the rising divorce rate). But the family has repeatedly been shown to be a major influence in Soviet society; and this fact is of crucial importance in any discussion about the realism or otherwise of planned political socialization from above.

One of the most frequently quoted pieces of Soviet evidence as to the influence of the family comes from a survey first reported in 1977 of 600 children aged 14–16. Half of them were pupils of vocational schools (PTU), mostly boarders. The other half were pupils at day-school. They were asked to indicate to whom they turned for advice on particular problems. Their answers are given in table 3. It will be seen that in no case did the teacher's advice decisively influence the majority of pupils. Moreover among the day-school children, the teacher's influence compared to that of family or friends was particularly low. This may be unremarkable in itself; what, perhaps, was more remarkable was the reaction of the author of the survey who described the findings as unexpected and 'particularly alarming'.[66] But this survey was only one of a number which pointed to the importance of the family in socialization. In another piece of research reported in 1979 a group of teenage children were asked: 'Which of your relatives or of the people close to you do you regard as an authority?' The replies in percentages are shown in table 4. The preponderant role of the Soviet family in socialization was again demonstrated by a local survey (carried out in the Vladimir province between 1976 and 1978 amongst a sample of 959 industrial and agricultural workers). When asked to say in retrospect which social factors they thought had most influenced them, the ranking order of their replies was: family; school; mass media; public organizations or work collectives; colleagues and friends; 'self-education'; and literature and art. At about the same time a questionnaire of students which drew 1,669 replies is also said to have confirmed the prime influence of the family. And, as the authors of the book which gave these findings observed:

These findings are profoundly indicative. Their reliability is authenticated by the fact that these opinions have been given retrospectively and by the fact that the respondents had the opportunity to set the influence of the family alongside that of other factors which formed and developed the personality. At the same time, the respondents

TABLE 3 Relative influence on school pupils of teachers, family and friends (replies %)

Who is your authority when deciding questions to do with:	Mother	Father	Brother/ sister	Friends of same age	Teachers	Older friends	Decide for myself
Study and social activity (i.e. school assignments)	48.0 (63.8)	24.6 (22.5)	26.0 (10.9)	14.6 (21.9)	34.6 (20.6)	15.3 (5.8)	0.6 (4.5)
Choice of friends and relationships with them	36.0 (44.4)	8.6 (16.7)	22.0 (12.2)	19.3 (22.5)	12.0 (1.2)	24.6 (7.0)	2.0 (16.7)
Evaluation of literature and art, television and radio programmes	16.6 (31.6)	14.0 (27.0)	21.3 (10.9)	30.6 (47.0)	36.6 (7.7)	20.0 (9.6)	1.3 (6.4)
Choice of career	46.6 (60.0)	43.3 (37.4)	20.6 (12.9)	12.0 (13.5)	25.3 (5.8)	15.3 (8.3)	2.6 (10.3)

Respondents were allowed to name up to three sources of influence: *Sotsiologicheskiye issledovaniya*, 3 (1977) p. 66. The first figure given in each case is for vocational school pupils; that in parentheses relates to day-school pupils. *Sources*: A. G. Kharchev (ed.), *Sem'ya v sisteme nravstennogo vospitaniya. Aktual' nye problemy vospitaniya podrostkov.* (Moscow, 1979), p. 142. The findings were originally reported by V. G. Alekseyeva in *Sotsiologicheskiye issledovaniya*, 3 (1977), pp. 60, 66.

TABLE 4 *School, family and friends as a source of authority for adolescent children*

	Father/ mother	Brother/ sister	Friend	Teacher	Total
Boys' replies:	51	31	10	8	100
Girls' replies:	58	17	10	15	100

Source: adapted from *Politichskoye samoobrazovanie*, 10 (1979), p. 109 (N. Kasyanov and V. Tokar). No details were given as to the size or social characteristics of the sample. However, in this survey, unlike the ones quoted above, the respondents must have been allowed to choose only one alternative, as shown by the fact that the totals add up to exactly 100. This brings into even sharper relief the relative importance of the various influences. (The questionnaire was also concerned with the relative influence of fathers and mothers, but this has been ignored as irrelevant for our purposes.)

generally link the family with most of their virtues as well as most of their shortcomings.[67]

There are other even more direct ways in which the family affects attitudes and behaviour. Not surprisingly, Soviet sociologists have noted a high correlation between problem families and juvenile delinquency: it has been estimated, for instance, that up to 65 per cent of juvenile first offences are due to abnormal conditions in the family.[68]

With regard, more specifically, to political socialization, Soviet research has increasingly pinpointed the family's role. It has shown, for instance, that a child's political awareness depends to a considerable degree on his or her reading habits, since 'a child obtains a significant proportion of political information from books and newspapers'; but reading habits in childhood, so it has also been shown, depend to a substantial extent on parental encouragement.[69] It has been suggested, on the evidence of children's school essays, that 'the significance [for children] of the events which occur in our country depends on the way the family reacts to these events.'[70] In one reported survey (of which precise details are not available) the question was asked: 'What has most contributed to the formation of your views and convictions?' Most of the respondents attached primary importance to 'discussions in the family of events ... taking place in the world'. It has also been said that 'Older schoolchildren themselves lay great emphasis on the influence of parents on the formation of their views and ideological convictions.'[71] One Soviet specialist on this subject has categorically stated that family influence, despite all other competing forces, 'remains the most important factor in the formation of a child's behaviour and world outlook', mainly because family relationships are 'more emotional by nature than relationships of any other kind (at school, . . . in the factory, amongst friends and so forth)'.[72]

There seems no reason to doubt the authenticity of these findings. They might even appear to be labouring the obvious; they have been quoted simply because they provide empirical confirmation of what many Western social scientists have assumed for many years. It is relevant to compare what has just been quoted with the conclusions – in relation to the world at large – put forward some years ago by Richard Dawson and Kenneth Prewitt in their book *Political Socialization*.[73] Having noted that the family is 'the most important source of primary relationships for most people in all societies' and that it is, in all political systems, 'a key agent through which the political culture is transmitted from one generation to the next',[74] these authors went on to point out one of the fundamental reasons why this was so:

> The relationships and personal ties developed in the family are among the most important and emotionally intense the individual ever develops. Few human relationships match the strength and depth of those between parent and child, and none compete with them during the early years of childhood. How much a person is affected by others depends heavily on the depth of the emotional ties between them. This notion is the key to understanding the particular potency of the family and of other primary relationships. The more intense and emotionally involved the relationship, the more influence it is likely to have on the development of social and political behaviour.[75]

So far as any one clue exists to the 'psychology of indoctrination', this passage probably provides it. It helps, indirectly, to explain why the impersonal or formalized Soviet political education courses are so often ineffectual. Above all, this passage highlights the fundamental psychological difference between the 'teaching' of values and the 'teaching' of such subjects as history or science, which essentially consist merely of imparting information or skills. Indeed, one of the basic shortcomings of the Soviet approach to propaganda, with its 'pedagogical' emphasis, is that it fails to give proper weight to this difference.

None of this is necessarily to say that the Soviet family is a force hostile to the system (of this, more in a moment); or that the Soviet authorities are trying to undermine the family. Earlier Soviet ideas of 'communal upbringing' have been dropped;[76] and today the authorities fully recognize the family's role, especially in view of their anxiety to arrest the fall in the birth-rate. Yet this raises yet another basic question about the realism of planned political socialization, because the family, however well-disposed towards the regime, still possesses a substantial degree of *de facto* autonomy from that regime. Dawson and Prewitt point to the obvious truth that 'the family is beyond the direct control of any centralized agency'; and that one result of the family's role is 'the diffuse and decentralized form that political socialization takes'. 'These factors,' they point out, 'render *much* of the most important socializing experiences free from manipulation by any centralized institutions, political or otherwise.'[77] This remains true, as the authors go on to say, even though the family will to some degree reproduce the values of society at large. These authors finally noted that the apparent Soviet encouragement for the family probably reflected a belief that the latter's political orientations were now 'congruent with the political order'.[78]

Granted, then, that at least one key element in political socialization – namely the family – is free from direct control from above, how can this be squared with talk about the 'management' of public opinion? It does, at all events, point to a flaw in official thinking at the level of theory. But it remains to consider how far family influences do, in practice, run counter to official values in Soviet society.

Some Western Sovietologists in the past appear tacitly to have assumed that the Soviet authorities have, by and large, been successful in neutralizing any resistance by the family. For example, a Sovietologist, writing in the early 1970s, said that, except probably in the case of minority groups, 'One must conclude . . . that the Soviet family tends to support and reinforce the political socialization carried on by the agents of the society and is relatively ineffectual in opposing or resisting such influence.'[79] Yet the real situation appears to be somewhat different. From the authorities' point of view, neutralizing the family would not necessarily help; the family is not only a potential rival but also an indispensable ally in the goal of successful socialization. Without its active assistance, the creation of socially committed and useful citizens is made infinitely harder. The rise in juvenile deliquency in the USSR, to take only one example, has led to calls for stronger rather than weaker parental supervision of children.[80]

It remains to consider how far the Soviet family strengthens or weakens the impact of official *political* ideas. Sometimes it no doubt strengthens them; and at other times it is an obvious impediment, as in the case of dissident, religious or nationalist families.[81] But it is in any case clear that political ideas are to a substantial extent *mediated* through the family. A Soviet educational specialist once illustrated this by quoting from an essay by a teenage schoolchild, who described how deeply impressed she was by the annual celebration of Victory Day (on 9 May) because of what she heard from her grandfather, a war veteran with military decorations.[82] A rather different example comes from an account in a more recent Soviet book on the impact of Western broadcasts on the Soviet home. Surveys, according to this book 'show . . . that members of the family take an active interest in domestic and international events, that they get information from the foreign mass media and discuss it.' But such discussions may take different forms:

> When asked ... which opinions carried the most authority in the family when assessing Western broadcasts, older schoolchildren gave such answers as the following: 'After an argument, everyone sticks to his own opinion'; or 'It all depends, sometimes it's my parents' opinion, sometimes it's my own opinion [which prevails]'; or 'My parents argue but I keep silent'; 'My father's opinion usually wins, it's always well-founded'; 'We read different journals and newspapers because our interests hardly coincide. We don't listen to the radio as a family.'

And the book then goes on to express concern that:

> Parents do not set themselves the conscious aim of inculcating an irreconcilable attitude towards bourgeois ideology and propaganda. Moreover, many adults have no idea of what forms or methods to use in such work, and think this is basically the business of the school.[83]

It does not, of course, follow that the Soviet family is necessarily an influence working against the system. But it is equally obvious that parents are not simply agents of the party's propaganda network. (It would be most surprising if they were.) There is not a great deal of empirical evidence about the family's political role. In the past, Soviet writers have often complained that parents give their children too *little* instruction in politics. Thus, according to *Pravda* in the late 1960s: 'Few fathers and only some mothers talk with their children on civic themes, apparently believing that our Soviet reality itself moulds one's communist world view.'[84] In a similar vein a Soviet book of 1984 remarked: 'As a rule, parents seldom talk to children on political topics.'[85] Sociological research concerning the attitudes of parents towards their children's activities in the Komsomol points in the same direction. According to one such study, the parents of younger pupils – up to the fifth class, that is, up to the age of about 12 – do generally work with the school in encouraging their children's participation in the 'Pioneers' (the organization immediately junior to the Komsomol). But after the child reaches the age of 12, 'the picture sharply alters'. Parents then become mainly concerned with their children's behaviour and educational progress and sometimes regard political assignments at school as a hindrance to study. One survey of schoolchildren in the ninth and tenth classes (aged 15 and 16) discovered that a child's Komsomol activity was seldom discussed at home; it came bottom of a list of 15 topics said

TABLE 5 *Political discussions between parents and children*

	Moscow		Vilnius		Baku	
	Mother	Father	Mother	Father	Mother	Father
Children discuss with:	28.7	55	26	52.4	23.6	51.8

Source: Vadim Titarenko, *Sem'ya i formirovanie lichnosti* (Moscow 1987), p. 297.

to have been discussed between parents and children.[86] Another survey of 240 older schoolchildren found that as many as 135 (that is, 56.2 per cent of the sample) did not know whether their own parents had ever belonged to the Komsomol.[87] Absence of family opposition to the system does not therefore mean that the family militantly propagates official values. One further indication of this is to be found in a book of 1979 about atheist education in the school. It remarks that this may be hampered not only by religious influences in the home but also by 'another category of parents who, whilst holding non-religious views, do not understand the harm caused by religion and are therefore indifferent to both religious and atheist propaganda. Their indifference is transmitted to their children.'[88]

The evidence just quoted may suggest that Soviet parents tend not to discuss politics with their children. But there is also evidence pointing in the opposite direction. A book published in Moscow in 1987 quoted the results of sociological surveys carried out in Moscow, Vilnius (the capital of the Soviet Baltic republic of Lithuania) and Baku (capital of the Soviet republic of Azerbaijan in the Caucasus). A question as to how many children discussed political events with their parents produced answers (in percentages) given in table 5. All these data tend to confirm the (in any case self-evident) proposition that the family – in the USSR as elsewhere – does have a key role in political socialization. Its influence helps to explain why official values are sometimes transmitted from one generation to the next and are at other times ignored or neutralized. But it would surely be wrong, in any case, to portray the Soviet family as nothing more than an agency of indifference or passive resistance. There are signs that parents do sometimes forcefully assert their own autonomous views. Thus in 1984 a parent who was a qualified psychologist wrote to the Moscow *Literaturnaya gazeta* to complain that her son was losing marks at school for originality and referring to a 'hidden rivalry' between parent and teacher.[89] Such public complaints from parents may be exceptional. But in the same year a *Pravda* article described how, at a parent–teacher day in a Moscow school, the parents on hearing that a lecture was about to be delivered 'on the upbringing of children in the family', immediately left. As the author of the article remarked: 'I shall never forget this because ... I was the lecturer the parents were running away from.' He went on to refer to research which showed, he said, that 'even the most successful lectures and seminars bring practically no improvement at all to the way children are actually brought up.'[90]

The late 1970s saw the very modest start of a new approach to family problems: the creation, mainly it seems on volunteer initiative, of a new 'Family Service' to give psychologically qualified advice about conflicts in marriage and in the home. In 1980 a group – of only nine staff – began to work in Moscow. It was reported that one of its guidelines in work was to 'avoid giving direct advice'.[91] The approach seems to make sense, and it deserves to be put on the record – because it was so utterly at odds with the traditional practice of the Soviet propaganda system.

The autonomous audience

Throughout this book we have been concerned, not primarily with the attitude of the Soviet public towards its government (important as that is), but with the realism or otherwise of the traditional Soviet approach to propaganda. These two issues, even though partly connected, need to be kept separate. There are indications, as we have seen, that official and unofficial opinions in the Soviet Union are to a significant extent in accord with each other: this is probably true, for example, with regard to nuclear arms control, the fear of China in the 1960s and 1970s, the maintenance of full employment and adequate welfare provisions at home and also, so it seems, with regard to support for 'collectivism'.[92] It would in any case be a fallacy to argue that if or insofar as the Soviet public supports its government, this must necessarily be the result of propaganda. Other factors may be far more important. But we have also seen that public opinion – in the Soviet Union as in other societies – must inevitably be shaped to a considerable degree by factors over which the authorities can have no direct control – such as the family, informal groups, and the personal experience and preferences of the individual citizen. If that is indeed so, then any official theory about the 'management' of public opinion from above is not only unrealistic, but inherently so. That is not to deny that propaganda and censorship sometimes have a major influence. But influence and control are two very different things. Perhaps the only successful strategy for the 'management' of opinion is for government to change the environment to satisfy the citizen's wishes, instead of simply trying to shape those wishes.

It would, furthermore, be wrong when discussing the role of the family or informal groups to portray the individual citizen as a purely passive entity torn this way and that by various pressures. Soviet sources contain impressive evidence that the citizen in the USSR is to a considerable extent autonomous in his or her judgements, and capable of initiative. The flourishing of the 'black economy', as well as the extent of listening to foreign broadcasts, are well-attested examples of personal initiative. The truth seems to be not that the Soviet system always stifles initiative, as is so often assumed, but that it has frequently failed to channel personal initiative along socially useful lines. And this is one of the basic problems which the Gorbachev reforms are trying to tackle.

Evidence that the Soviet citizen has a mind of his own was noted in a Soviet book of 1981 which said that, as a result of media research, 'Journalists discovered that the reader or viewer is not just a passive consumer of information, but is active in the way he makes his choices: that he often displays a 'recalcitrant' nature and quite often has no liking at all for what journalists think important.'[93]

Meanwhile, the autonomy of the Soviet citizen has been further assisted in recent decades by two social changes, both of long-term importance. The first was that in the USSR, as elsewhere in the world, television vastly expanded and by 1984 was said to be available to 95 per cent of Soviet families.[94] Many Soviet citizens were, naturally enough, unenthusiastic about attending political lectures when they could follow the news through television at home.[95] Indeed, in 1984 a survey of schoolchildren in the Moscow area reported that 85 per cent followed events through television, whilst only 14.8 per cent found political study sessions at school interesting.[96]

A second and no less important change in the Brezhnev years was the growth of education, which, whatever its problems, was a solid achievement. Ten-year education became compulsory in the 1970s; whereas in the mid-fifties it embraced only 40 per cent of school-leavers.[97]

There can be no doubt that Western broadcasts beamed to the Soviet Union were also a factor in affecting audience attitudes. But it was the authorities themselves who helped to produce a growing body of better educated and therefore more critical citizens. And this, rather paradoxically, created a new challenge to the traditional propaganda system – as was being pointed out as far back as 1974:

Being a propagandist in present-day conditions has become immeasurably more difficult than it was, say, 15–20 years ago [that is, in the 1950s]. The propagandist used, as a rule, to be a good deal more erudite than his audience; he was often in the position of having a monopoly of information. The changed social situation, the general educational, political and cultural level of the working people, the new aspects of the ideological struggle on the international arena, the rapid growth of the material and technical opportunities for education (the mass information media) substantially alter the demands made on the propagandist in present-day conditions.[98]

Borrowing from Soviet terminology, one is tempted to describe the problem as a 'contradiction' between the primitive political education system and the growing knowledge of the Soviet public.

Notes

1   B. A. Grushin and L. A. Onikov (eds), *Massovaya informatsiya v sovetskom promyshlennom gorode* (Moscow, 1980), p. 282.
2   A. A. Tarasenko, *Obshchestvennoye mnenie i povedenie lichnosti* (Minsk, 1975), pp. 131, 132.
3   V. K. Paderin, *Obshchestvennoye mnenie v razvitom sotsialisticheskom obshchestve: sushchnost' i zakonomernosti formirovaniya* (Kazan', 1980), pp. 58, 59.
4   See Stephen White, *Political Culture and Soviet Politics* (Macmillan, London, 1979), esp. ch. 6.
5   V. S. Korobeinikov (ed.), *Sotsiologicheskie problemy obshchestvennogo mneniya i deyatel'nosti sredstv massovoi informatsii* (Moscow, 1979), p. 19. Fuller details of these results can be found in Angus Roxburgh, *Pravda: Inside the Soviet News Machine* (Gollancz, London, 1987), p. 279.
6   For further details, see White, *Political Culture*, ch. 6.
7   M. F. Nenashev, *Ideino-vospitatel'naya rabota KPSS* (Moscow, 1980), p. 78.
8   Grushin and Onikov, *Massovaya informatsiya*, p. 250.
9   G. P. Davidyuk and V. S. Korobeinikov (eds), *Effektivnost' sredstv massovoi informatsii* (Minsk, 1986), p. 77.
10 See R. Eugene Parta, 'Soviet Area Audience and Opinion Research (SAAOR) at Radio Free Europe/Radio Liberty' in K. R. M. Short (ed.), *Western Broadcasting over the Iron Curtain* (Croom Helm, London, 1986), pp. 227ff.
11 See Radio Liberty Soviet Area Audience Research and Program Evaluation, 'Samizdat, the Soviet public, and Western radio', Analysis Report 9–77, esp. p. 14. Amongst an estimated 43.8 per cent of the Soviet population who had heard of *samizdat*, 24.5 per cent were reported to be favourable towards it, but only 8.6 per cent strongly favourable. But these favourable responses were more than offset by reactions of the opposite kind. Amongst those who were aware of *samizdat*, 38.2 per cent had an unfavourable attitude, of which 25 per cent were strongly unfavourable. The proportion of favourable attitudes was, in general, highest amongst the under-thirties age group and amongst the most highly educated. Favourable responses exceeded unfavourable ones in four regions: Leningrad, Moscow, the Baltic states and the Caucasus. In

no case, however, did positive reactions to *samizdat* amount to an absolute majority of the sample.

12 See Parta, in Short, *Western Broadcasting*, p. 233, quoting SAAOR Analysis Report 6–84 'Civil liberties and the Soviet citizen: attitudinal types and Western radio listening', issued in September 1984. The report tentatively estimated that amongst this sample attitudes towards civil liberty broke down as follows: liberal 13 per cent; 'moderates' 29 per cent; conservative 28 per cent; hardline 12 per cent; indifferent or uninterested 19 per cent.

13 David Shipler, 'The view from America', *New York Times Magazine*, 10 November 1985, pp. 33ff, esp. p. 82.

14 Viktor Zaslavsky, *The Neo-Stalinist State: Class, Ethnicity and Consensus in Soviet Society* (Harvester, Brighton, 1982), p. 10.

15 See Martin Walker, 'One step back to Stalin', *Guardian*, 21 December 1984.

16 G. L. Smirnov et al. (eds), *Voprosy teorii i praktiki partiinoi propagandy* (Moscow, 1971), p. 243.

17 *PS*, 6 (1970), p. 97 (N. Klepach).

18 See the resolution 'On the further improvement of ideological, political-educational work', summarized in *Pravda*, 6 May 1979, pp. 1ff.

19 *Pravda*, 15 June 1983, p. 3.

20 See P. K. Kurochkin et al. (eds), *Kommunisticheskya propaganda: voprosy teorii i metodiki* (Moscow, 1974), p. 124.

21 N. S. Nazarova, *Formirovanie kommunisticheskoi ubezhdyonnosti molodyozhi* (Kiev/ Odessa, 1981), p. 62.

22 Nenashev, *Ideino-vospitatel'naya rabota KPSS*, p. 102, where it is also stated that 7.5 per cent of the sample mentioned 'the authoritative vocation of a lecturer' as one source of job satisfaction, whilst 1.1 per cent mentioned the lecturer's remuneration as an incentive.

23 Ibid., p. 103. In the survey there quoted, 21.6 per cent mentioned the burden of other public assignments as a handicap to their lecturing work, whilst 37.4 per cent mentioned as a hindrance the burden of their main job. See also White, *Political Culture*, ch. 6, pp. 132–3.

24 See *Pravda*, 23 June 1978 (leading article); see also, 'The manager makes a report' ibid., 26 November 1979, p. 2, which criticizes those managers who think that their sole function is to manage and that propaganda should be left to 'ideological workers'.

25 *Pravda*, 26 November 1979 (n. 24); see also 'What will you say, comrade propagandist?', ibid., 5 April 1980, p. 2; and 'Today there is a lecture', ibid., 15 April 1980, p. 3, where a lecturer was criticized for simply reading aloud a 20-page mimeographed lecture distributed by the local party committee.

26 Ibid., 5 April 1980: 'What will you say?'

27 See E. M. Tyazhel'nikov (ed.), *Za vysokoye kachestvo i deistvennost' ideologicheskoi raboty. Materialy vsesoyuznogo seminara-soveshchaniya ideologicheskikh rabotnikov. Moskva 20–5 aprelya 1981 g.* (Moscow, 1981), p. 81 (M. V. Zimyanin).

28 A. K. Uledov et al. (eds), *Obshchestvennoye mnenie i propaganda* (Moscow, 1980), pp. 130–1.

29 See V. K. Egorov (ed.), *Iskusstvo vospitaniya* (Moscow, 1981), pp. 142–4 (V. A. Titov).

30 L. P. Buyeva, *Sotsial'naya sreda i soznanie lichnosti* (Moscow, 1968), p. 132, quoted in Paderin, *Obshchestvennoye mnenie*, p. 34.

31 This was shown by the enactment during the Andropov period of a series of measures to tighten up labour discipline, the most important of which were published in *Pravda* on 7 August 1983.

32 *Pravda*, 22 June 1978, p. 3.

33 *Pravda*, 10 September 1979, p. 3. The size of the factory's work-force was given in ibid., 12 September 1981, p. 4.

34 Ibid., 21 December 1979, p. 3.

35 A. S. Zakalin, *Sotsial'naya mikrosreda i organizatsiya ideologicheskoi raboty* (Moscow, 1984), pp. 34–6.

36 See *Sotsiologicheskie issledovaniya*, 4 (1984), p. 6, which also stated that the total labour-force in the USSR numbered 129 million people.

37 T. N. Mal'kovskaya, 'The spiritual interests of older schoolchildren', *Chelovek i obshchestvo*, 6 (Leningrad, 1969), pp. 89, 95, 96.

38 V. G. Alekseyeva, 'Informal adolescent groups in urban conditions', *Sotsiologicheski issledovaniya* 3 (1977), pp. 61–2.

39 I. S. Kon, *Psikhologiya yunesheskogo vozrasta* (Moscow, 1979), p. 95.

40 Ibid., p. 102.

41 See Urie Bronfenbrenner, *Two Worlds of Childhood: US and USSR*, (Allen & Unwin, London, 1971). The author outlines the school authorities' use of peer group pressure as a method of maintaining discipline (see esp. pp. 51–69) and suggests (p. 90) that Soviet children of the future will continue to be more conforming than those of the United States.

42 Kon, *Psikhologiya yunesheskogo vozrasta*, p. 103, quotes Soviet research indicating that among schoolchildren aged 15 and over, 'the higher the . . . status of the young person in the spontaneous group, the lower it is in the official class collective.' See also Hedrick Smith, *The Russians* (Sphere Books, London, 1976), p. 205. The author, who was Moscow correspondent of the *New York Times* in the 1970s and sent his own children to a Soviet school, came to the conclusion that most children aged over 11 or 12 refused to inform on their class-mates to their teacher.

43 Jerome Gilison, *British and Soviet Politics: A Study of Legitimacy and Convergence* (Johns Hopkins Press, Baltimore, 1972), pp. 175–6.

44 *LG*, 2 July 1986, p. 3.

45 Ibid., 14 May 1986, p. 2.

46 Ibid., 22 January 1986, p. 10.

47 See, most notably, Alex Inkeles and Raymond A. Bauer, *The Soviet Citizen*, (Harvard University Press, Cambridge, Mass., and Oxford University Press, London, 1959), esp. pp. 159–88. See also Gayle Durham Hollander, *Soviet Political Indoctrination: Developments in Mass Media and Propaganda since Stalin* (Praeger, New York, 1972), pp. 181–2.

48 *Zhurnalist*, 6 (1970), p. 19 (Vladimir Derevitskii).

49 *LG*, 5 December 1979, p. 11.
50 Ibid., 20 October 1982, p. 13.
51 *Pravda*, 16 October 1979, p. 2.
52 V. S. Korobeinikov (ed.), *Pressa i obshchestvennoye mnenie* (Moscow, 1986), p. 157.
53 V. A. Losenkov, *Sotsial'naya informatsiya v zhizni gorodskogo naseleniya* (Leningrad, 1983), p. 8.
54 Ibid., p. 79–81.
55 Ibid., pp. 74, 95–6.
56 Ibid., p. 73.
57 Ibid., p. 87.
58 See Parta, 'SAAOR at Radio Free Europe/Radio Liberty', in Short, *Western Broadcasting*, p. 231.
59 These figures are taken from Ellen Propper Mickiewicz, *Media and the Russian Public* (Praeger, New York, 1981), p. 142, quoting Radio Liberty Soviet Area Audience Research and Program Evaluation, 'Soviet audience to Western radio', Analysis Report 2–79, pp. 4–5.
60 N. S. Nazarova, *Formirovanie kommunisticheskoi ubezhdyonnosti molodyozhi* (Kiev/Odessa, 1981). The figures on students and foreign radio are on p. 119.
61 Ibid., p. 65.
62 Ibid., pp. 65–6.
63 It has been said that 'the closer one observes the workings of the mass media, the more it turns out that their effects depend on a complex network of specialized personal and social influences': see Paul F. Lazarsfeld and Herbert Menzel, 'Mass media and personal influence', in Wilbur Schramm (ed.), *The Science of Human Communication* (Basic Books, New York, 1963), p. 95.
64 I. S. Kon, *Psikhologiya starsheklassnika* (Moscow, 1980), p. 177.
65 Yu. V. Sychev, *Mikrosreda i lichnost'* (Moscow, 1974), p. 151.
66 *Sotsiologicheskie issledovaniya*, 3 (1977), p. 66 (V. G. Alekseyeva).
67 *Sem'ya i obshchestvo* (Moscow, 1982), pp. 17–18.
68 See Zh. T. Toshchenko et al. (eds), *Teoriya i praktika kommunisticheskogo vospitaniya* (Moscow, 1980), p. 157, quoting N. Belyayev, *Pravda*, 25 January 1979.
69 See *Sovmestnaya rabota shkoly, sem'yi i obshchestvennosti po vospitaniyu u uchashchikhsya kachestv grazhdanina v svete reshenii XXV s"yezda KPSS* (Moscow, 1977), pp. 61ff. (T. P. Lausova), where it is stated that about 90 per cent of schoolchildren with a high standard of social-political awareness have an active attitude towards reading; whilst over 92 per cent of children with a developed interest in reading come from families whose parents 'devote a great deal of attention' to developing their children's interest in reading.
70 Ibid., p. 135 (T. K. Zaichikova).
71 A. G. Khripkova et al. (eds), *Vzaimodeistvie shkoly, sem'yi, obshchestvennosti v kommunisticheskom vospitanii* (Moscow, 1978), pp. 34–5.
72 *Sovmestnaya rabota*, pp. 128–9 (V. I. Sikorova). This finding was based on a comparative survey by the author of 250 adolescents in Leningrad, drawn

from both stable and maladjusted families.

73 Richard E. Dawson and Kenneth Prewitt, *Political Socialization* (Little, Brown, Boston, 1969).

74 Ibid., pp. 106, 107.

75 Ibid., p. 108.

76 Already in the early 1960s, the idea of 'communal upbringing' was attacked in the Soviet press: see Bronfenbrenner, *Two Worlds of Childhood*, pp. 82–4.

77 Dawson and Prewitt, *Political Socialization*, p. 122.

78 Ibid., p. 126.

79 Gayle Durham Hollander, *Soviet Political Indoctrination*, p. 11.

80 See, e.g. Toshchenko et al., *Teoriya i praktika kommunisticheskogo vospitaniya*, p. 258, which notes that working mothers do not have enough time to devote to the family and suggests that part of the solution probably lies in 'greater responsibility of the father for the upbringing of the children'. See also N. G. Yurkevich, A. G. Kharchev et al. (eds), *Sem'ya v sisteme nravstennogo vospitaniya. Aktual'nye problemy vospitaniya podrostkov* (Moscow, 1979), p. 177. Yurkevich emphasizes the 'decisive importance' for adolescent behaviour of the family structure (i.e. whether the family has two parents or only one), the 'personal qualities' of the parents, their degree of contact with the adolescent and 'the presence or absence of supervision' by them over the child.

81 See, e.g. T. N. Mal'kovskaya (ed.), *Aktual'nye problemy kommunisticheskogo vospitaniya shkol'nikov* (Moscow, 1980), p. 76, which states that 'the surmounting of nationalist survivals among pupils, and especially among their parents, is a difficult and complex task.'

82 *Sovmestnaya rabota* pp. 135–6 (T. K. Zaichikova).

83 I. F. Vydrin and S. V. Myagchenkov (eds), *Vospitaniye u shkol'nikov neprimirimosti k burzhuaznoi ideologii i propagande* (Moscow, 1985), p. 53.

84 *Pravda*, 2 February 1969, quoted in Gayle Durham Hollander, *Soviet Political Indoctrination*, p. 11.

85 Zakalin, *Sotsial'naya mikrosreda*, p. 65.

86 Khripkova et al., *Vzaimodeistvie shkoly*, p. 23.

87 *Sovmestnaya rabota*, p. 163 (F. Fonotova).

88 R. M. Rogovaya (ed.), *Ateisticheskoye vospitaniye v shkole. Voprosy teorii i praktiki* (Moscow, 1979), p. 140.

89 *LG*, 22 February 1984, p. 11.

90 *Pravda*, 31 July 1984, p. 6 (S. Soloveychik, 'The parents fled from the lessons').

91 *LG*, 5 August 1981, p. 13 (Lidia Grafova).

92 Soviet unofficial attitudes are discussed in Stephen White, *Political Culture*, esp. ch. 8, pp. 185–8; and in his article 'Continuity and change in Soviet political culture: an émigré study', *Comparative Political Studies*, 11 (1978), pp. 381–95. See, for a more recent study of this subject, James R. Millar (ed.) *Politics, Work and Daily Life in the USSR: a Survey of Former Soviet Citizens* (Cambridge University Press, 1987).

93 See E. P Prokhorov (ed.), *Sotsiologiya zhurnalistiki* (Moscow, 1981), p. 14.

94 *LG*, 23 May 1984, p. 11.

95 Cf. *Pravda*, 26 March 1973, p. 2, where a geophysicist with higher education wrote to question the value of political information sessions intended for an already well-informed audience, noting that 'Naturally not everyone willingly attends such functions.' The paper rejected his argument, partly on the ground that these meetings helped people 'to get their bearings in the situation'.
96 *Sotsologicheskie issledovaniya*, 2 (1984), p. 82.
97 *Pravda*, 14 August 1982, p. 3 (B. Stukalin). See also L. M. Voladarskii (ed.), *Naselenie SSSR, Spravochnik* (Moscow, 1983), p. 115, which records that between 1959 and 1982 the number of people with a completed higher education rose from 3.8 million to 17 million, a more than fourfold increase.
98 See Kurochkin et al., *Kommunisticheskaya propaganda*, pp. 120–1.

7

Persuasion, Soviet Politics and East–West Relations

Let us re-examine our attitude toward the cold war, remembering that we are not engaged in a debate, seeking to pile up debating points ... We must, therefore, persevere in the search for peace in the hope that constructive changes within the Communist bloc might bring within reach solutions which now seem beyond us.

> Address by John F. Kennedy, 'Towards a Strategy of Peace', June 1963

If we are talking about deficits in modern civilization, there are many of them. But the greatest is the deficit of new thinking.

> Mikhail Gorbachev, October 1986; printed in *LG*, 5 November 1986

At the start of this book, we explained its purpose as being to examine the Soviet approach to method in relation to persuasion, and also to explore the wider issue of the relation between the nature of Soviet beliefs and the nature of persuasion. It only remains to gather the threads of the argument together and briefly to consider the more general implications and lessons which have a wider importance – for Soviet politics as a whole, for the understanding of persuasion and public opinion in general, and for East–West relations. It is to these topics that we now turn.

Propaganda, public opinion and Soviet politics

In the past, the control of public opinion was widely assumed – both by Soviet communists and by anti-communists – to play a key role in the Soviet political system. It is not hard to see how this notion gained acceptance in the West. What appears to have happened is that (1) the Soviet system was portrayed in the West, for most of the period since 1917, in overwhelmingly unattractive terms, whilst (2) that system did not seem to be based on force alone and apparently faced no widespread domestic opposition. Therefore (3) it seemed plausible to assume that the Soviet authorities had indeed evolved some method of opinion control based on psychological manipulation. Added to all this was (4) the undoubted fact that the Soviet Communist Party has always devoted an enormous amount of energy to propaganda, which is a vast and highly organized activity in the USSR. Finally (5) there was the traditional 'Iron Curtain' mentality of the Soviet authorities who, particularly in the past, sometimes went to extreme lengths to prevent contacts between their own citizens and foreigners. From all this it might have seemed to follow not only that propaganda and censorship were vital to the stability of the Soviet system, but also that if that system were exposed to competing ideas from the outside world, it could be fatally weakened.

This picture of a 'propaganda state' was often only implicit. But it seems to have had a pervasive influence on many people in the West (as well as on Soviet ideologues, though for different reasons). It would naturally be wrong to dismiss these assumptions as totally groundless. Yet at the same time they need to be looked at a little more closely – both for academic and for practical political reasons.

Just how important, then, are propaganda and secrecy to the stability of the Soviet system? One cannot be absolutely sure. But the question should at least be asked because, as already noted, the USSR particularly in the 1970s did become *de facto* a considerably more open society. Closely guarded state secrets – whether about agriculture or about the siting of nuclear missiles – became the property of the outside world, thanks largely to American spy satellites. Foreign travel became less of a rarity for Soviet citizens. And it may not be as much of a threat to the system as is sometimes thought – because Soviet citizens, even if sometimes impressed by Western living standards, may be less impressed by Western political ideas, as we saw in the last chapter. Moreover, foreign broadcasts beamed to the USSR could be widely heard in spite of jamming. In 1982, according to one Soviet writer, there were at least 40 million short-wave radio sets in the country, which would be enough in itself to create a mass audience for foreign radio.[1] Over and above that, the Soviet authorities in 1987 suspended (or ended) the jamming of (often highly critical) broadcasts in Russian by the BBC and Voice of America; and in 1988 they also stopped jamming Radio Liberty.[2] They would hardly have done so had they believed that foreign ideas seriously threatened the stability of the system.

The question then arises: what are the other sources of stability in the

Soviet system, unconnected with propaganda? It is notorious, of course, that authoritarian regimes can sometimes survive for long periods without the support of public opinion. The history of the Warsaw Pact countries in Eastern Europe is a well-known example. Soviet-style propaganda methods manifestly failed to shape public opinion which, during some periods at least, was influenced to a far greater degree by broadcasts from the West. True, this created serious difficulties for the governments concerned; and anti-regime sentiment in Eastern Europe is bound to be a matter of serious concern to Moscow. But Western broadcasts – whatever their value or impact – did not prevent the regimes of Eastern Europe from surviving. Perhaps the most striking case in point is that of the German Democratic Republic, which has achieved a degree of stability and a respectable economic performance. Whatever the reason, it cannot be the result of official propaganda – because most East Germans for at least a generation have chosen to watch West German television in preference to the television provided by their own government.

One might be tempted to explain all this simply by reference to foreign (that is, Soviet) domination or to sheer armed force. Both are obviously important; but one may doubt if they fully explain why authoritarian regimes stay in power. Foreign domination cannot account for the survival of the Greek military dictatorship for seven years, between 1967 and 1974, nor for the survival after the 1940s of the communist regime in neighbouring Albania; nor for the long life of the Franco regime in Spain (which in its later years was remarkably open to contact with the outside world and did not rely on extreme repression, even though it clearly lacked popular support). So far as Russia is concerned, foreign domination is not a factor. Armed force may explain how the Bolsheviks retained power after the revolution, but even this is not quite the whole story. Sheer physical force can explain the power of the Soviet armed forces and secret police, but it obviously cannot explain how they in turn came to be so completely under the control of one man, namely Stalin.

All this highlights one further key element in the power-base of a dictatorship; the physical control of communications. A regime which controls the radio, television and press, and which can intercept telephone calls and letters and can keep its citizens under surveillance, has an overwhelming advantage in neutralizing opposition because *it can prevent its potential opponents from organizing*. This is in no sense a uniquely communist weapon. It is no coincidence that military coups, when they occur, almost always begin with the rebel seizure of the local broadcasting station. It is equally significant that when the Jaruzelski government imposed martial law in Poland on 13 December 1981, it immediately paralysed opposition by banning all inter-urban telephone calls as well as suspending contact with the outside world.[3] This illustrates the close link which exists between the control of communications and the exercise of power. But it has to be emphasized that the control of communications in this sense has *no* necessary connection with opinion control or indoctrination. Indoctrination played no part whatever in the consolidation of the Jaruzelski regime. And similarly, Stalin's total power over the Soviet armed forces and secret police rested neither on mere persuasion nor on physical force. It relied on a system of surveillance which prevented potential conspirators from organizing. The result was that no individual would have been able to make the first move against the dictator, because to do so would have been too risky.[4]

When considering sources of stability, there is a further more general factor to be remembered: the difficulty, in any society, of actually carrying out a revolution. That is to say, it would be very hard to overthrow not just the Soviet, but the British, French or American political systems. Professsor John Kenneth Galbraith once pointed out that successful revolutions require determined leaders and disciplined followers (neither of which are usually found in practice). And victory is only possible over an already weak regime: 'All successful revolutions,' as he said, 'are the kicking in of a rotten door.' Therefore, he implied, stability is something much harder to shake than might at first appear: 'The word revolution comes easily to the tongue; revolutions are always being threatened. If we knew how hard it is to have one, we might use the word less, and conservatives might fret less about the danger. They are far, far, safer than they know.'[5]

We have so far, when discussing stability, assumed a regime exercising power over an alienated, indifferent or hostile public. Amongst Russia's allies in Eastern Europe this may sometimes reflect the true state of affairs. But, as explained in the previous chapter, one cannot assume the same thing with regard to the Soviet public itself. There are a number of ways in which Soviet official and unofficial opinion coincides, which probably have nothing to do with propaganda. For one thing, some (although not of course all) ordinary Russians may take pride in what they see as Soviet achievements, especially in the Second World War. And the acceptance by many Russians of authoritarian rule cannot be accounted for merely in terms of the Russian psyche or Russian history. It stems from problems which lie not just in the past but in the present. Economic reform based on greater decentralization and greater personal initiative could, for many people, have painful side-effects, including unemployment and inflation. Another problem which exists very much in the present arises, of course, from the multi-ethnic nature of the USSR. She is the only major power in the world where the main ethnic group constitutes no more than about half the country's total population. Political liberalization entails at least the potential danger of the country's being dismembered – supposing that the various non-Russian republics demanded to secede, as they are theoretically entitled to do under the 1977 Soviet Constitution (article 72). Even this would not resolve the nationalities problem because, partly as a result of the extensive migration within the USSR, all the republics contain ethnically mixed populations and it would therefore be quite impossible to redraw national boundaries along ethnic lines. (The crisis which erupted in 1988 over the province of Nagornyi Karabakh highlighted this problem.) One cannot in any case assume that the mass of ordinary Russians would be willing passively to accept the disintegration of their state. It follows that there is a potential price to pay for liberalization. Dilemmas exist – but they exist not only for the leadership but for the public as well. And it would therefore be wrong to portray the Soviet government and public as having diametrically opposed interests.

For all these reasons, it is possible to account for much of the stability of the Soviet system on the basis of factors which have nothing directly to do with propaganda or secrecy. This is naturally not intended to imply that propaganda and secrecy have played no part in the Soviet system's survival. A totally uncontrolled press – almost unknown in Russian history – would naturally have unpredictable consequences. And the effect of the system's traditional media controls must have been enormous. Misleading information will have been widely believed, especially where it did not run counter to the personal experience or personal sympathies of the audience. Vast areas of ignorance will have been artificially created – on subjects ranging from American living standards to the history of Stalin's purges. The highly organized network of propaganda and censorship will have had a powerful negative effect – in preventing opposition ideas from crystallizing and thus in keeping public opinion in a kind of limbo.

A critic of this book might object that it had given too little prominence to the purely coercive (or, in the past, terroristic) aspects of Soviet rule; and that only if these things are experienced can anyone fully appreciate the impact which official propaganda must have made. But such criticism would arise from misunderstanding. It is no part of the present argument to minimize the role of coercion in the recent Soviet past, or of terror in the more distant past. The question is not whether coercion existed, but how far if at all it served as an instrument of positive indoctrination. It is precisely here, according to our argument, that theories of 'brainwashing' become implausible. No doubt, the overwhelming power of the Soviet state over its citizens will tend to induce a certain conformism. But it is unlikely, taken on its own, to produce the kind of stable political beliefs which the authorities say they want. Indeed the evidence points in the opposite direction. The use of massive coercion in Eastern Europe during the last years of Stalin's life not only failed to mould public opinion, but alienated even the minority which had originally been sympathetic to the Soviet Union.

For all the reasons presented in this book, our conclusion about Soviet propaganda of the traditional kind is that, whatever successes it may have had, it was nevertheless based on a flawed theory – which consistently overrated the role of organization, whilst neglecting the role of psychology. The Soviet system may indeed enjoy significant popular acceptance for reasons already mentioned. But public support for a system is determined far more by the system's performance – particularly over the economy – than by propaganda from above. No doubt the concern with organization is important in a negative sense – when it involves depriving opponents of the right to organize. However, the notion of 'scientific management' of public opinion is – like the notion of 'thought control' – dubious in the extreme. There is no visible basis in common sense for the idea that the constant exposure of an audience to an unsolicited message will of necessity win that audience over; and the Soviet findings quoted in chapters 5 and 6 all tend to confirm this common sense view. Taken as a whole, propaganda and censorship in the Soviet Union seem to have been more effective in a negative than in a positive sense. Paradoxically, they represented far *more* than the Communist Party needed in order to remain in power, but far *less* than it needed in order to win hearts and minds. This is the incongruous feature. And it is precisely this 'overkill' approach which provides one of the main clues to the faulty rationale of traditional Soviet thinking about propaganda.

Given the irrational elements in the propaganda system, why did it survive so long and why, under Brezhnev, was it even expanded? There may be several reasons. For one thing, the weakness of the traditional thinking may not have been apparent to the leaders; and may have been largely camouflaged owing to the fact that the regime (as we have just argued) owes much of its stability to quite different factors. Another explanation may have had to do with bureaucracy – a long-recognized evil of Soviet (and, indeed, of earlier Russian) society which was attacked with renewed vigour after Gorbachev came to power. Bureaucracies are notoriously resistant to change and have often helped to perpetuate systems in which no one any longer has any genuine belief. The vast bureaucracy associated with Soviet propaganda is probably no exception. Finally, when seeking to explain why outdated approaches to this subject survived, one has to bear in mind Soviet neglect of psychology, to which we shall return shortly.

If the above analysis is correct, then propaganda and secrecy are less essential to the Soviet system than might at first appear and have a role different from what the leadership intends. But this leads on to the related question: what independent influence, if any, is exercised within the system by Soviet public opinion? How far is it valid to assume – as Soviet leaders have done implicitly and Western observers have done explicitly – that the political system in the USSR does not in fact need the support of public opinion?

One can understand what is meant by this claim. The Soviet government did not, certainly up to the late 1980s, depend on the *electoral* support of public opinion. There was never any opportunity for Soviet voters to dismiss their leaders. Nor, for the reasons just given, is there any probability of the system being overthrown by force. It is true that, within certain limits, the system has always sought to encourage 'criticism from below' and that the volume of suggestions and complaints from ordinary citizens apparently grew during the Brezhnev period.[6] But the complaints system was subject to a number of drawbacks; and in any case it did not touch on major political issues.

Does it therefore follow that power in the USSR flowed in one direction only – from the top downwards? Is it true that Soviet public opinion had no way of asserting itself except through the ballot-box or through revolution? And could the Soviet leaders ignore their own public opinion with impunity? These questions have had less attention in the past than they deserve. But they have already been partly answered by the specific examples given in chapter 2 of this book: the problems of alcoholism, a falling birth-rate, poor labour discipline – to which may be added the best-known problem of all, corruption. It would be wrong to treat them as signs of political opposition, but they do reflect the unwillingness of a large section of the Soviet public to act in the way the authorities want them to. Moreover, none of these problems is of marginal importance: they represent a potentially very serious obstacle to the achievement of the leadership's policy goals.

In the early 1970s, one Sovietologist, Jerome Gilison, aptly put all this into the context of public opinion when he noted: 'The ultimate sanction that followers can impose over leaders in the Soviet system is poor performance – perfunctory implementation of and lethargic reaction to the leadership's policies – the most wasteful and demoralizing way of assuring long-term responsiveness of the party-state.'[7] That sanction is not necessarily a minor one, as the record of the Brezhnev era eventually showed. Poor performance was seen to extend not only to the economy but to other areas of society, including the media. The penalty for letting poor performance continue would not necessarily be the collapse of the system but a steady decline in the system's status and influence both at home and abroad. The Soviet media, Soviet ideology and Soviet consumer goods were increasingly becoming unprestigious, even within the USSR; and this was hardly a prospect which any Soviet leadership could passively accept. This as much as anything must surely have been one of the precipitating factors behind the Gorbachev reforms.

Yet it seemed unlikely that alcoholism or corruption or any of the other problems just mentioned could be solved purely by measures from above, however necessary. Solutions would almost certainly be impossible without a high degree of co-operation at grass-roots level. Getting that co-operation meant allowing a significantly greater role for public opinion. It also made it necessary, among other things, for the leadership to find an antidote to cynicism and to create public confidence in the honesty of the system. This no doubt explains the growing emphasis on reform. And it also explains the importance attached to openness (*glasnost'*) in the media, whose own influence had been damaged by poor performance in the recent past. Taken as a whole, it represented a change not of mere style, but of substance; not just another shift in the party line, but an experiment in the redistribution of influence, and perhaps of power, within the Soviet system.

Public opinion, persuasion and the 'consent factor'

If the above argument is right then it follows that (1) the past Soviet propaganda effort was not, on the whole, one of the systems' major strengths, although (2) it was probably less important to the system's stability than was often supposed. However (3), this whole subject does repay study because of the clue which it provides to the thinking of past Soviet leaders. They obviously assumed that, given the necessary preconditions, they could either control or disregard their own public opinion. They made this the foundation of their entire propaganda effort; and, paradoxically, they ignored or suppressed any findings from psychology or the social sciences which cast doubt on their basic assumption. The end result of the sustained propaganda effort was not the 'thought-control' of Orwellian fantasy, nor indeed was it the downfall of the system. The end result was poor performance – in the media as elsewhere – which was later publicly admitted and which undermined the system's prestige. At least part of the explanation for all this does, indeed, seem to lie in the official attitude towards psychology. For not only did the leaders ignore the findings of psychology in the narrow, professional, sense: they seemed to have remarkably little interest in the empirical study of human motivation. This may be one of the reasons why they overrated their own ability to control public opinion. And this in turn may have impelled them in the past towards policies which were at times not only ruthless but also lacking in realism. If this is so, then it would be misplaced to credit the Soviet leaders with special psychological skill. Rather the opposite: it was the official disregard for psychology which can provide an insight into Soviet politics in the past.

The issues just raised have, so one could argue, a relevance not only in the context of Soviet politics, but also in a wider context. To overrate the power of propaganda whilst underrating the autonomy of public opinion can, at least sometimes, be a costly mistake. And this in turn raises further questions. How far, in any society, is public opinion a power in its own right? How far is it persuasible? What does effective persuasion involve? And are there any useful insights to be gained by contrasting the different Soviet and Western answers to these questions?

Public opinion: an autonomous force

In no society is public opinion expressed only through the ballot-box. Familiar examples came to mind where such opinion has to be heeded by government as a matter of sheer practical necessity. This is especially true when leaders require not just passive acceptance of their policies, but affirmative public support. Relations between Hitler and Stalin provide an illustration. The Soviet–German non-aggression pact of August 1939 was a classic instance of secret diplomacy in which public opinion played no role whatsoever. But as soon as war broke out between Germany and the Soviet Union, the grass-roots commitment to the war-effort on each side assumed great importance. Another relevant example is that of Britain's crash programme of re-armament in the summer of 1940. Without grass-roots public support it could hardly have succeeded; and the continuation of the war would have been impossible. Again on D-Day in June 1944, public attitudes in German-occupied Europe were of crucial military importance. If the allied forces led by General Eisenhower had been met by the local populations not as liberators but as a hostile invading army, then the invasion would have cost many more allied lives and would have had to be carried out in an entirely different way. Cases like these are so self-evident as to seem like truisms. But there have been other cases where the importance of public opinion became apparent only later on, or too late. It may be suspected that the root cause of the US defeat in Vietnam was that South Vietnam (even if not pro-communist) was simply not motivated to fight; and that it was beyond all the power and resources of the United States to supply the South Vietnamese with motivation.

These examples once again bring into relief the question raised at the outset of this discussion, namely the role of consent as a practical necessity. The point which concerns us here is not how far governments ought in a moral sense to rely on consent, but how far they can realistically afford not to do so. There are many cases, needless to say, when governments do not have to reckon with public opinion. It can be argued that politicians should not invariably succumb to opinion polls. It can even be argued that in some conditions (including perhaps those which at present exist in the Soviet Union) total democracy would not work. But the point being argued here is not that the 'consent factor' always overrides everything else, but simply that it needs to be taken explicitly into account and treated as a distinct issue in its own right. The price for disregarding public opinion can be high, and this proposition holds good for regimes of all kinds, not just for liberal societies where consent is built into the system. Soviet history tends to confirm this view – as regards not only domestic, but also foreign policy.

One familiar example was Stalin's disregard for public opinion in Eastern Europe after 1945. Even if, as we have suggested, the governments in the Eastern European countries are unlikely to fall, public opinion in those countries remains a strong (even if hidden) factor in the power balance and a potential threat to Soviet security. A more recent example was the war in Afghanistan, where the Soviet-backed regime could almost certainly have held its own, even against a Western-armed resistance movement, if that regime had had the bulk of local public opinion on its side. The original Soviet decision to back the regime and send troops into the country evidently involved among other things a failure to give due weight to Afghan public opinion.[8] The Soviet leadership consequently found itself in a predicament very similar to the one faced by America in Vietnam: hence its decision to withdraw its forces on terms far short of Soviet victory.

It is the 'consent factor' – rather than the overall merits of particular ideologies or policies – which concerns us here. For instance, the present argument is not directed against collectivism or economic planning as such, but merely seeks to underline the importance of consent as one factor to be reckoned with when assessing how they will work.

But if public support is sometimes essential for the success of a policy, this leads on to the further question raised earlier: how far is public opinion amenable to control from above? And what does effective persuasion involve? We touched briefly in chapter 2 on the different nuances sometimes associated with the terms 'propaganda' and persuasion; we noted that the Nazis, for instance, might be said to have believed in the former but not in the latter. There *is* a difference between the two; but it is a conceptual not just a semantic difference; and it hinges precisely on the issue of consent. There is nothing intrinsically wrong, or indeed unrealistic, about attempts by governments or anyone else to change public opinion in a radical fashion. Such changes do occur – as graphically shown by the anti-Nazi and pro-democratic shift of public opinion in West Germany following the overthrow of Hitler in 1945. But genuine shifts of opinion cannot by definition occur without consent. If consent is obtained by force, fraud, threats, concealment or (arguably) by manipulation, then one may say, as lawyers do, that the consent is not genuine, i.e. that it was never given at all or was only given as a result of misunderstanding. No strategy of persuasion is likely to prove realistic in the long run, if it fails to address itself to this 'consent factor'.

'Coercive' versus 'manipulative' persuasion

It was in this context that we sought to compare and contrast the evolution of propaganda doctrine in the Soviet Union and the West. The two doctrines *are* radically different. Yet they cannot adequately be contrasted in purely moralistic or political terms (such as 'freedom' versus 'censorship') because, so we have argued, this is liable to result in a disregard for other important differences between them. It could be said, (at the risk of slight over-simplification) that the traditional Soviet approach to propaganda in practice greatly relied on 'coercive persuasion', that is pressure from above. By contrast, the prevalent approach to propaganda in the West has tended to rely on 'manipulative persuasion'. Each involves different implicit assumptions about how consent is to be won.

As we noted in chapter 3, neither Marx nor Lenin ever subscribed to the belief that propaganda was all-powerful. Lenin stressed the crucially important role of personal experience in the formation of mass opinion, although he did eventually advocate a strategy of winning power first and converting public opinion afterwards. It cannot be said that this strategy was inherently bound to fail: it all depended, as Lenin recognized, on the experience of the masses *after* the new regime had taken power. Indeed, the overthrow of Hitler and the subsequent conversion of West German public opinion to democracy on the basis of the personal experience is an example of just such a strategy succeeding. In practice, things did not work out in the USSR according to theory; and most of this book has been concerned with trying to explain why.

It only remains to add that Stalinist-style persuasion could never have become a substitute for force, because it involved the suppression of inconvenient information and therefore perpetuated the need for censorship. Besides that, the issue of consent was eventually fudged, by blurring the distinction between what people actually wanted and what was in their 'objective interests'. Finally Stalin and his successors – instead of arguing, as they might have done, that dictatorship was for the time being unavoidable – tried to dispose of the problem by denying that conflicts could spontaneously arise in Soviet society, that is, by pretending that consent existed when it plainly did not. For a time this approach may have seemed viable. But the end result was that the official ideology – with its talk of a 'unanimous public opinion' – became increasingly mythological and therefore increasingly unpersuasive even in Soviet society itself. This was just one example of the gap between 'word and deed', of the discrepancy between theory and observed reality, which – as later Soviet leaders admitted – had merely served to erode public commitment to the system.

In total contrast to all this, the techniques of mass persuasion in the West appear to make the winning of consent the foundation of their strategy. The whole idea is to make the audience *want* to comply with the persuader's wishes; and to get this result by methods which have no necessary connection with coercion or censorship. This can be termed 'manipulative persuasion'. It involves carefully identifying the desires (or fears or prejudices) of members of the public and then trying to harness or exploit them in accordance with the persuader's purposes. Most propaganda of this kind (such as advertising or appeals to marginal voters) is targeted on minorities and is done on an *ad hoc* basis. But no one familiar with advertising or the use of public relations consultants in election campaigns can imagine that 'manipulative persuasion' is a small-scale activity in Western society. And the refinement of opinion research techniques has made it a far more powerful instrument than in the past.

The basic premise of this approach seems to be that no message will make an impact (at least with an adult audience) unless related in some way to the predispositions of that audience. This strategy has inbuilt limitations as well as the inbuilt dangers. There are, of course, situations in which large groups of people do become receptive to false information or apparently impervious to rational argument; this is particularly true in times of crisis, when people fear that their vital interests are threatened. It is these situations which provide an opportunity for demagogues – whose method consists in telling the public what many of them want to hear. And it is in cases like these that manipulative propaganda can have a powerful, apparently 'brainwashing' effect. But it must again be pointed out that 'brainwashing' of this variety has virtually nothing in common with traditional Soviet indoctrination techniques, which smacked of the 'schoolmaster state' and were not greatly concerned with what people wanted to hear. The implicit assumption of persuaders in the West might be put in a slightly different way: that a message to an adult audience is unlikely to have an effect unless it caters for a *demand* (in the psychological, rather than the commercial, sense); from which it would follow that communications whether good or bad – video-nasties, anti-semitic propaganda or environmentalist propaganda – will become a force to be reckoned with only if they do cater for such a demand. The proposition may never have been expressed in quite that form, but it does appear to have had a powerful influence on Western persuasion techniques.

The moral problems which all this raises will be discussed in a moment. But first, something further needs to be said about the propaganda techniques themselves. These, as already indicated, seem themselves to have become the centre of cold war myth and misunderstanding – because neither side fully understood the other's approach. Westerners tended to give credence to the 'thought-control' image of Soviet propaganda and implicitly credited the Soviet authorities with psychological skills which they clearly did not possess. Soviet ideologues, for their part, denounced Western 'manipulative' techniques; but they were totally unwilling or unable to recognize that the effectiveness of these techniques is based on an appeal (even if sometimes less than scrupulous) to audience demands. Apart from that, the Western finding that propaganda is of generally limited power was hardly something which Soviet ideologues would find helpful.

Given the disparate natures of Soviet and Western persuasion, is there any meaningful yardstick for comparing them? Can one, for instance, compare the Soviet campaign aimed at creating a 'New Man' with the commercial advertising campaigns in the Western world? What can perhaps be said is that whereas Soviet communicators used primitive methods in the pursuit of ambitious goals, those in the West used important psychological discoveries often in the pursuit of trivial goals.

Propaganda and ethics

All this takes us from the technology of persuasion to the ethical issues to which it gives rise. One may doubt whether the two sorts of issues can in practice be totally separated; that is, whether an entirely 'value-free' discussion of propaganda method is possible. The reason for this is simple: that the long-term success of any appeal, especially moral or political, depends on the persuader winning the trust of his audience. (Substantive trust is not the same as cosmetic credibility.) Persuaders who are known to rely on less than totally honest methods (or to be cynical, or contemptuous of their audiences) can therefore, in the long run, defeat their own objectives.

The moral and political case against the monopolistic control of the media is too well known and too self-evident to need re-stating here. The morally objectionable features of the Soviet media in the past do not therefore need to be set out at length; nor do the virtues of a pluralistic political system which can, at least in principle, ensure genuine freedom of debate.

All the same, this book was not intended to seem like an apology for Western-style manipulative persuasion. It is, needless to say, a much less disagreeable thing than the indoctrination techniques traditionally attempted by the Soviet authorities. But it may, for that very reason, sometimes be far more effective. Moreover, psychological manipulation is not as innocuous as its practitioners may claim. And one does not have to believe in the dangers of 'thought-control' in order to see this.

The concern here is not with 'dirty tricks' or lies. It hinges on the increasing reliance on non-rational forms of mass persuasion. This highlights yet another contrast with the Soviet approach. The official Soviet ideology (as noted in chapter 3) has in principle relied heavily on an appeal to reason – although this was virtually nullified over many decades by the effective banning of debate. As against this, Western persuaders have always laid enormous stress on pluralism, though this has by no means always resulted in a more rational level of political debate. The non-rational approach has steadily gained ground – as shown by the increased reliance on 'images' rather than issues in Western election campaigns. Competition has not always proved an effective antidote to this non-rational approach: for example, if one political party uses professional advertisers in an election campaign, the others have little choice but to follow suit.

Moreover, it seems a little too facile to respond with the argument that 'nothing can be done' or that the media, with all their faults, are merely giving the public what it wants. The public – as Soviet experience shows – does feel a need for reliable information, especially in times of crisis. If commercial interests find it unprofitable to satisfy that demand, one might suggest at least two quite different ways of improving matters. One way might be to develop and strengthen genuinely autonomous public service broadcasting – so as to give the public guaranteed access to at least one source of untendentious information which it can trust. A second way might be to encourage a greater psychological 'immunity' (to borrow a Soviet expression) against techniques of non-rational persuasion.

Graham Wallas, who in 1908 was apparently the first to use the term 'image' in relation to political propaganda, is widely remembered as a pioneer thinker in this field. It is less often remembered, however, that Wallas was not an advocate of manipulative persuasion. He allowed of the possibility that:

> the change in political science which is now going on will simply result in the abandonment by the younger politicians of all ethical traditions, and the adoption by them, as the result of their new book-

learning, of those methods of exploiting the irrational elements of human nature which hitherto have been the trade secret of the elderly and the disillusioned.[9]

However, Wallas was optimistic that it would be possible to avert this danger; he clearly believed that an understanding of the non-rational elements in political opinion would help to promote debate on a more rational level. He proposed the teaching of 'a very simple course on the well-ascertained facts of psychology' to children aged 13 to 14 as one practical step in this direction.[10] His proposal seems as relevant today as it was in 1908.

Dialogue, confrontation and the cold war

It remains finally to consider how far the subject of our discussion has any bearing on the much broader questions of East–West relations.

The cold war was (or is) by its nature a conflict pursued on both sides by methods short of all-out war. In that conflict propaganda inevitably came to occupy a prominent place – because it is both inexpensive and relatively free of risk. It is naturally tempting to try to assess the impact which propaganda has had in the cold war. No proper assessment is possible here, however, because propaganda cannot be evaluated in isolation from all the other elements – political, diplomatic, economic and military – which have shaped East–West rivalries. Thorough examination of all these other factors would take the discussion far beyond the scope of this book.   What can perhaps be suggested, however, is that 'cold war propaganda' has done much more to reinforce existing attitudes (by convincing the Soviet and Western publics of an external threat, real or imagined) than it has done to win converts. Western broadcasts to the Soviet bloc have had a certain inbuilt advantage over Soviet foreign propaganda, because they have, certainly in the past, helped to remedy an unsatisfied demand for information amongst the audience caused by censorship. In Eastern Europe they have helped to sustain (although not create) anti-regime opinions. There is, however, little sign that propaganda has ever shifted the East–West power balance – which, when it was changed, has changed for other reasons. It is, moreover, obviously true that 'cold war propaganda' was to a considerable extent the result rather than the cause of tensions. At the same time, this kind of propaganda has, only too often in the past, become an obstacle to meaningful, productive debate.

The merits or otherwise of 'cold war propaganda' have been much argued about. To a considerable extent this reflects the disagreements between so-called doves and hawks as to where the blame for the cold war lies. It also reflects the basic issue of East–West relations, debated on both sides, namely attitudes towards confrontation. Under what conditions is confrontation something to be avoided, or won, or ultimately eliminated? On this fundamental issue, a whole spectrum of answers have been put forward.

The point on which I wish to end is, however, quite separate from the 'dove–hawk' dispute. It does not have to do with apportioning blame for the cold war – but is simply concerned with the relevance of an understanding of psychology to East–West relations.

If psychology could contribute to conciliation this would be welcome – though it would perhaps be too optimistic to count on this happening in any direct fashion. What psychology may, however, be able to do is to contribute on both sides to *realism*. Without offering any panacea solutions, psychology may still be able to highlight certain common, but very avoidable, mistakes in East–West communication. And there are three kinds of mistakes which deserve to be mentioned.

The first – as we have argued throughout this book – is the tendency to overrate the power of propaganda and to underrate the autonomy of the audience. This can lead to many misconceptions – for example, the supposition that if ordinary Russians reject Western ideas they must necessarily have been 'indoctrinated'; or equally, that American anti-communism is simply the result of propaganda. The reality may be a good deal more complex. And the impact of a propaganda message usually depends far more on the substance of the message and on the autonomous views of the audience than on the psychological skill of the persuader.

However, if persuasion ever is to make an impact, there are, again, certain pitfalls to avoid. This highlights a second avoidable mistake – namely the mistake of disregarding the 'consent factor' as we argued earlier in this chapter. No would-be persuader who ignores the crucial importance of winning consent is likely to prove very realistic in the long run.

The third mistake is to disregard the role of 'empathy' (as distinct from sympathy) in the handling of conflicts of whatever kind. The 'empathy factor' is a crucially important prerequisite of realism. And it is important quite regardless of whether the aim is to win in a confrontation or to resolve it.

To advocate empathy is not necessarily to take a charitable view of the adversary. It can hardly be denied that Winston Churchill had a more realistic insight into the mind of Hitler than did Neville Chamberlain. But one could quote examples of a different kind. Those who see themselves as 'hawks' often lack empathy; and for this reason, their claims to realism cannot be uncritically accepted at face value. It is worth recalling that

Richard Crossman, who was directly involved in allied propaganda against Nazi Germany during the Second World War, specifically mentioned 'empathy' as one of the key prerequisites for propaganda effectiveness; and he once described how British leaflets dropped over German lines were carefully drafted to take account of Nazi psychology but were classified as 'secret', for fear that if the British public got to know what was in them this might lead to accusations that the allies were 'appeasing' the enemy.[11] Appeasement, of course, had nothing to do with it. Crossman's point about empathy was solely related to the issue of professional competence. Lack of empathy results in the inability to foresee how others will respond to one's own actions. It is therefore never an asset to one's own side, and can sometimes become a serious obstacle to effectiveness in the conduct of policy. From this it follows that where empathy is lacking in East–West relations, it has to be seen as a complicating factor *in addition* to whatever substantive disputes exist. And here the study of propaganda can itself provide insights. Insofar as propaganda indicates a lack of empathy on the part of the communicator, it has, apart from anything else, a *symptomatic* significance which may be very important.

It might have seemed banal to end by stressing the role of empathy – had its importance not been so frequently disregarded by politicians over the decades. Most of this book has focused on the Soviet example – which is only one illustration of a much more general phenomenon – for the historical record of Soviet propaganda, whatever else it may prove, demonstrates virtually beyond doubt that empathy was not a characteristic of the Soviet political mind. One of the first Westerners to draw attention to this was Bertrand Russell, who was received by Lenin in Moscow in 1920. In an account of this meeting, published shortly afterwards, Russell recorded:

> When I suggested that whatever is possible in England can be achieved without bloodshed, he [Lenin] waved the suggestion aside as fantastic. I got little impression of knowledge or psychological imagination as regards Great Britain. Indeed, the whole tendency of Marxianism is against psychological imagination, since it attributes everything in politics to purely material causes.[12]

Lack of empathy is something more than mere misjudgement, and need not stem from stupidity or ignorance. (Lenin had stayed in England before the revolution and spoke English well.) It usually stems from a blind spot rooted in emotional or temperamental causes. And if the Soviet leaders did have such a 'blind spot' in relation to Britain and other Western countries, then the price in Soviet foreign policy terms may have been considerable.

In a more general sense, lack of empathy on both sides helps to explain the patterns of cold war behaviour: the moralizing propaganda which hardly ever appeals to the unconverted, the absence of genuine debate (which is usually inversely related to the volume of propaganda) and the pursuit of verbal or diplomatic confrontations which, to all appearances, exacerbate an antagonism without visibly promoting the victory of either side. It is no part of the present argument to suggest that lack of empathy is a defect peculiar to the Soviet leadership. One of the best-known *non*-Soviet examples was the protracted confrontation between the United States and communist China between the late 1940s and the beginning of the 1970s. The apportionment of blame has largely ceased to matter because it is now seen that the conflict did not serve the interests of either side and stemmed at least in part from misperception. The once strongly held American belief that China was, in effect, a Soviet dependency, and that the war in Vietnam was part of a joint Sino-Soviet conspiracy, has long since been shown to be groundless. Yet had it not been for this American misperception, it is doubtful whether the United States would have become so deeply involved in Vietnam in the first place.

The above argument does not presuppose that all conflicts arise from misunderstanding or that conflicts never have to be won. It merely seeks to show that lack of understanding or empathy, insofar as they exist, can – both in theory and in practice – make conflicts needlessly unproductive and protracted, if not dangerous. One might hope that this view is acceptable to Marxists, anti-Marxists, liberals and conservatives alike; and recent signs suggest that the Soviet leadership is beginning to take the principle seriously. The fostering of empathy is not a panacea; it is only one ingredient in the search for solutions. But it does have practical implications, particularly in the long run. It involves more thought about the stereotypes and rhetoric which undermine empathy: the assumption that 'empathy equals appeasement' has to be tackled head-on. It involves the encouragement of greater research and feedback to enable conventional wisdom to be more rigorously scrutinized. It makes it desirable to discuss fundamental differences (for example, involving ideology, not just disarmament) – at informal East–West meetings which have recently become much easier because of changes on the Soviet side. Finally, it involves the fostering of a more informed, discriminating and critical public opinion; and even if that happened only in the West, it would still be an important gain. The results of these efforts might be modest, but the efforts would still have been worthwhile – for the simple reason that they involve little cost and no risk. There are in any case signs that the climate is changing in this direction of its own accord.

But the principle of empathy can sometimes have a much more immediate, practical application. One statesman who came to take it very seriously indeed in the context of East–West relations was President John Kennedy. In his speech of 10 June 1963, partly quoted at the beginning of this chapter, he urged Americans to re-examine their own attitudes to peace, the cold war and the Soviet Union; and he set out what he saw as a fundamental rule of conduct for the leaders of the superpowers in the nuclear age: 'Above all, while defending our own vital interests, nuclear powers must avert those confrontations which bring an adversary to a choice of either a humiliating retreat or a nuclear war.' He added, a few sentences later, that United States diplomats had been 'instructed to avoid unnecessary irritants and purely rhetorical hostility.'[13]

Belief in empathy was implicit in this entire speech. Perhaps the best evidence that this was indeed in the President's mind is to be found in the account of the 1962 Cuban missile crisis, written after the President's death by his brother Robert Kennedy. Robert Kennedy made the point very forcefully indeed:

> The final lesson of the Cuban missile crisis is the importance of placing ourselves in the other country's shoes. During the crisis President Kennedy spent more time trying to determine the effect of a particular course of action on Khrushchev or the Russians than on any other phase of what he was doing. What guided all his deliberations was an effort not to disgrace Khruschev, not to humiliate the Soviet Union, not to have them feel they would have to escalate their response because their national security or national interests so committed them.

It was precisely the gravity of the confrontation and the unwillingness of the United States to back away from it that made empathy so important. As Robert Kennedy went on:

> Miscalculation and misunderstanding and escalation on one side bring a counter-response. No action is taken against a powerful adversary in a vacuum. A government or people will fail to understand this only at their great peril. For that is how wars begin – wars that no one wants, no one intends, and no one wins.[14]

The role of empathy, or the ability to place oneself in the other person's shoes, is seldom mentioned in discussions about politics, yet its importance is hard to doubt. Empathy helps to explain President Kennedy's effectiveness in beginning to establish a rapport with Nikita Khrushchev. And, in the much more recent past, it almost certainly helps to explain why Mikhail Gorbachev made such a totally new impact on the Western world (though it may be noted that neither Gorbachev nor Kennedy were seen as weak

Corybatrue
orgo, brubach

leaders). It seemed to be clear in the case of Gorbachev that, quite apart from the specific policies which he helped to launch, his entire approach involved a capacity to empathize with points of view other than his own. We saw in chapter 1 how he condemned 'the arrogance of omniscience' and how, in 1987, a Soviet newspaper even went so far as to print an article explaining why the USSR was so widely distrusted in the United States. Yet Gorbachev, somewhat paradoxically, seems to have been less interested than his predecessors in propaganda activity as such. He repeatedly expressed the view that exhortation was no substitute for reform; and that propaganda, if seen to be at odds with reality, could have no persuasive impact.

One cannot yet know how far the momentum of reform which began in the Soviet Union in the 1980s will be sustained. But regardless of what the future may hold, there are lessons – not least in regard to propaganda – which can be learned from the Soviet past. In the preceding chapters, we have taken a sceptical look at the whole notion of 'opinion control'. We set out to explore the Soviet approach to propaganda methods – and came to the conclusion that that approach, far from being motivated by any concern with psychology, was conspicuously deficient in empathy. That, so it could be argued, says something about Soviet politics, at least in the past. It also raises a much broader issue, for it would be hard to deny the importance of empathy in situations which may have nothing to do with Soviet politics; in the success of persuasion, debate, dialogue, negotiation or indeed crisis management of whatever kind. But it would be even harder, in the nuclear age, to deny the crucial importance of empathy in the conduct of East–West relations – if real progress is ever to be made in the search for lasting settlements.

Notes

1   Vladimir Yaroshenko, '*Chernyi efir*'. *Podryvnaya propaganda v sisteme burzhuaznogo vneshnepoliticheskogo radioveshchaniya* (Moscow, 1986), p. 192. In this context, the book's author said: 'In the Soviet Union practically all the radio sets produced have short-wave bands and they are sold without restriction. Furthermore the price of such sets is no higher than that of others. The Soviet Union occupies first place in the world with regard to the number of short-wave radio sets used by the population and capable of picking up broadcasts from foreign countries.'

2   The discontinuance of Soviet jamming was reported, with regard to the BBC, in the British press of 22 January 1987 and, with regard to the Voice of America, in the press of 26 May 1987. The cessation of the jamming of Radio Liberty was reported in the press on 1 and 2 December 1988.

3 *Guardian*, 14 December 1981, p. 1 (report by Hella Pick).

4 A Stalinist-type system, which effectively prevents individual citizens from communicating openly with one another, can of course inhibit the crystallization of public opinion, since, as W. Phillips Davison has pointed out, 'If people are unaware of the attitudes of others, public opinion cannot grow.' The inhibiting of public opinion in this sense naturally strengthens the power of government; but it is clearly not the same thing as successful indoctrination. This author immediately goes on to quote the case of Hungary in 1956, where immediately before the uprising in that year, most workers were opposed to the regime, but could not be sure of the attitudes of others, because fear of informers made it difficult for them to discuss politics outside their immediate circle of friends. See W. Phillips Davison, *International Political Communication* (Praeger, New York, for the Council on Foreign Relations, 1965), p. 67.

5 John Kenneth Galbraith, *The Age of Uncertainty* (Deutsch, London, for the British Broadcasting Corporation, 1977), p. 96.

6 A detailed review of evidence available on this subject in the early 1980s can be found in Stephen White, 'Political communications in the USSR: letters to party, state and press', *Political Studies*, 31 (1983), pp. 43–60. A well-documented examination and critique of grievance procedures in the Soviet Union can be found in Nicholas Lampert, *Whistle-blowing in the Soviet Union: Complaints and Abuses under State Socialism* (Macmillan, London, 1985).

7 Jerome Gilison, *British and Soviet Politics: A Study in Legitimacy and Convergence* (Johns Hopkins Press, Baltimore, 1972), p. 119.

8 In early 1988 a Soviet writer seemed to confirm this. Whilst denying that the Soviet intervention had been pointless, he conceded that 'the original aims [of the Kabul regime] were not achieved.' He went on to say: 'There was a wrong prognosis. The experts who assessed the situation in the country were mistaken; mistakes were made by specialists in Islam, by diplomats, by politicians and by the military.' See Aleksandr Prokhanov, 'Afghan questions', *LG*, 17 February 1988, pp. 1–9.

9 Graham Wallas, *Human Nature in Politics*, 2nd edn (Constable, London, 1910), pp. 176–7. The first edition of this book appeared in 1908.

10 Ibid., p. 189.

11 R.H.S. Crossman, 'Psychological warfare', *Journal of the Royal United Service Institution*, 587 (August 1952), pp. 327–8.

12 Bertrand Russell, *The Practice and Theory of Bolshevism* (Allen & Unwin, London, 1920), p. 38.

13 John F. Kennedy, 'Towards a strategy of peace: Commencement Address at the American National University, Washington, DC, 10 June 1963', reprinted in Richard P. Stebbins (ed.), *Documents on American Foreign Relations: 1963* (Harper & Row, New York, for the Council on Foreign Relations, 1964), pp. 117–120.

14 Robert Kennedy, *13 Days* (Macmillan, London, 1969), pp. 121–2.

Index

237

**DO NOT REMOVE
SLIP FROM POCKET**